WINDOWS AZURE® HYBRID CLOUD

Windows Azure® Hybrid Cloud

Danny Garber

Jamal Malik

Adam Fazio

wrox™

A Wiley Brand

Windows Azure® Hybrid Cloud

Published by
John Wiley & Sons, Inc.
10475 Crosspoint Boulevard
Indianapolis, IN 46256
www.wiley.com

Copyright © 2013 by John Wiley & Sons, Inc., Indianapolis, Indiana
Published simultaneously in Canada

ISBN: 978-1-118-70867-5
ISBN: 978-1-118-70893-4 (ebk)
ISBN: 978-1-118-74974-6 (ebk)

ACQUISITIONS EDITOR
Mary James

PROJECT EDITOR
Kevin Kent

TECHNICAL EDITORS
Bruce Johnson
Cory Fowler

SENIOR PRODUCTION EDITOR
Kathleen Wisor

COPY EDITOR
Luann Rouff

EDITORIAL MANAGER
Mary Beth Wakefield

FREELANCE EDITORIAL MANAGER
Rosemarie Graham

ASSOCIATE DIRECTOR OF MARKETING
David Mayhew

MARKETING MANAGER
Ashley Zurcher

VICE PRESIDENT AND EXECUTIVE GROUP PUBLISHER
Richard Swadley

VICE PRESIDENT AND EXECUTIVE PUBLISHER
Neil Edde

ASSOCIATE PUBLISHER
Jim Minatel

PROOFREADER
Nancy Carrasco

COVER DESIGNER
Ryan Sneed

I dedicate this book to my loving dad who sadly passed away last year. Growing up, my father taught me many valuable lessons, specifically: to be kind to everyone, always learn from my mistakes, and to never give up.

– Danny

To my father whom I love and adore greatly. You provided me with the inspiration and encouragement to follow my dreams and stop at nothing until I achieved them.

– Jamal

For my kids and teachers: London, Bella, and Willow.

– Adam

ABOUT THE AUTHORS

 DANNY GARBER is a Latin America and Canada regional lead in the Worldwide Windows Azure Modern Apps Center of Excellence (Azure Modern Apps CoE) of Microsoft Worldwide Services. The Azure Modern Apps CoE's main objective is to drive Windows Azure adoption, knowledge, skills and implementation in the enterprise customers market space.

Danny is responsible for planning and execution of the services' sales and technical pre-sales Windows Azure platform adoption strategy for customers worldwide. He leads the Windows Azure discovery and Bring-Your-Own-PoC (BYOP) workshops, application assessments, architecture design sessions and oversees the implementation and quality of customer Proof-of-Concepts.

Danny often speaks at the external and internal customers' conferences, such as TechEd, DevConnections, TechReady, and Cloud Summits.

 JAMAL MALIK is a Business Solution Architect with Microsoft's Modern Datacenter of Excellence based out of Microsoft Headquarters in Redmond, WA. As a board certified Architect (CITA-p - IASA Global) Mr. Malik envisions, designs, and oversees the deployment of cloud solutions, which help organizations execute against their strategic business goals and initiatives.

He has developed and published several thought leadership papers around migrating to Cloud Solutions and also delivers training of Cloud Solutions and Capabilities to both internal and external resources to Microsoft. He has a passion for public speaking and regularly presents at internal and external Microsoft events.

Mr. Malik is also very comfortable and experienced with analyzing an Organization's Business Drivers and Investment Objectives and translating them into solutions that help businesses realize benefits, such as Increased Revenue, Improving Efficiency and Productivity, Reducing OpEx\Capex, Winning Market Share, and Improved Decision Making.

 ADAM FAZIO, Microsoft Corporation, is a Solution Architect in the Worldwide Modern Datacenter Center of Excellence organization with a passion for evolving customers' IT infrastructure from a cost-center to a key strategic asset. With focus on the broad Core Infrastructure Optimization model, his specialties include: Private & Hybrid Cloud, Datacenter, Virtualization, Management & Operations, Storage, Networking, Security, Directory Services, People & Process.

In his 14 years in IT, Adam has successfully led strategic projects for Government, Education Sector, and Fortune 100 organizations. Adam is a lead architect for the Microsoft's *Private Cloud Fast Track* and *Datacenter Services* programs. Adam is a course instructor, published writer, and regular conference speaker on Microsoft Cloud, Datacenter, and Infrastructure solutions. He can be reached at http://aka.ms/BuildingClouds and http://twitter.com/adamfazio.

ABOUT THE TECHNICAL EDITOR

PATRICK BUTLER MONTERDE is a Cloud Architect at Microsoft. In his current role he is responsible for developing Cloud strategy solutions and IP for Microsoft Services. Prior to this role, Patrick worked as the Worldwide Windows Azure Technical Sales where he was responsible to support global enterprise customers to successfully adopt the Windows Azure platform.

Prior to joining Microsoft, Patrick held a number of positions from development, management and software architecture. He brings thirteen years of experience spanning multiple industries including; military, health care, oil and gas, government, and legal. He specializes in the Windows Azure platform, .NET, Microsoft SQL Server, and project management. Patrick holds a B.S. in Computer Science from The Evergreen State College and an M.S. in Computer Information Systems from Phoenix University. He is fluent in Spanish and French. Read Patrick's latest at: http://www.azuretribes.com.

ACKNOWLEDGMENTS

Writing a book is by necessity a solitary process. However, co-authoring, on the other hand, has very little to do with solitude. It is a dynamic, exciting process where things can go wrong, or right, at countless junctures. I am extremely lucky to be surrounded by some of the best people in the business. Adam Fazio and Jamal Malik, my co-authors — you are all top-notch. Without your dedication, top knowledge, and creative minds there would be no way I could have pulled off this book by myself.

To our publishing team: Kevin Kent, Rosemarie Graham, and Mary James for continuing to push the boulder up the hill–I do not know how you do it.

To my friend Patrick Butler Monterde, who helped us with technical reviews of most of the chapters in this book, for straightening me out with some of his accurate comments and suggestions.

And to all those who choose to remain in the shadows, thank you. To those whom I may have forgotten — my sincere apologies.

And last, to you, the reader. I hope this book will answer some of your questions on the number of false and truth mythical promises hybrid clouds have managed to stir in the enterprise community. Thank you for your support and enjoy the reading.

DANNY GARBER

I'd like to thank my incredible co-authors (Danny and Adam). Working with you both has been a fantastic experience and I am in absolute awe of your expertise and technical knowledge. To the Wiley Press editors and staff that assisted in polishing this book and ensuring that it actually made sense. To my family, friends, and co-workers for showing support when working on the book had me waking up early in the morning or staying up later than usual at night. Finally, to all of the fantastic customers, clients, and businesses I have had the pleasure of working with and inviting me along on your journey to cloud, for without you this book would not have been possible.

JAMAL MALIK

There are so many people that make a book like this possible. The countless experts inside and outside Microsoft, the bloggers, tweeters, and really anyone who takes the time to write stuff down and share it out. I have grown immeasurably over the years as a direct result of working with some amazing people, such as Joel Yoker, David Ziembicki, Jeff Baker, Bryon Surace, Suzanne Morgan, Allen Stewart, and others. Of course, when I shared an outline for a book with Jamal a couple of years ago, I really had no intention of writing it, so he deserves special thanks for pushing me, inspiring me, and demonstrating what excellence looks like on a daily basis. While I'm new to working with Danny, his deep knowledge and ability to explain things in an easily digestible way has really influenced me.

ADAM FAZIO

CONTENTS

INTRODUCTION TO THE WINDOWS AZURE BOOK SERIES

It has been fascinating watching the maturation of Windows Azure since its introduction in 2008. When it was announced, Azure was touted as being Microsoft's "new operating system." And at that level, it has not really lived up to its billing. However, if you consider Azure to be a collection of platforms and tools that allow you to cloud-enable your corporation's applications and infrastructure, well, now you're on the right track.

And, as it turns out, a collection of co-operating tools and services is the best way to think of Azure. The different components that comprise Azure become building blocks that allow you to construct an environment to suit your needs. Want to be able to host a simple Website? Well, then Azure Web Sites fits the bill. Want to move some of your infrastructure to the cloud while leaving other systems on premise? Azure Virtual Networking gives you the capability to extend your corporate domain to include machines hosted in Azure. Almost without exception, each twist and turn in your infrastructure roadmap can take advantage of the building blocks that make up Windows Azure.

A single book covering everything that encompasses Azure would be huge. And because of the breadth of components in Azure, such a book is likely to contain information that you are not necessarily interested in. For this reason, the Windows Azure series from Wrox takes the same "building block" approach that Azure does. Each book in the series drills deeply into one technology. If you want to learn everything you need to work with a particular technology, then you could not do better than to pick up the book for that topic. But you don't have to dig through 2,000 pages to find the 120 pages that matter to you. Each book stands on its own. You can pick up the books for the topics you are care about and know that's all that you will get. And you can leave the other books until desire or circumstance makes them of interest to you.

So enjoy this book. It will give you the information you need to put Windows Azure to use for you. But as you continue to look to other Azure components to add to your infrastructure, don't forget to check out the other books in the series to see what topics might be helpful. The books in the series are:

- ➤ *Windows Azure and ASP.NET MVC Migration* by Benjamin Perkins, Senior Support Escalation Engineer, Microsoft

- ➤ *Windows Azure Mobile Services* by Bruce Johnson, MVP, Partner, ObjectSharp Consulting

- ➤ *Windows Azure Web Sites* by James Chambers, Product & Community Development Manager, LogiSense

➤ *Windows Azure Data Storage* by Simon Hart, Software Architect, Microsoft

➤ *Windows Azure Hybrid Cloud* by Danny Garber, Windows Azure Solution Architect, Microsoft; Jamal Malik, Business Solution Architect; and Adam Fazio, Solution Architect, Microsoft

Each one of these books was written with the same thought in mind: to provide deep knowledge of that one topic. As you go further into Azure, you can pick and choose what makes sense for you from the other books that are available. Constructing your knowledge using these books is like building blocks, which is just in the same manner that Azure was designed.

Bruce Johnson
Azure Series Book Editor

INTRODUCTION TO *WINDOWS AZURE HYBRID CLOUD*

The three authors of *Windows Azure Hybrid Cloud*, Adam, Danny and Jamal, belong to special groups within Microsoft. Adam and Jamal work for the Global Datacenter and Private Cloud Center of Excellence (CoE), and Danny is part of the Global Azure Modern Apps CoE. When Microsoft looks to develop its capabilities within a specific area they stand-up CoE's to blaze the trail and train other resources within that area (not unlike other large organizations).

Their charter is simple. It is to Evangelize and Grow Microsoft's Private and Public Cloud Strategy. It's a fairly broad charter; however, it is that way for a reason. It is stated that way because there are multiple points of entry to a Microsoft Cloud solution and they execute against this charter through three key areas:

➤ Solution and Opportunity Identification (Pre-Sales)

➤ Cloud Solution Development (IP — intellectual property)

➤ Internal and External Field Enablement (Readiness)

Jamal's area of focus is working with business decision makers (CIO's mostly) and understanding the motivations and business strategies for large (typically Fortune 1000) organizations and identifying opportunities or solutions which Microsoft can assist in enabling them to achieve their strategic business goals and imperatives. If it isn't already obvious, there is an incredible amount of effort that goes into analyzing and understanding a Fortune 1000 Company's business strategy (more on that later). In any event, when Jamal has these initial conversations he then looks to pass off these private and public cloud opportunities to the Datacenter and Azure Modern Apps CoE's, respectively. Increasingly over the last year Jamal has come across opportunities where organizations would actually benefit more from Hybrid Cloud Solutions (a mixture of public and private cloud technologies). That is really how the idea of this book was born. Microsoft knows and understands that Hybrid Cloud Solutions are the path to the future. Their teams are continuously encouraged by management to collaborate more and find different ways to work together. So here they are.

Adam, Danny and Jamal are really excited to put this book together for the benefit of organizations everywhere. They wholeheartedly believe that the future of Information Technology is smack dab in the middle of this phenomenon called Cloud and are happy to do whatever they can to demystify or bring clarity to organizations that are looking to make this journey. This book is the outcome of months' worth of collaboration between these three and they can honestly say it was much easier than they thought it was going to be. Working together was such a motivator within itself and they feel incredibly fortunate to be given the opportunity to be at the very cusp of a brand new revolution that is taking place within the IT world and are even happier to share the insights they have gained while operating in this space with you.

As you thumb through the pages (or click or swipe for that matter) of *Windows Azure Hybrid Cloud* remember that this is just the first phase of your organization's journey to Hybrid Cloud Solutions. As you work through this exercise within your company you will learn that there are unique characteristics to your organization (whether people, process, or technology). The purpose of this book is to reduce or account for the risks associated with migrating towards a Hybrid Cloud Solution; however, it is unrealistic to assume that all risks can be accounted for completely. Frankly, we must balance the amount of planning that we as business and IT decision makers do in preparing for initiatives such as these. At some point we must decide and firmly set in our minds that this will happen, and we will move forward. Otherwise we get caught up in "Analysis Paralysis" as it is called in the consulting world. The best thing to do in order to avoid Analysis Paralysis is to set a deadline with go\no go criteria. We will discuss this and various other methods, approaches, and strategies in this book; however, bear in mind that you either write your own organization's destiny, or it will be written for you. Thank you again for reading this book. Adam, Danny and Jamal wish you the best of luck on your journey towards a Hybrid Cloud!

WHO THIS BOOK IS FOR

Although this book can be read by just about any IT Professional (Architects, Sys Admins, Support Staff, etc.) it is primarily focused on addressing the concerns and needs of Business and Technical Decision Makers. We call out specifically CIO's, SVP of Infrastructure, and VP's of Operations and Engineering. We specifically targeted Business and Technical Decision Makers because frankly, many of the changes an organization must make in order to realize the benefits that can be gained through adopting cloud solutions require some form of organizational or behavioral change. These changes typically require executive sponsorship and will have an impact on both business and IT operational activities for the organization.

This doesn't mean, however, that other roles within a business cannot benefit from this book (far from it). We provide guidance on how to build business cases, gain executive sponsorship, and pinpoint the changes that will be needed by the business to adopt a hybrid cloud solution. Therefore, we highly recommend that a wide array of individuals read this book. Regardless of your role, you will gain deep insight as to what the proper motivation should be to move to a cloud solution and be provided with the proper guidance to ensure that the approach used to discern whether a cloud solution is a right fit, as well as architecting, designing, and operating the cloud solution is done in a consistent and standardized manner.

WHAT THIS BOOK COVERS

The chapters in this book address the aspects of moving your organizations to cloud solutions in a systematic and pragmatic approach that will look to reduce the risk and account for the different dimensions in which making this transition will have on your business and organization. We will cover all three Cloud Service models (IaaS, PaaS and SaaS), provide details to help you decide which models are most appropriate for your organization, and also provide guidance that will aid not only in the transitioning of your organizations to adopting cloud solutions but also provide a very structured approach to operating and maintaining this new solution as well.

As a note, we will mainly focus on providing guidance to organizations that wish to leverage Hybrid Cloud solutions. It is of our viewpoint that pure Private Cloud solutions (although applicable to many organizations) are most beneficial to organizations who wish to provide cloud services to other businesses (i.e. Hosters, Solution Integrators, etc.). The reason for this is because the up-front investment needed to plan, build and design an on-premises cloud solution is fairly substantial and could possibly take many organizations over a decade to fully realize their return on investment just from a cost perspective. Does this mean that organizations can't realize the benefit of a truly Dynamic Datacenter? Of course not. We would suggest however that organizations look to leverage cloud capabilities offered by other more established Service Providers before turning to a Private Cloud to satisfy those needs. This doesn't mean, however, that some organizations (regardless of their size) will also need a Pure Private Cloud solution. Adopting a Private Cloud is an entirely another subject altogether, and therefore the focus of this book will be providing guidance to adopting Hybrid Cloud solutions and offerings (regardless of organization composition and size).

HOW THIS BOOK IS STRUCTURED

Although we have written this book to be read linearly you may find that certain portions of this book may seem more interesting or relevant to you than others (and that is perfectly OK). We suggest that regardless of your background you should try to read every chapter. This is because it will put you on equal footing with other resources in your organization regardless of their background on why, how, and when to adopt a Hybrid Cloud Solution. With that being said we would also like to provide some guidance on what chapters you should pay particular attention to based on your role:

- ➤ C-Level Executives
  - ➤ Chapter 1
  - ➤ Chapter 2
  - ➤ Chapter 10
- ➤ Technical Decision Makers
  - ➤ Chapter 1
  - ➤ Chapter 2

- ➤ Chapter 3
- ➤ Chapter 10
- ➤ IT Architects
  - ➤ Entire Book
- ➤ System Administrators
  - ➤ Chapter 1
  - ➤ Chapter 5
  - ➤ Chapter 8
  - ➤ Chapter 9
  - ➤ Chapter 10

This is not an exhaustive list of roles and suggested chapters; however, you get the idea that the beginning few chapters really cover the motivation and reasoning to adopting a Hybrid Cloud Solution, and Chapter 4 onward is focused more on the "what" and "how" of achieving it.

Chapter 1: What Is Hybrid IT?

Discover an overview of the motivations, deployment models, and characteristics of a Cloud Solution. We set expectations around what are some of the benefits an organization can look to achieve through adopting cloud and also cover what are some un-realistic expectations as well.

Chapter 2: Why Is the Hybrid Cloud Important to My Business

Learn how to properly define and state the proposed benefits that adopting a Hybrid Cloud Solution will provide, as well as the business and organizational change that must take place in order to realize those benefits.

Chapter 3: Project Planning

Understand the approach, scope, and activities related to architecting, designing, and building a Hybrid Cloud Solution.

Chapter 4: What You Need to Know About Azure As a Platform

Take a closer look at the capabilities and features available through the Microsoft Azure Platform. Azure offers more than just Platform as a Service, and now provides features such as Infrastructure as a Service, Media Services, and SQL as a Service.

Chapter 5: Private Cloud Components and Services That Help to Build Hybrid Clouds

Learn the on-premise capabilities that will be needed in order to properly deploy a Hybrid Cloud Solution. This chapter covers not only the components available through Microsoft System Center but also covers networking and identity management topics.

Chapter 6: Hybrid Options in Windows Azure

Distinguish the different methods, scenarios, and approaches that can be used in building a Hybrid Cloud Solution.

Chapter 7: Designing for Resiliency and Scalability

After pulling the capabilities of System Center and Azure together, we are now able to offer guidance on building workloads that are resilient, highly available, and elastic across both Private and Public Clouds.

Chapter 8: Optimizing for Performance

Once workloads have been defined, learn about application architecture performance fundamentals, and storage and networking performance considerations for a Hybrid Cloud Service model.

Chapter 9: Monitoring and Management for Successful Operations

See that as the Workloads and Applications begin moving into deployment, we cover the operational and management principals that govern a hybrid cloud environment, including people and process implications.

Chapter 10: Final Hybrid Cloud Considerations

You are about to pull the trigger on the Hybrid Cloud Solution. What are a few things to think about not only from a technical perspective but from an organizational change perspective as well? Your journey to the cloud will be an on-going one, and we will talk through the process of easing your organization to leverage cloud solutions in a much more open fashion, as well as discuss techniques to handle objections, concerns, and other roadblocks that may arise during the process of adopting Hybrid Cloud.

CONVENTIONS

To help you get the most from the text and keep track of what's happening, we've used a number of conventions throughout the book.

> **NOTE** *Notes, tips, hints, tricks, and asides to the current discussion are offset and placed in italics like this.*

As for styles in the text:

➤ * We *highlight* new terms and important words when we introduce them.

➤ * We show keyboard strokes like this: Ctrl+A.

➤ * We show filenames, URLs, and code within the text like so: `persistence.properties`.

➤ * We present code in two different ways:

```
We use a monofont type with no highlighting for most code examples.
```

We use bold to emphasize code that's particularly important in the present context.

ERRATA

We make every effort to ensure that there are no errors in the text or in the code. However, no one is perfect, and mistakes do occur. If you find an error in one of our books, such as a spelling mistake or a faulty piece of code, we would be very grateful for your feedback. By sending in errata you may save another reader hours of frustration and at the same time you will be helping us provide even higher quality information.

To find the errata page for this book, go to `www.wrox.com` and locate the title using the Search box or one of the title lists. Then, on the book details page, click the Book Errata link. On this page you can view all errata that has been submitted for this book and posted by Wrox editors. A complete book list, including links to each book's errata, is also available at `www.wrox.com/misc-pages/booklist.shtml`.

If you don't spot "your" error on the Book Errata page, go to `www.wrox.com/contact/techsupport.shtml` and complete the form there to send us the error you have found. We'll check the information and, if appropriate, post a message to the book's errata page and fix the problem in subsequent editions of the book.

P2P.WROX.COM

For author and peer discussion, join the P2P forums at `p2p.wrox.com`. The forums are a Web-based system for you to post messages relating to Wrox books and related technologies and interact with other readers and technology users. The forums offer a subscription feature to e-mail you topics of interest of your choosing when new posts are made to the forums. Wrox authors, editors, other industry experts, and your fellow readers are present on these forums.

At http://p2p.wrox.com you will find a number of different forums that will help you not only as you read this book, but also as you develop your own applications. To join the forums, just follow these steps:

1. Go to p2p.wrox.com and click the Register link.

2. Read the terms of use and click Agree.

3. Complete the required information to join as well as any optional information you wish to provide and click Submit.

4. You will receive an e-mail with information describing how to verify your account and complete the joining process.

NOTE *You can read messages in the forums without joining P2P, but in order to post your own messages, you must join.*

Once you join, you can post new messages and respond to messages other users post. You can read messages at any time on the web. If you would like to have new messages from a particular forum e-mailed to you, click the Subscribe to this Forum icon by the forum name in the forum listing.

For more information about how to use the Wrox P2P, be sure to read the P2P FAQs for answers to questions about how the forum software works as well as many common questions specific to P2P and Wrox books. To read the FAQs, click the FAQ link on any P2P page.

1 What Is Hybrid IT?

Forget for one moment all of the rhetoric you hear today from analysts and researchers about the growth and increased adoption of this thing they call the *cloud*. Focus instead on you: the individual, the business owner, CIO, IT director, IT professional, or consultant. In particular, focus on some of the challenges you face today. Chances are good you are responsible for the health of your business's IT environment (either directly or indirectly). Maybe you are even accountable for the performance or achievement of the earnings your business is expected to produce. Chances are you are constantly trying to balance day-to-day operational activities with projects or special initiatives.

THE THING THEY CALL THE "CLOUD"

So in your situation, the question you must ask yourself is this: "Will leveraging cloud solutions really assist my organization in achieving its business plans and objectives?" Although it seems obvious, that answer (interestingly enough) is a resounding *no*. There is no shortage of traditional solutions that provide capabilities to help your organization achieve its business goals. In fact, these solutions have been doing just that for quite some time now. Just because cloud solutions are the new hype, it doesn't leave all existing (or traditional) solutions irrelevant.

That said, it's important to consider what will happen if you don't take advantage of some of these cloud solutions and your competitors do. Will they find new levels of efficiency in their organization or streamline their operational processes to a point where they now have an advantage over your organization in terms of agility, control, and execution? The answer here is a resounding **YES**. The benefits that cloud solutions bring to an organization are very apparent. The impact and provided benefits in terms of resilience and reliability (due to the expertise and economies of scale achieved by service providers) and potentially shifted cost structures will easily outweigh the cost\capability battle when compared to similar functions provided by your traditional (on-premises) technologies and solutions.

So, what is all this excitement about the cloud anyway? In this chapter we'll try to share some insight as to why so many organizations are looking to cloud solutions to transform their organizations. First, however, we want to make sure that we are all talking about the same thing. A plethora of solutions and offerings in the market claim to be cloud-centric, or something within that realm, so we will first explore the anatomy of a cloud to help you differentiate between solutions that actually provide cloud capabilities and those that do not.

CLOUD SERVICE MODELS

In this section, we want to explain the three following cloud service models:

- ➤   Infrastructure-as-a-Service (IaaS)
- ➤   Platform-as-a-Service (PaaS)
- ➤   Software-as-a-Service (SaaS)

We'll begin with the analogy that everyone can understand and relate to — transportation. If you are like most, two of your main requirements of transportation are as follows:

- ➤   It must be available to you whenever you need it.
- ➤   It must take you from point A to point B.

So, with those requirements in mind, you drove to the dealership and bought a new car. Congratulations! Now, assuming you know how to drive, you can drive it anywhere, anytime, and for as long as you can, as long as you stop for rest and refueling your gas tank.

At the same time, you must take care of your car so that it stays usable and operational. And if you think of your personal vehicle as the investment you have made for many years to come, you are wrong. The very minute that you drive a new car off a dealer's lot, it loses value. On average, cars depreciate about $3,000 annually. So does the hardware you bought for your datacenter.

Here comes the first comparison. Think of the traditional IT and the hardware (servers, network switches, hubs, etc.) as if it were your own car you bought, you drive, and you take care of (maintenance, service checks, etc.). If you draw the parallel line, you could quickly appreciate the common pattern of having full control over where it goes and when, and the depreciation of value over the time (see Figure 1-1).

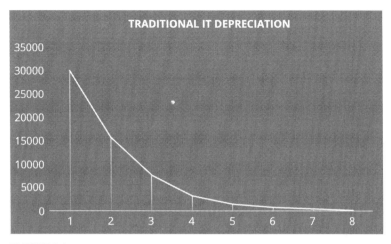

FIGURE 1-1

Infrastructure-as-a-Service — The Leasing Option

Now, consider the car leasing option. There are a few striking key differentiators from the previous model — your own car (a.k.a. traditional IT datacenter). Those differences can be outlined as:

➤ You pay monthly fees during the entire lease period, which sum in total to 50-60 percent of the new car's manufacture price tag.

➤ You can still drive whenever you want and wherever you wish, but with imposed mileage limits (for example: a lease contracts may have 36 K miles maximum per 36 months of lease).

➤ There's also a limitation of cars/models types that are available for lease.

➤ You still have to take care of your leased car as if it were your own (service maintenance, refueling, changing the tires, etc.), but because you don't own it you can't modify it in any way.

And that's exactly, or almost exactly, what you are going to get when you "lease" the *Infrastructure-as-a-Service (IaaS)* from the public cloud provider (the "dealership"). This is equivalent to leasing a virtual server on which the tenant can install their own operating system and administer the server themselves. Like when you lease a car, in the case of leasing VMs from your public cloud service provider you will observe the following "+" and "-" that may affect your business decision on when to choose what cloud service model:

Pros:

➤ You can use pre-installed VMs containing some of the most common software packages installed and ready for you to configure per your business needs. Windows Azure IaaS includes a standardized VM Image Gallery for consistent workload deployment and hosting. The VMs you can find in this gallery are available for "pick-up" to serve as the starting point (in many cases it puts you on the accelerated path) for your IaaS deployment environment. Note that only Microsoft Windows Azure IaaS cloud services offers the Image Gallery at this moment. No other cloud vendors currently have that. Think about the pre-installed navigation and sound systems in your leased car.

➤ You pay only for the time you use your VM in IaaS. Note that the Azure VMs must be shut down (turned off) in order for billing charges to stop. More on Azure VMs later.

➤ Can easily scale-up and scale-down whenever you need it to.

Cons:

➤ Have the limited choice of what guest OSs are currently supported by cloud vendors. For example, you can't bring your own VM containing Windows Server 2003 32-bit OS.

➤ Have limitation on the VM formats supported by a cloud provider's IaaS platform. For instance, Microsoft doesn't support VMWare VM images on their Windows Azure IaaS, while Amazon only supports its own proprietary VM format forcing customers to convert their original on-premises VM formats into Amazon's format.

➤ Have restrictions imposed on you by a cloud provider on what software licenses you can bring to the public cloud. For example, Oracle DB isn't supported on Windows Azure IaaS VMs due to the licensing restrictions imposed by Oracle.

So far so good, right? Now it's time to look at the other two popular public cloud hosting models: *Platform-as-a-Service (PaaS)* and *Software-as-a-Service (SaaS)*.

Platform-as-a-Service — The Rental Option

PaaS is analogous to another transportation option: a rental car. In this case, you need to go from point A to point B for the T duration (in most cases from 1 to 7 days, sometimes longer). Does it make sense for you to go and buy a new car? No, and we proved it with our car depreciation analysis. Does it make sense to lease a car for a short period of time, say, in some place you came for vacationing or for a business? Absolutely not! First of all, no one will lease you a car for such a short period of time, and secondly — and most importantly — you wouldn't want to pay heavy costs associated with a leased car (down payment, residual depreciation fees, dealership, and car delivery fees). It's not worth it.

Thankfully, rental car agencies allow you, for a nominal fee, to use a rental car per day, to drive wherever you want and whenever you want without worrying about the car maintenance, tires, and sometimes even filling the gas tank. It's all included in the rental price. "It's all included" is the key phrase. Because, when you draw the parallel line from the car analogy back to the public cloud, you can see that PaaS has most of the features owned or leased to you by a cloud vendor included in its hosting model. In other words, when you "rent" a piece of cloud — that is, deploy your application to the PaaS flavor of the public cloud — you will observe the following:

Pros:

➤ Pay as you go, or pre-pay for the specific period of time/consumption.

➤ Use the cloud only when you need it.

➤ Have no need to worry about infrastructure maintenance, OS, and security upgrades, patches, networking, load balancing.

➤ Can easily scale-up and scale-down whenever you need it to.

Cons:

➤ Have the limited choice in what you can rent (read: "deploy").

➤ Have restrictions imposed on you by a cloud provider on what you can bring to the public cloud and in what capacity.

By now, you should have if not a completely clear picture, at least a partially cloudy picture of how an IaaS cloud model is different from a PaaS cloud model. Both models have their own Pros and Cons and the absolute right to co-exist and/or be your preferable choice for your business cloud solution.

Now, let's review the third cloud hosting model, SaaS, while comparing it to the other two you have just finished reading about.

Software-as-a-Service — The Public Transportation Option

Finally, what transportation options do you have when you don't know how to operate the vehicle or simply don't want to? You choose public transportation. To use public transportation you buy a ticket, day pass, monthly pass, or Oyster card (if you're in London), and use it every time you get onboard the train, bus, subway, or airplane.

It still can take you from point A to point B, but cannot take you to point C if the bus's route doesn't go there. At the same time you don't have to know how to drive the bus, and of course, you have no maintenance headaches, need to fill the gas, or requirement to be always alert when operating the vehicle. Once again, drawing the parallel line from transportation analogy back to the public cloud, you can see the same pattern realized in the *Software-as-a-Service (SaaS)* public cloud deployment model. As you have tradeoffs when you use public transportation, running the software package such as Office, Mail Exchange, SharePoint, CRM, etc., on someone's else cloud without investing in infrastructure hardware, software licenses, and operational maintenance cost has its obvious perks as well as some disadvantages:

Pros:

- ➤ You pay on a per-user basis.
- ➤ No software licenses are required.
- ➤ You can easily scale-up and scale-down whenever you need to.
- ➤ No skills to run and operate third-party software are required.
- ➤ The system is always highly available.
- ➤ SLAs are guaranteed.

Cons:

- ➤ SaaS is typically a multi-tenant, shareable environment, where you share physical resources with others tenants (customers). Theoretically, if someone messes up the physical ecosystem you happen to share, you and your customers are impacted as well.
- ➤ There is a limited list of SaaS packages available today.
- ➤ You can always make some limited configuration changes in the product you "rent" as part of your SaaS subscription, but rarely can you customize or tailor to your own business needs.

By now, you should have made the obvious connection in the parallel patterns we tried to draw here through the transportation analogy, and we hope you can see the differences as well as the pros and cons of each public cloud hosting model. We believe that drawing parallel lines between the cloud service models and the various options you have when choosing a specific type of transport whether it is your own vehicle, a lease car, rental car, or public transportation, would help you better understand the common traits and differences that exist between these three cloud service models. However, by providing such an analogy we certainly do not aim to give you a recipe or instructions on how to choose between the cloud service models. Obviously, whatever reasons that affect your decision in choosing between lease, rental, or public transportation cannot be and shouldn't be applied to the cloud service models decision making process. Our aim was merely to give you the perspective on various factors that can be applied for each cloud service model, and which, to some degree, can be explained in more accessible, plain English understood by virtually every reader of this book.

To clarify the differences each public cloud hosting model has even more, take a look at Figure 1-2:

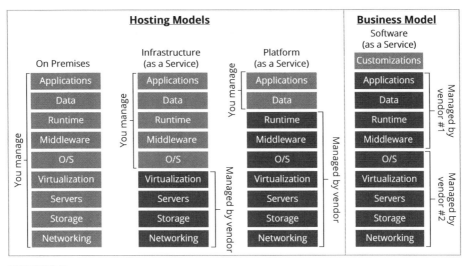

FIGURE 1-2

Whether you are buying our public cloud computing story or not, enterprise application developers are finding the self-service, pay-as-you-go, instant deployment values of cloud computing platforms appealing. Developers can go to a web page, sign up with a credit card, and instantly instantiate any number of virtual machines and applications without any IT ops involvement. Just remember, IT ops processes and procedures, and enterprise architecture rules, for that matter, exist to ensure that the overarching needs and policies of the business are followed and fulfilled. Allowing time in the deployment process to accommodate these demands may hinder time-to-market, but often there are very good reasons to do so. Later in this book, in Chapter 10 we review some of these reasons and provide our own thoughts on when it is good for business to go to the cloud and when it is bad.

WHAT ARE THE TRENDS THAT YOU SHOULD WATCH?

If you ever hear that organizations are flocking to the cloud service model and looking to leverage this offering for every part of their business, you should take that with a grain of salt. The truth of the matter is that every organization which has some established business and IT processes are taking baby steps toward cloud solutions — and rightfully so. In this section we talk about some small steps that organizations can take to begin their journey toward cloud solutions and share a few examples of organizations that have already taken those steps. This will also be covered in greater detail in Chapter 3 where we cover planning for the cloud.

Ideally, and taking the size of the organization into account, efforts to leverage cloud solutions should be done so that risk is mitigated and accounted for as much as possible. Hinging the success of an entire business unit on an offering that is still rapidly maturing and evolving in the market is probably not the best business strategy. Additionally, removing all risk from an initiative is not realistic either, as low risk often also means low returns. The trend thus far has been divided into two categories:

➤ Identify low risk areas of your business that can potentially benefit from adopting cloud capabilities.

➤ Find a business unit that you have a strong relationship with to pilot the new cloud service.

Of course, this decision also depends on the cloud service model that is being leveraged (IaaS, PaaS, or SaaS).

Trends towards IaaS

Organizations are applying the IaaS model to business units that require rapid provisioning of virtual machines or operating systems. This rapid provisioning however, associated with certain limitations and differences IaaS infrastructure presents, coupled with challenges related to people's mind shift in dealing with a new paradigm, can create negative side-effects that often slow down the adoption of such a model by issues within these business units. Therefore, finding an IaaS solution that is able to tie into an existing organization's technology, operational and culture practices, can be a bit challenging. When it comes to IaaS, there is usually one of three ways (covered throughout this chapter) in which it can be deployed: private, public, or hybrid. A private cloud IaaS solution is the most common form found in the "wild." If you are reading this book and looking to leverage a private IaaS solution, it is most likely being provided by an internal IT Services department (common in government, financial, and retail sectors). If that is the case, the private IaaS solution will most likely already provide the capability to host virtual machines while still part of either your domain or Active Directory environment (assuming you are using Active Directory), or limit the access to your virtual machines to just your organization or business unit. If that is the case, consider yourself lucky.

For all other organizations that choose to leverage public IaaS solutions (Azure IaaS), there are a few more things to take into consideration. Although we will cover this in greater depth in Chapters 4 through 9, a few of the considerations include the following:

➤ Connectivity and access

➤ Disaster recovery

➤ Data isolation and sovereignty

➤ Identity management

After addressing some of these considerations, some business units first look to leverage IaaS solutions for their development environment, while others look to host non-mission critical application and data (freeing up their own datacenters for more critical workloads). It is not common to see organizations moving to cloud solutions in giant leaps. However taking small steps toward IaaS gives the organization an opportunity to see how this new service model will affect their organization and also to test the waters in terms of stability and flexibility as they look to increase their adoption of IaaS.Trends towards PaaS.

Although PaaS can be deployed as either public or private, most organizations look to leverage PaaS in a public cloud model. Organizations interested in PaaS in a private cloud scenario are mostly hosters and solution integrators that want to extend PaaS into a SaaS solution. We do not cover that scenario in detail in this book, but note that the capability to deploy a PaaS as an on-premises solution typically is not useful unless it will be used to provide services to other organizations (hence, the interest of hosters or at least very large organizations, which must provide IT services to other business units or IT agencies).

So, in terms of consumers looking to leverage a public PaaS solution, what are typically the trends? As far as critical applications are concerned or business units that require the rapid deployment of line of business (LOB) applications, we haven't really seen a great deal of adoption in those key areas. Instead, PaaS solutions are used by organizations which are looking to move away from managing the infrastructure required to host LOB applications or deliver elastic workloads to external consumers (retail chain websites, government web-based portals, or externally facing LOB applications). One of the more popular public PaaS solutions is Microsoft Azure, which we of course will cover extensively later in this book.

Trends towards SaaS

Although this is the most sophisticated of the cloud service models, SaaS is probably the most common form of public cloud solution available. A common misconception about SaaS is actually derived from its name. The term *software* usually denotes some form of middleware, which is really closer to what PaaS offers. SaaS typically entails offering a feature or functionality within an application. An example of this would include a mailbox within Microsoft's Office 365 suite. Whatever the middleware, SaaS assumes the management of the middleware by the service provider, and the only thing that the service consumer is aware of or concerned about is the feature that is being provided to them.

SaaS is also the most popular cloud service model because it means that service consumers can get out of the middleware and infrastructure management "game" and leave it completely to the service provider. From a cost benefits perspective this is the most appealing, as it allows service consumers to dramatically scale back the physical server footprint of hosting such middleware in their datacenters and reduces the need for expertise of that middleware application in-house, instead delegating those management responsibilities to the service provider.

You have to be very careful here, however, because moving to a SaaS solution often leads to a fairly disruptive change within an organization's IT environments. In short, IT professionals look at SaaS as a threat to their job security. It is not uncommon to see or hear about efforts to move to a SaaS solution being sabotaged or slowed down due internal politics or fear of IT professionals losing their positions.

As organizations begin to realize the benefits of moving to a SaaS model of operations, they typically do so first by either augmenting their internal on-premises solutions or using the SaaS model as "spillover." Meaning all new users' mailboxes (customer accounts, SharePoint Sites, and so on) are a part of this new off-premises SaaS cloud solution. This can be challenging, however, from an architectural perspective, as the technical specifics and configuration of enabling this scenario can be fairly complex or often take more effort to set up than they provide value to the organization. For these cases, a hard cutover is often necessary. In either scenario, a fair amount of planning and preparation is required to move to an off-premises SaaS solution. As a tradeoff, your organization will lose one very large benefit that an on-premises middleware solution provides: flexibility. We will cover in more depth why this is a necessary tradeoff and whether it's worth making some minor operational changes to help offset these limitations or re-thinking instead what capabilities are most important for your business.

WHAT ARE THE CHARACTERISTICS OF A CLOUD?

So, what are the characteristics of a cloud? The National Institute of Standards and Technology (NIST) sums it up fairly well. NIST defines all cloud solutions as having the five following essential characteristics:

- ➤ Broad network access
- ➤ Resource pooling
- ➤ Elasticity
- ➤ Chargeback (measured service)
- ➤ Self-service

NOTE *You can find the NIST definitions at* `http://csrc.nist.gov/publications/nistpubs/800-145/SP800-145.pdf`.

These characteristics are found in one of three cloud service models, which were described earlier:

- ➤ Infrastructure as a Service (IaaS)
- ➤ Platform as a Service (PaaS)
- ➤ Software as a Service (SaaS)

And these cloud service models can be deployed in one of four ways:

- ➤ Private cloud
- ➤ Community cloud
- ➤ Public cloud
- ➤ Hybrid cloud

What we want to focus on first are the cloud attributes and the benefits they can have to your organization. Second, we want to talk through the different ways you can leverage or consume cloud solutions. Lastly we will take a look at where these cloud solutions "live" and ultimately the cost of everything in between you and your cloud solution. In the next few sections we will delve into each of the NIST defined attributes, not only in definition but also in terms of the benefits these attributes can have to your organization. In doing so, you will come to understand the textbook definition of each attribute and how it relates to the potential impact that attribute will have on your business. Ultimately, understanding the potential impact to your business is what matters most, and this is what all business decisions should be based on. Some attributes will impact organizations more than others, and the potential changes that cloud solutions will bring to your organization will be based on what benefits your business feels are most important.

Broad Network Access

NIST defines broad network access as follows:

> *Capabilities are available over the network and accessed through standard mechanisms that promote use by heterogeneous thin or thick client platforms (e.g., mobile phones, tablets, laptops, and workstations).*

This is a fantastic definition, but we want to expand it in the following ways:

- ➤ In order to ensure that access to a cloud solution is perceived as being stable and reliable, broad network access is required *to* the solution.

- ➤ In order to ensure that the solution is capable of enabling the other cloud characteristics, broad network access must be available *within* the solution.

- ➤ In order to properly maintain and administer a cloud solution, broad network access *to* the solution from a service provider's perspective must be available.

The following subsections walk through what potential changes must be made from the perspective of the service consumer and the service provider in order to fully realize the value of broad network access.

Service Consumer

Changes:

- ➤ Increase throughput or bandwidth to service provider's cloud solution.

Benefits:

➤ This will ensure that network access is never the bottleneck to the solution. Additionally, it enables the capability to leverage all the other cloud characteristics.

Service Provider

Changes:

➤ Increase throughput to tenant or service consumers (may just be to the Internet).

➤ Increase throughput within the cloud solutions (read as throughput to switches and routers).

➤ Increase throughput for managing the solution (aside from the backbone, access to the solution from a management perspective must also be robust).

Benefits:

➤ Eliminates network access as the bottleneck in providing the service

➤ Enables all other cloud characteristics within the cloud solutions

➤ Eliminates the bottleneck of ever having to manage the solution in the event of network saturation

As you can see, ensuring that broad network access is available in all aspects of a cloud solution is essential to enabling all the other cloud attributes. Without broad network access (or redundant access to cloud services, for that matter), the service consumer's experience will be limited — and could be the sole reason why consumers may not want to leverage a service any longer.

Resource Pooling

NIST defines resource pooling as follows:

> The provider's computing resources are pooled to serve multiple consumers using a multi-tenant model, with different physical and virtual resources dynamically assigned and reassigned according to consumer demand. There is a sense of location independence in that the customer generally has no control or knowledge over the exact location of the provided resources but may be able to specify location at a higher level of abstraction (e.g., country, state, or datacenter). Examples of resources include storage, processing, memory, and network bandwidth.

This is another great definition provided by NIST. We would, however, like to take a moment to really dig into this characteristic, as it is the subject of much of the controversy regarding cloud environments. Many organizations that must comply with federal, state, or industry regulations around data sovereignty and isolation will not be very comfortable with this characteristic because this characteristic is founded on the principle that many organizations or business units (tenants) will essentially share a common hardware or resource footprint. In and of itself this doesn't sound very troubling; however, when you consider the impact this characteristic has on complying with specific mandates and regulations regarding the location and control of data, you are faced with a few challenges. For example, if a specific industry mandate states that customer or client data must be either stored, journaled, or isolated from another customer's data, you can quickly see how resource pooling begins to lose its benefit.

Needless to say, we have assisted countless organizations with building cloud solutions that are built to comply with the strictest industry, state, and federal regulations; however, be aware that these segregated or isolated resource pools will most likely be much more expensive to operate, stand up, and maintain, and therefore, will be much more cost-intensive to consume, hence losing some of the benefit of leveraging a cloud solution. Some organizations have counteracted this dilemma by building an on-premises cloud solution. This is still somewhat of a workaround because, as stated earlier, the upfront investment and the level of planning required to deploy a private cloud solution can potentially erase the benefits that resource pooling provides.

So what can be done here? It is simple: If you or your organization is comfortable with hosting your data on a cloud solution that, through resource pooling, enables economies of scale (and therefore can provide you with cloud services cost effectively), and there aren't any regulations or mandates that govern the location and isolation of your data, you are free and clear. Consider yourself lucky.

Now, just because you don't have to worry about mandates and regulations, does that mean you should just start migrating to a public cloud solution tomorrow? Absolutely not. You still need to ask the cloud service provider certain questions, including the following:

- ➤ What mechanisms ensure and enforce the separation of information within the cloud environment?
- ➤ How is data backed up and protected?
- ➤ What site resiliency mechanisms are in place for the solution?

In regards to the changes that must be adopted by the service consumer and the service provider, from a service provider's perspective the changes are more *physical*, whereas for a service consumer the changes are more *organizational*:

Service Consumer

Changes:

- ➤ Potentially releasing control of data
- ➤ Allowing a service provider to secure and protect data
- ➤ Potentially allowing data to coexist with other tenant data

Benefits:

- ➤ Decreases in capital expenses and investment needed in hardware

Service Provider

Changes:

➤ Logically and potentially physically separate tenant information and data from one another.

➤ Create resource pools that enable various service levels and enforcement of regulations and mandates.

Benefits:

➤ Enables economies of scale and services that come at a lower cost, savings which are then passed on to service consumers.

The primary and driving force behind organizations not considering moving to public cloud solutions today revolves around security and compliancy concerns. There are methods you can use to alleviate those concerns, however, as well as data classification strategies that may enable your organization to leverage or move a portion of its data to cloud services.

(Rapid) Elasticity

The NIST definition of elasticity states the following:

> *Capabilities can be elastically provisioned and released, in some cases automatically, to scale rapidly outward and inward commensurate with demand. To the consumer, the capabilities available for provisioning often appear to be unlimited and can be appropriated in any quantity at any time.*

However simplistic this concept seems, we assure you it is much more difficult to implement and realize within a solution than you can imagine. We are not saying it is not possible, but it takes a lot more planning and design than most organizations anticipate. Regardless, having the capability to quickly provision and assign resources to an application or workload when the need arises and then release those resources when the need is no longer there is the focal point of this characteristic.

Elasticity is also very tightly intertwined with the characteristic of resource pooling, in part because the idea of growing and shrinking a workload of resources also insinuates that the resources being assigned all come from a single pool of resources (hence elasticity's connection with resource pools). Therefore, several workloads or applications can pull from the same pool of resources when required; but once the resources are no longer needed, they can be released and freed up for another workload or application to use.

From a service consumer's perspective, how does elasticity affect you? Well, as always, the answer is, "It depends." In this case, it depends on the type of cloud service model your organizations will use. The following summarizes the responsibility of elasticity based on the three cloud service models:

Elasticity in IaaS

Service Consumer

➤ Instructs the cloud environment to grow or reduce the number of virtual machines needed to host a workload.

➤ Responsible for monitoring resource utilization of the virtual machines as well as installing or expanding workloads or applications onto virtual machines.

➤ Also responsible for releasing the resources back into the resource pools after they are no longer required.

Service Provider

➤ Enables the service consumer (in an automated fashion) to grow and reduce the number of virtual machines consumed by the tenants (typically provided through some form of portal).

Elasticity in PaaS

Service Consumer

➤ Must inform the service provider or build\leverage a mechanism that triggers the increased resource assignment to the platform.

Service Provider

➤ Responsible to accept or receive requests from the service consumer to assign additional resources to the platform.

➤ Also responsible for managing the platform and adding additional resources as required.

Elasticity in SaaS

Service Consumer

➤ Makes request to the service provider for the increased utilization of applications and workloads or even specific items with workloads.

Service Provider

➤ Responsible for all aspects of adding and removing resources at the IaaS, PaaS, and SaaS layers.

➤ Ensures that adding resources to the three cloud layers is done with governance, risk, and compliance in mind.

Ultimately, you can see more and more functions shift to service providers the higher in the cloud service layers you go (that is, the more you move from IaaS and PaaS to SaaS). Therefore, it is easy to understand that organizations who do not wish to invest in internal IT departments or operations should look to SaaS models to provide the capabilities they are looking for in their business. It should be noted, however, that as consumers go higher in the cloud service layer, the service provider tends to be more rigid and offer fewer features.

Elasticity in Your Organization

With all of this talk about responsibilities and functions, you should also consider what shift in your organization's service consumers and service providers must make in order to provide elasticity in the cloud service model you choose. As you can guess, some system or mechanism must be put into place in order to properly gauge the resource utilization of the services being provided to the end user or consumer. The following breaks down the potential shift in activities related to elasticity that organizations may have to make.

Service Consumer

Changes:

➤ Implement a system that monitors the consumption of workload or application utilization.

➤ Implement a system that processes requests for resources, either dynamically or manually.

Benefits:

➤ Although at some layers service providers typically are responsible for implementing such systems on behalf of service consumers, service consumers should also try to implement a system for themselves that they can govern and use to validate the service-level agreements agreed upon with the service provider. Such systems will ensure that only the resources required are being consumed and therefore the service consumer is being charged only for the resources required to provide the services needed.

Service Provider

Changes:

➤ Build a system that enables the service consumer to request or release resources if required.

➤ Build a system that can dynamically grow and shrink workloads based on resource utilization thresholds.

Benefits:

➤ Depending on the service offered to consumers, service providers can automate much of the provisioning and de-provisioning of resources, thereby reducing the operational overhead associated with administering and managing dynamically changing workloads.

As you can see, for each cloud service model both the service consumer and the service provider have their fair share of responsibilities. IaaS provides the least amount of automation in terms of elasticity, in that the service consumer must trigger the increase in virtual machines needed, whereas in SaaS, the service provider is responsible for everything from patching and maintaining the service to growing or shrinking the application footprint based on the needs and requests of the service consumer.

Chargeback (Measured Service)

NIST's definition of chargeback includes the following:

> *Cloud systems automatically control and optimize resource use by leveraging a metering capability at some level of abstraction appropriate to the type of service (e.g., storage, processing, bandwidth, and active user accounts). Resource usage can be monitored, controlled, and reported, providing transparency for both the provider and consumer of the utilized service.*

Chargeback, or measured service, is probably one of the least thought about NIST cloud characteristics (after broad network access, of course). That's because many organizations (big and small) find it very challenging to consider their IT department as anything more than an arm of the organization that enables certain technical capabilities (messaging, collaboration, etc.). Within the cloud space, however, IT departments can become a profit-generating component of a business. To do this, they must make the transition from service manager to service provider. Over and over again we have seen organizations underestimate how much effort this will actually require.

"How does this all relate back to chargeback?" you may ask. Well, chargeback is the ability to "charge" (or at the very least show) to service consumers the amount of service or resource that they are consuming. In order to get to a point where organizations can explicitly charge for a service, they must also create what is called a *service description*. A service description contains all the details and parameters governing the relationship between a service provider and a service consumer. It must contain the type of service that is being provided; the service-level agreements associated with the service (level of uptime and so on); as well as the pricing guidelines for the offering. The latter, of course, must be created with a solid understanding of what the cost of providing the service will be to the service provider with the right level of margins inserted to make selling the service profitable to the business.

What does this all translate to from the perspective of the service consumer? Know what you are paying for and understand the relationship or binding agreement you are entering into with regard to the service provider. When transitioning to a cloud-based SaaS solution, many service consumers assume that they will receive the same level of functionality from a similar on-premise solution, but nine times out of ten that is not the case. In order to make selling the solution profitable and keep operational costs down, service providers must create offerings that can be built as *scale units*. These scale units are often standardized and often very rigid (not allowing for much customization) so that the operational overhead of managing a cloud environment is kept to a minimum. This is how large service providers attain what is known as *economies of scale*, which can be defined as reducing cost per unit by increasing production of units. Essentially, the more of the same unit you can build and deploy, the less the cost of producing the unit becomes over time. In order to achieve this, however, the unit must be standardized, and customization has to be rare or offered at a much higher rate.

This affects the service consumer because the consumer must be cognizant of the tradeoffs they will be making by moving to this new cloud service offering. The financials, however, do lean in favor of the SaaS solution due to the reduction of maintaining and operating similar on-premises solutions for organizations. Additionally, most organizations don't have the contract vehicles in place to leverage an "outside resource" in delivering IT services. The following describes the typical changes a service consumer and service provider must make in order to move to a successful cloud service offering.

Service Consumer

Changes:

➤   Set up a contract vehicle that enables the business to pay for IT services provided by an external organization.

Benefits:

➤   Removes the cost of maintaining and operating on-premise solutions, and shifting off-premises can greatly reduce the IT budget of an organization.

Service Provider

Changes:

➤   Build a service description for the solution that is being offered to its consumers.

Benefits:

➤   Contains the parameters of the solution being offered to consumers and serves as a binding agreement governing the relationship of the service consumer and service provider

For service consumers, chargeback (or show back) also has a very interesting ancillary benefit. In a traditional IT environment, resources are typically provisioned at every request made by business units. However, when chargeback is implemented, business units become much more conscious around the resources that they are consuming. This practice incents the responsible use of resources and keeps business units from requesting unnecessary resources. More importantly, it also incents them to always ask themselves, "Do we really need the systems\resources provisioned to us?" and "Can we reduce the number of resources we are consuming?"

Self-Service

NIST's definition of self-service includes the following:

> *A consumer can unilaterally provision computing capabilities, such as server time and network storage, as needed automatically without requiring human interaction with each service provider.*

The notion of self-service is a very powerful enabler for service consumers and service providers alike. It gives service consumers the capability to provision and de-provision resources based on the needs of their organization. This very simple capability also gives service consumers something that they would not otherwise have prior to the cloud service model: choice. Of course, every organization can choose from the various means of provisioning resources; but in a cloud service model, the choice can be made with little or no interaction with the service provider. Herein lies the benefit to service providers. Service providers simply set up the parameters that service consumers can choose, and within those boundaries or guidelines, service consumers can provision and de-provision systems and resources as required.

This, however, can only be set up after a service description is agreed upon and the business and IT process automated, orchestrated, and aligned. This in itself is not an easy endeavor. The organizations or IT departments that interact with a "self-service" portal must be granted the authority by the business to bring up or take down the resources necessary to fulfill the business' needs. From a service consumer perspective (and the service model being consumed), the persona or part of the organization that will interact with this self-service portal will vary. For example, in an IaaS model, an organization's IT department is likely the department that provisions and de-provisions virtual machines or systems so that applications and workloads can be installed on them. In a SaaS model, however, a business' help desk staff might be given the authority to provision mailboxes on behalf of end users which after they are configured and properly provisioned can be handed over to the actual service consumer.

This kind of self-service represents a major shift in the way an organization's IT department interact with a cloud system, and everything hinges on the service consumer's experience and expectations in regards to leveraging a cloud service model. The following outlines some of these expected changes on the part of both the service consumer and service provider. Because the type of cloud model being leveraged directly impacts the service consumer's experience, all three models are represented.

Self-Service in IaaS

Service Consumer

➤ Build or designate a persona that will manage the provisioning and de-provisioning of virtual machines.

Service Provider

➤ Build a set of virtual machine templates that may or not be modifiable during the time of provisioning (add/remove CPUs, memory, storage, and network).

Self-Service in PaaS

Service Consumer

➤ Inform the service provider when additional resources are needed, or build\leverage a mechanism that can trigger the increased resource assignment to the platform.

Service Provider

➤ Responsible for accepting, or receiving, requests from the service consumer to assign additional resources to the platform

➤ Responsible for managing the platform and adding additional resources as required

Self-Service in SaaS

Service Consumer

➤ Makes a request to the service provider for the increased utilization of applications and workloads or even specific items with workloads

Service Provider

➤ Responsible for all aspects of adding and removing resources at the IaaS, PaaS, and SaaS layers

➤ Ensures that adding resources to the three cloud layers is done with governance, risk, and compliance in mind

PRIVATE CLOUDS

Whereas the cloud models described in the previous sections are public clouds made available to the general public, the private cloud infrastructure is *operated solely for an organization*. It may be managed by the organization or a third party, and it may exist on or off the premises, but in most cases it is built off the base of virtualized infrastructures. Both are composed of a collection of x86 servers topped with either a grid engine or a virtual infrastructure based on hypervisors. So, what is a private cloud? A private cloud is a dynamically provisioned and optimized infrastructure with self-service developer deployment, hosted within the safe confines of your own datacenter. The following sections describe the key aspects of private clouds.

Developers Deploy to the Private Cloud via a Self-Service Portal

Long time to market (TTM) schedules have traditionally created tension between application development and IT ops, which created the market opportunity for cloud computing platforms.

Ease of deployment has been a big part of this; cloud platforms appeal to organizations because they provide fast, easy controls and configuration options that quickly deploy apps. For example, a cloud-savvy developer can stand up a SharePoint farm on Windows Azure IaaS in under 20 minutes. Your server administrators would probably never be able to match this time to market, but in the private cloud no server admin is involved — that's the difference.

The Private Cloud Has an Automated Workload Distribution Engine

To realize the value of the private cloud, not only do developers need autonomy, but your system administrators need to be free of extra work, such as determining the best placement of new workloads and optimizing the virtual pool to make room for more applications. This is where an automated workload distribution system comes in. Grids have them, and similar tools are available for your virtual infrastructure, such as Microsoft System Center Virtual Machine Manager, Puppet, and Chef. These tools manage the pool of resources dedicated to the cloud by following high-level policies or guidelines set by IT ops. The less IT ops has to be involved in managing the cloud, the more cost-effective it becomes.

Private Clouds Are Multitenant Resource Pools and Metered as Such

The economic value of the private cloud rises with its use, which normally means inviting as many applications as possible. That means sharing the cloud among business units, divisions, and other groups that may not currently share other resources. To account for the use of the virtual pool, internal cloud infrastructures usually provide a method of metering and tracking resource use that feeds chargeback or direct billing for the resources consumed. Although you may not choose to bill back to the business units or to do so with fine-grained resource tracking, as is typical on public clouds, this mechanism helps justify investment in the private cloud and its future expansion.

Private Clouds Can Enforce Internal Standards and Policies

Another way in which private clouds can differ from public clouds is that they can be tailored to follow your organization's internal standards and procedures. For example, your application and program management leaders may want applications built only using your standard applications or application infrastructure layers or only from preapproved VM images — and even then they still may want to approve the final applications before they are deployed.

Private Clouds Are Highly Customizable

When constructing any cloud for your organization, the first thing to keep in mind is that not every organization needs or wants all aspects of what is possible. Again, you need to first understand your business and let those drivers play the proper role in determining the necessary architecture. Once that is accomplished, you should have a good list of what specific cloud characteristics will bring about those business benefits. You might even go so far as to have a weighted list to help you prioritize the financial and people investments that you put toward constructing your private cloud.

Microsoft offers a free tool to help you do this. The tool has gained significant praise and attention in the industry and rightly so. Significant investments have been made into this tool both financially and by bringing real customer experiences to the process. Called the Cloud Analysis Tool (Figure 1-3), it is part of the Infrastructure Optimization Assessment. The Infrastructure Optimization process has been continually developed and matured for many years. One advantage the Cloud Analysis Tool has is that literally hundreds of customers have already used it and provided valuable feedback about what cloud capabilities organizations require to assist them in achieving their business goals and objectives. In addition, many architects and engineers have invested their time into the Cloud Analysis portion, which helps you focus on the cloud characteristics that matter to you. We highly suggest you take a moment to view the introductory video for the Cloud Analysis Tool and take a moment to try it out for yourself at http://www.microsoft.com/optimization/tools/overview.mspx.

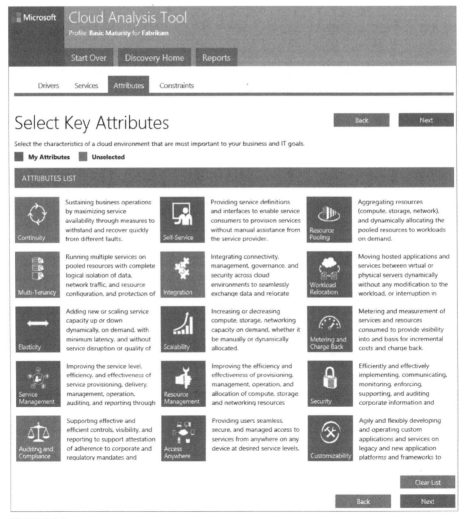

FIGURE 1-3

HYBRID CLOUD

Now, that you know what public and private clouds are, it is time to get back from the clouds into the reality of the world we live in and ask ourselves, "Is it possible — balancing the obvious benefits of getting scale and cost savings that the public cloud offers with the complexities related to security, privacy, and legacy hardware and software platforms some applications still run — to forecast that many, if not all, enterprise organizations would endorse either public or private cloud for their businesses?" It should be a no-brainer that the answer is "No." Instead, given the desire to tap the cloud for its enormous scale and low cost, coupled with concerns over availability and security, it shouldn't be a surprise that many organizations are looking to split the difference with a hybrid architecture. As such, we believe it is time to define what a hybrid cloud is.

> **NOTE** *A hybrid cloud is an integrated approach, combining the power of both public and private clouds. Customized rules and policies govern areas such as security and the underlying infrastructure. In this scenario, activities and tasks are allocated to internal or external clouds as required.*

Hybrid clouds represent the best way to maintain control over data environments while gaining the flexibility and operational efficiency of a dynamic data infrastructure. Building them, however, is not an easy task, particularly if the underlying internal physical and virtual infrastructure is not ready. Later in this book, we will describe some best practices and recommendations for planning a hybrid cloud, and what things to consider before deciding on the hybrid cloud architecture for your business.

One way to best position what your hybrid cloud will consist of would be to take on the following capability-based view: "Hybrid clouds are a mixture of capabilities enabled through both public and private resources." Simply put if you are leveraging a private cloud solution to enable self-service, resource pools, and broad network access and are leveraging a public cloud to enable chargeback and elasticity, as long as the cumulative solution consists of the essential characteristics mentioned by NIST you have a cloud solution. And because the solution is enabled through public and private cloud resources it is considered a hybrid cloud.

The following sections explain why/when you would want to enable certain cloud attributes through public cloud solutions and why/when you would want to keep certain attributes located on the premises (or enabled through a private cloud).

Hybrid Cloud Scenarios

For many various reasons, CIOs are increasingly looking to hybrid clouds in order to find a solution that blends the benefits of private clouds with public clouds. The ways in which this is achieved are myriad, but the following sections describe four major scenarios.

Sharing Workloads across Clouds (Cloud Bursting)

By way of analogy, think of this scenario as if you needed an extra battery for your phone when you are out of charge and didn't have time to plug the phone back in to charge. You need an extra battery to take over at that point. Similarly, consider the unexpected or unplanned peaks in demand for your business, as illustrated in Figure 1-4.

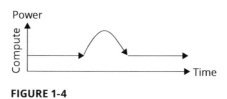

FIGURE 1-4

Sudden spikes could impact performance and cause outages in your business operations, and you can't always provision for extreme cases.

Another spike might be caused when you do know about forthcoming demand, an example could be businesses that provide services with micro seasonality trends. Think of the online flower shops around Valentine's Day or Christmas.

In addition, some businesses may experience peaks due to periodic increased demand, as shown in Figure 1-5.

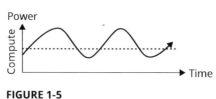

FIGURE 1-5

One example that comes to mind is Microsoft's case study on the Windows Azure customer solution for the RiskMetrics Group.

NOTE *You can find this case study at:*

```
http://www.slideshare.net/msitpro/microsoft-windows-
azure-risk-metrics-enhances-capabilities-with-dynamic-
computing-case-study
```

In this study, RiskMetrics Group, in order to deliver risk management services to its customers and to meet increasing market demand for risk analysis, needed to accommodate increasing peak loads on its computing infrastructure for a specific period of time. The company therefore used Microsoft's hybrid cloud solution, based on Windows Azure and the company's on-premises infrastructure, to support bursts in computing activity as required.

Running Sensitive or Data-Intensive Workloads on Private Clouds and Other Workloads on Public Clouds

Some companies prefer to have their mission critical business applications deployed within their own highly virtualized datacenters and keep both the critical-to-the-application sensitive data and the front-end content management system on the premises. However, this model often requires up-front capital expenditures (Capex) investments and therefore might prove to be very costly — especially for those who seek economically affordable on-going operating expenditures (Opex) that are offered by pay-as-you-go cloud service providers.

Therefore, those companies chose to leave on the premises only data-sensitive data and workloads while the front-end content management applications are often migrated to the public cloud. Of course, some complexity and technical restrictions may apply. For example, sensitive data must be encrypted both at rest and in transfer, and it could be decrypted either in memory for processing in the cloud fabric or always brought back on-premises for computation workloads.

Using One Cloud as a Backup for the Other

This type of hybrid cloud workload can be effective in both scenarios. That is, when the public cloud is used as a backup and the private cloud is used as a master, it provides protection for hot or cold failover disaster recovery (DR) and/or enables data archiving workloads. Similarly, when the private cloud is used as a backup and the public cloud is a master, it builds a good business case for those who believe that even public clouds can't avoid disruptions.

Develop on a Public Cloud; Deploy on a Private Cloud

It is no secret that many development testing (dev/test) efforts are poorly served by existing infrastructure operations. If you think about it for a minute, that makes perfect sense for the following reasons:

➤ **Dev/test is underfunded with respect to hardware.** Operations get budget priority. Companies naturally devote the highest percentage of their IT budget to keeping vital applications up and running. Unfortunately, that means dev/test is usually underfunded and cannot get enough equipment to do its job.

➤ **Infrastructure objectives differ.** Dev/test wants to be agile, while operations want to be deliberate. When developers want to get going, they want to get going *now*. Operations, however (if it's well-managed), has very deliberate, documented, and tracked processes in place to ensure that nothing changes too fast and that anything that does change can be audited.

➤ **Infrastructure use patterns differ.** Dev/test use is spiky, while operations seek smooth utilization to increase hardware use efficiency. A developer will write code, test it out, and then tear it down while doing design reviews, whiteboard discussions, and so on. By its very nature, development entails a spiky use of resources. Operations, of course, are charged with efficiency, with an aim of lowest total cost of operations.

➤ **Operations don't want dev/test to affect production systems.** Putting development and test into the production infrastructure, even if quarantined via VLANs, can potentially affect production app throughput, anathema to operations groups. Consequently, dev/test groups are often hindered in their attempts to access a production-like environment.

➤ **Dev/test scalability and load testing affect production systems.** If putting dev/test in a production environment can potentially affect production apps, what about when dev/test wants to see how well the app under development responds to load testing or variable demand? Not having access to a production environment means that some of the most necessary development tasks — assessing how well an application holds up under pressure — are difficult or impossible to assess in many environments. Many of the most important bugs surface only under high system load; if they aren't found during development, then they will surface in production. Moreover, in constrained environments it's difficult to reproduce a production environment topology, which means it's hard to assess, prior to going into production, the impact of network latency, storage throughput, and so on.

We want to emphasize that these issues are not the result of personal antagonism or contrary people; they reflect the fact that, in most organizations, two groups with conflicting objectives are asked to share a common resource. Naturally, it is hard to mutually satisfy both parties; more important, given the very reasonable prioritization of production app availability, dev/test is frequently starved of the resources it needs to do its job effectively. Of course, the challenges are not limited to the interaction between operations and the development group as a whole. There are even challenges within the development organizations — specifically, between development (one might call it software engineering) and QA.

One frequently used solution to these issues is virtualization. For sure, virtualization ameliorates many of the intra-development issues. Because a single server can support multiple virtual machines, a complex application topology can be mirrored with much less physical hardware. In addition, of course, the portability and "cloneability" of virtual machines means that apps can be handed off to QA without requiring component installation from scratch.

However, virtualization does nothing, absent sufficient hardware availability in a production environment, to address the ability to evaluate scalability and load stress testing. Furthermore, putting virtual machines into a production environment presents the same issues just outlined regarding a very natural reluctance to affect production applications negatively.

The hybrid cloud can help for several reasons:

➤ **No contention for resources** — Development and QA can each get as much computing resource as needed. This means they no longer have to contend for a limited pool of boxes.

➤ **Agile development and spiky usage is supported** — One can use just what is needed at one point in time, and then release the resources with no further commitment.

➤ **QA can be more productive** — Because cloud computing environments are typically based on virtualization, it is easy to clone virtual machines and re-create an application. Development can hand over a virtual machine (or indeed a collection of virtual machines) that have been cloned, which QA can begin testing. This obviates the issue noted earlier, whereby a component residing on a development machine is overlooked in the install instructions, which results in causing the application to fail to run. Of course, when it is time to put the app into production, should the application target environment be the public cloud, the same clone/handover process can be reproduced between QA and production.

➤ **Scale and load can easily be tested** — Infinite resources means that setting up a stress test is easy. One company that we helped to build and launch a very large website used by millions of users needed to test its web application under circumstances when a large number of users (approximately 40,000 concurrent connections) simultaneously initiated contact with the system. This is the kind of test that drives a development organization crazy, as obtaining enough hardware resources to host the user sessions is extremely difficult. Then, when the test is over a few days later, there's a big teardown effort as well. Instead, we fired up a large number of Windows Azure VM instances, ran them for a few days, and then shut them down. Total cost? Around $100 — versus ten thousands of dollars they would have to pay to typical load-testing companies such as Gomez.

➤ **Dev/test avoids the common concerns about public cloud** — Most of the previously cited issues regarding the public cloud don't apply to dev/test use. Application use of the cloud is ephemeral, the data is not production information, and the application is sandboxed in a cloud. Therefore, security and availability level issues are not impediments to use to support dev/test.

This should give you a perspective on why dev/test is a good initial application for the cloud.

Motivation and Issues behind Hybrid Cloud

Integrating both public and private clouds into an amalgam of resources that can be deployed and configured to specifications has a tremendous appeal. However, the complexities involved and the capabilities that are available today, as opposed to those that are somewhere between the conceptual stage and the drawing board, should give many organizations pause — at least for the moment.

Earlier, we mentioned that some companies have a variety of business applications deployed in their own data center, remember? Let's suppose, at the last business strategy meeting of Company X, along with the strategy goals of reducing the time to market and minimizing the capital expenditures while making more for less — sound familiar? — the CIO demanded that his business and IT organizations modernize the IT by moving its business critical applications to the cloud.

Which cloud? Public or private? The public cloud's cost efficiency and elasticity of scale definitely appeal to the CIO, but the sensitivity of the data, which may contain some personally identifiable information (PII) and therefore cannot leave the premises, presented a serious obstacle in the path of IT modernization.

Early on, our risk-averse CIO got comforting words from a private cloud vendor that all the company's sensitive data wouldn't be hosted in a public cloud and that Company X could get all the benefits of cloud computing by building its own private clouds — because, he was told, datacenters, among other things, deliver perfect uptime and are impervious to security breaches. Or are they?

Could the private cloud have been the right solution for Company X? Consider that for a moment. Today, most organizations run highly virtualized datacenters. While this technology has been a great enabler of standardization and in some cases has yielded savings, this is by far *not* the case for most organizations when you dig a bit deeper (see Figure 1-6).

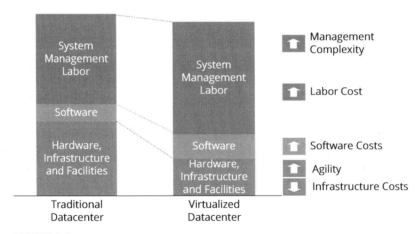

FIGURE 1-6

The promise of virtualization was that through savings on physical hardware great savings and rapid ROIs would be realized. Unfortunately, cost has been driven up in many areas. On the hardware side, many organizations chose to invest in very expensive servers and expand their SAN capacity. Whereas before they had only I/O-intensive and very critical workloads on a SAN, because of virtualization all workloads suddenly consumed expensive SAN storage. In addition, software costs increased because a new technology, along with licenses, was introduced. Even though many physical servers were removed, administrative overhead still increased because a new technology was introduced that needed to be managed. Finally, all the virtualized workloads still needed to be patched and secured, and because deployment is easier in a virtual environment there were more servers than ever. Many of the benefits of cloud computing go out the window the minute a CIO runs a cloud behind their firewall.

So, what does this leave our CIO with? Hybrid cloud. Based on our analysis, we strongly feel that private clouds don't actually make a lot of sense unless they have a hybrid capability. Yes, there are and will always be some specific private clouds that are private and only private — government agencies, for example. (However, even government agencies begin realizing cloud benefits via so called government clouds — community clouds built and dedicated specifically to government agencies.) In addition larger public cloud providers are arguably better positioned to invest in uptime and security than isolated enterprises.

SUMMARY

We've now reached the end of Chapter 1, and our hope is that you have a much clearer understanding and view of the different cloud service models, trends, and capabilities that compose a cloud solution. This is definitely a lot to take in, so make sure to come back to the chapter when you need a reference or refresher on a specific area. Trust us, you will find yourself doing this fairly often — we still do ourselves! As you progress further in this book be sure to highlight, note, and bookmark the specific references called out and find the scenarios that match your organization the closest. We have found that organizations that learn from others and take modest steps in their journey to the cloud tend to have higher chances of success. As you do begin your journey, you may find yourself faced with a scenario that you may have thought was not relevant to you or your businesses at first, but now that you have started your initiative, you recall stories that seem to match what your organization is facing (gaining executive sponsorship, instituting organizational change, or justifying the initial investment of the first cloud solution, for example).

In any event, we hope you will find that once you finish reading this book you will come back to it fairly often to either re-read or reference portions of it. We hope that we laid the book out in a fashion that will make this easier to do. In Chapter 2 we will take our next step in specifically defining and understanding why you would want to move to a hybrid cloud solution. That chapter covers the foundational reasons why you would make that choice.

2 Why Is the Hybrid Cloud Important to My Business?

Originally, the content for this chapter was part of Chapter 1, but after some long discussion, we decided the topic merited its own chapter. After some long discussion we decided that it required its own section. Delving into this topic will have a deep and lasting impact on the justification of moving to a hybrid cloud solution. Although there are myriad reasons to begin an organization's journey toward leveraging hybrid cloud solutions, it is best practice to specifically pinpoint the reasons that will justify the initial investment, operational costs, or transitional changes that are often necessary when migrating or leveraging these solutions. In doing so, your business will have a well laid out plan in expanding your service addressable market, lowering operational costs, or simply becoming more agile in your day-to-day operations. In any case, here are a few reasons that *do not* justify moving to a hybrid cloud solution:

- ➤ Because everyone else is doing it
- ➤ To cut costs for the short term
- ➤ To outsourcing data security responsibilities

So before we delve into reasons why your organization should move to a cloud solution, we want to look at these reasons that *do not* justify that course of action.

THE VALUE OF GAINING EXECUTIVE SPONSORSHIP

Near the end of 2010 we were working with a large government organization that was looking to implement an enterprise security and auditing solution that could collect, parse, and analyze event log information, which would then be used to show that the organization was compliant with a federal compliance regulation (NIST 800-53). We started the project by jumping directly to soliciting the technical requirements of the solution. Everyone on the team "knew" what the intent of the project was. However, it was never documented nor was the purpose of the project relayed to senior business decision makers. After about three months of effort (we reached the build phase of the project), word was sent that funding for the project was being cut. After inquiring as to the reasoning behind the decision, we found that budget cuts were forcing the organization to prioritize the portfolio of projects that were currently underway and that this specific project did not meet the requirements for continued funding.

It was an interesting predicament to be in because canceling the project put the organization in a place where it was no longer compliant with a number of security and compliance regulations. Instead, funding continued for projects that did not have a real business impact for the organization (for example, deploying a new systems management solution when one already existed). The difference between the two projects was that one had executive sponsorship and the other did not. The event log auditing project we were working on was born out of an IT initiative that was commonly a priority for the organization, and therefore, we did not look to gain executive sponsorship at the beginning of the project. Everyone assumed it was the right thing to do. In other words, when budget cuts needed to be made, the event log auditing solution got the axe because the business justification was not performed and relayed to the CxO level and the business decision makers who could save the project.

Although it may seem trivial and unnecessary, always try to gain some form of executive sponsorship for transformational-type projects because when hard decisions need to be made, those that lack business justification are commonly the first ones to go. It would have taken us around a week or so of additional work to put together a business case for the project, and it might have saved it.

EVERYONE ELSE IS DOING IT

When we were young our parents would always say, "If everyone jumped off a cliff, would you?" Although that line never seemed to work on us because jumping off a cliff sounds fairly exciting, they were right in making this very simple point: What is right for others isn't necessarily right for you. Before embarking on a new project, we like to perform an exercise using what is called a *Benefits Dependency Network*. It is a tool used by Enterprise Architects to first understand an organization's mission and business objectives and then relate projects and initiatives to those objectives (whether IT-related or not). What we have seen over the course of the last decade is that most (if not all) business initiatives are somehow joined or related to IT initiatives.

NOTE *You can read more about a Benefits Dependency Network at* `http://www.som .cranfield.ac.uk/som/dinamic-content/research/documents/peppardwarddaniel07 .pdf.`

For example, a business objective such as "growing the marketing presence within a new region" eventually translates into an advertising campaign that will be carried out over the Internet. How does this business objective tie to an IT initiative? Well, follow the dependencies to see.

➤   First, the marketing campaign must be created.

➤   A resource in the marketing department may want to create a new team site and invite the resources that will be working on this campaign.

➤   That marketing resource can request a new site through a portal, and the workspace can dynamically be generated based on the type of initiative.

➤   The members of the initiative can be dynamically granted access to the site based on the marketing resource identifying the member user credentials during the creation of this site.

➤   After the marketing campaign has been created, it must be sent to a publisher that will make final edits and polish the collateral, or media, for end-user consumption. The collateral must be shared with the publisher, even though the publisher is external to the organization. They can be granted access temporarily to the internal marketing campaign workspace.

We are going to stop here, but this process or workflow can go down a few more levels. Analyze for a moment all the IT systems and capabilities that would have to be in place to make this scenario possible:

➤   Dynamic workspace creation portal

➤   External access capabilities

➤   Application of rights and security based on sensitivity of marketing collateral

➤   Document rights management

Each of these technical systems and capabilities then translates to either a feature within a product or a solution. Will a cloud solution enable this scenario? Possibly, however by performing this exercise, you now have clear traceability of the benefits that will be realized by implementing or leveraging the technical solutions. Always, always, always understand the business benefit of implementing a technical solution and how it directly impacts your organization. Only through this exercise can an organization understand the value and return it will receive on its investment. Most important, such understanding can help continue the funding of IT projects when difficult decisions need to be made in terms of prioritizing certain initiatives and dropping others. We will walk you through the process of building your own Benefits Dependency Network in Chapter 3 of this book.

CUTTING COSTS FOR THE SHORT TERM

As with most initiatives, it is often necessary to make an up-front investment to receive some form of return over a given period of time (ROI). Making a move toward adopting cloud solutions is no different. One common misconception, however, is that the return on this investment will come overnight or almost immediately. It is true that farming out certain IT functionalities to service providers will reap benefits in terms of costs; however, it may take a much longer time to realize despite what many service providers would like you to believe.

It is true that organizations might see an immediate decrease in operational or licensing costs by moving, for example, to a Software-as-a-Service (SaaS) messaging solution. What most organizations will see an increase in, what is often not mentioned by many service providers, is an increase in the operational investment that organizations must make to ensure that the migration or adoption of this cloud solution is either seamless or causes the least amount of disruption to the business.

Actual migration costs of data are another factor that can add to the expense of migrating to cloud solutions. Migrating to a cloud solution should be a long-term strategy and investment. This long-term planning will fundamentally change the way your organization relies on technology, and failing to account for these transitional changes and costs can often catch many organizations by surprise, erasing whatever financial benefit adopting a cloud solution was supposed to provide. If the strategy does account for these transitional costs, and the organization understands that the financial benefits will be realized in the second, third, or fourth year (and beyond), then economical decisions can be made today that account for expected savings in the short term as well the long term.

The one caveat here, however, is if your organization is adopting a new service or application and there is no need to "migrate" users, data, or applications to a cloud platform. Then you can perform a cost analysis of provisioning a similar service on-premise (within your datacenter) in comparison to standing it up in the cloud with a service provider. The points to look at include the cost of hardware required, licensing, and operational staff (and so on) that will not be required because the service is delivered through a service provider. The total cost of ownership (TCO) in the cloud solution should include what is consumed through operational expenses only (in some cases, however, certain cloud solutions may require a small physical footprint within your datacenter to consume). When understanding the TCO of a solution, try to understand and account for all direct and indirect costs of consuming the solution.

INDIRECT COSTS OF MIGRATING TO THE CLOUD

In 2011 an organization we were working with decided to make that big leap into Office 365 (Microsoft's SaaS messaging, communication, and collaboration solution) from an enterprise perspective. It was an unprecedented event and would touch every dimension of this organization (people, processes, and technology). One of the main drivers for this initiative was the benefit in regards to reduced operational and capital expenses. Operational expenses would be reduced due to less need for Microsoft Exchange experts on staff to support the on-premises Exchange environment. Capital expenses would be reduced due to decommissioning the on-premises Exchange environment, which at the time consisted of hundreds of physical servers.

In order to undergo the transition, the organization would need to begin initiatives to clean and prep its messaging environment for the migration. This by itself proved to be very involved and costly. The cost was so high, in fact, that it pushed the organization to cut funding for other projects, including vendor support, to make the initiative fit within the fiscal year's budget. Even though the Office 365 initiative was sold as a cost-cutting measure, it actually ended up costing the organization much more in migrating to the solution than initially anticipated. As we already stated, when you are putting together a risk adjusted cash flow statement that analyzes the acquisition costs of the solution and is coupled with the costs of operating and migrating the environment, you should take into account the financial benefits and "cost avoidance" of capital and operational expenses. For example, for this government organization to fully realize the financial benefit of Office365 they would have to realistically look to the fourth or fifth year of consuming the service. However, that doesn't mean there isn't strategic value to moving to Office365; that is why we cover in depth non-financial benefits as a key factor in moving to a hybrid cloud.

OUTSOURCING DATA SECURITY RESPONSIBILITIES

"We just don't want to deal with the headache of managing the security of our data anymore."

We can't tell you how many times we have heard that before. Some service providers claim that you can offload or move your data into their datacenters and they will manage and maintain your information in a secure and reliable manner, thereby alleviating your organization's need to "worry about such things." The fact of the matter is that even if a service provider is managing and hosting your data and information, the ultimate responsibility for that data still belongs to your organization. Your business should still make efforts to classify, sanitize, and ensure the security of your information regardless of its location (either on-premises or off-premises), bearing in mind that your organization's data and information is ultimately the responsibility of your organization. There is no overcoming this simple truth, so embrace it.

We have worked in the government and public sector for the bulk of our careers (Adam and Jamal almost exclusively), and if there is one thing that we have both learned it's that every organization looks for a tool or a new technology that will solve its security and data protection concerns. In fact, many vendors and organizations would like you to believe that their products, technologies, and solutions are all you and your organization need to keep your data secure — and prevent the bad guys from accessing it. We wish it were that easy. The truth of the matter is that, in terms of security, what is much more beneficial to an organization is due diligence and validation. What we mean by this is that the most secure organizations don't always have the shiniest new technology or solution, but they are often the most disciplined when it comes to processes and procedures. What is the reason for this you may ask? Well, for starters, a technology or technical solution can never ensure that the people in your organization are not trying to either bypass it or find some other alternative to achieving what they wish. Such solutions are effective only when they are being used.

For example, your organization may have put in place a ticketing system or *configuration management database* (CMDB) that tracks that the appropriate security and vulnerability testing is performed on a technical solution before it is deployed to your organization's network. That doesn't mean that someone will try to find a way to bypass this system. In fact "personal favors" are performed even in the largest organizations every day, or special concessions are made to bypass these security scans because of a zero-day vulnerability and a patch must be released immediately. Name a process and someone will always find a way around it. The most successful migrations to cloud solutions typically involve a security "custodian" or manager who can track, validate, and continuously monitor the security of data located within a service provider's datacenter. Having someone perform this function helps establish a regular process within your IT organization and builds a regular procedure to ensure that data is stored, accessed, and maintained in a manner that is consistent with the security requirements for your business.

ALL SECURITY PROCESSES ARE NOT CREATED EQUAL

While working for one government organization, we were helping deploy a systems management solution that was to be used enterprise-wide. We were almost a year into the project and just getting through the stabilize phase, in which the solution was being assessed for any security vulnerabilities (right before we would be looking to deploy the solution). The project had taken almost a year to complete because during the test phase of the initiative a separate agency within the organization was responsible for ensuring that the solution was fit for the enterprise. We would often travel to visit this group to see if we could assist with issues that came up during the testing phase.

One evening we learned that another systems management solution had to be deployed because of a federal mandate. It was "all hands on deck" until the solution was deployed. In order to speed up the deployment, this other systems management solution was given a waiver to bypass testing and go straight to production. Needless to say, a number of issues hindered the deployment; and ultimately, operating this solution costs the organization countless man hours, late nights, and emergency calls with the vendor.

After it was all said and done, the organization had to manage two systems management solutions, one of which continuously caused downtime and unplanned outages. This case was one of the last times a system or solution would be deployed without having to pass through the proper gates before deployment. It may take more effort and cycles to pass a solution into production; however, take the advice that many carpenters and architects use in similar scenarios: "Measure twice, cut once."

A CASE FOR HYBRID CLOUD

Now that we have talked about a few reasons you might choose *not* to move to a hybrid cloud solution, we want to take some time to talk through why it *is* a good reason to move to a hybrid cloud solution. As you likely noticed, we put a large emphasis on ensuring that the reasoning to move to a cloud solution is based on specific business benefits. We continuously try to hammer this message home because ultimately there will be some need for some business changes to occur in order for a hybrid cloud solution to be adopted successfully. During our time in working with businesses worldwide we have found the following business-led justifications for moving to a hybrid cloud environment:

➤ Differentiating yourself from the competition

➤ Enhancing strategic position (reducing nonperforming assets)

➤ Easing mergers and acquisitions (M&As)

As we step through each of these areas, please keep in mind there can be myriad reasons that can propel an organization to leverage a hybrid cloud solution. We will actually go over what it takes to uncover some of those business motivators in Chapter 3. For now, we'll stick with these three, as they are typically the most popular reasons that came up during our conversations with customers.

Differentiating Yourself from the Competition

In today's competitive business environment the need to differentiate yourself from competitors is sometimes key to whether your business will succeed or fail. Global organizations that are looking to grow to new and emerging markets or looking to grow their brand know this story all too well. How do you make the appropriate investments to ensure that your core business is able to separate itself from the other players in your industry?

Well, for starters you look to streamline and create efficiencies around processes that are core to your business but do not give you a distinct advantage over your competitors. Actually, you should try to offload non-core business processes and capabilities that don't provide you with a competitive advantage to service providers who can provide those capabilities at much better economies of scale and reliability than you can (think messaging, collaboration, and so on).

However, those business processes and capabilities that are core to your business and set you apart from your competitors should be digitized and made available to the business through proper means. They should also go through the proper security protocols and measures. This is not the same as outsourcing. Many organizations that turned to outsourcing for core business capabilities (such as call centers for telephone companies) quickly retreated from those strategies. That's because the quality of the call centers could not be held to the standards that could have been applied internally given the appropriate access to or control of the call center operators. The lesson to this story? Don't outsource core business capabilities, especially when you are trying to differentiate from competitors. Instead, look to enhance existing capabilities through cloud solutions and optimize, streamline, or create more reliable services leveraging a hybrid cloud.

The benefits associated with differentiating through hybrid cloud solutions can be accessing more customers, attracting new clients, attracting new top tier employees, and winning market share.

LEADERSHIP THROUGH DOMINANCE

There was a large bank in Canada that we had the very good fortune of working with, and one of the things that we were most impressed with in this bank was that they had one of the best business strategies we ever had the pleasure to analyze. We remember mentioning to them during an Executive Roundtable (a meeting usually with a CIO of a company where Microsoft would validate our understanding of our customer's business) that if we didn't work for Microsoft, we would have liked working for them. As a leading bank in Canada their business strategy was to continue winning market share both within Canada and abroad. They did this through differentiating their customer experience by focusing on technology and innovation. There were other strategies as well, such as continuing to drive efficiencies, focusing on managing costs, growing specific business lines, and building a strong and collaborative corporate culture.

This financial institution understood and believed deeply in the power of leveraging technology to differentiate itself in the marketplace. When other banks were lagging in the areas of customer care and experience they "doubled down" on digitizing these core processes and bringing to consumers a rapid and reliable customer service experience. This no doubt has some financial and non-financial benefits such as increasing access to customers and attracting new clients. They found that when they looked to grow certain parts of the business (specifically in new and emerging markets) that key to differentiating was operational efficiency.

This in turn spurred a slew of IT projects focused on IT and business operational efficiency, centralizing IT operations and virtualization initiatives, and green IT mandates. Instead of just leveraging traditional means of provisioning IT services for new and emerging markets, they leveraged a mixture of public cloud and internal private cloud capabilities, which enabled them to quickly deploy IT services required by new areas of the business. Additionally, they were able to reduce the time it typically takes to bring new products to market by leveraging development and test capabilities through public cloud Infrastructure-as-a-Service (IaaS) solutions. Needless to say, this organization is still one of the most successful banks in their market.

Enhancing Strategic Position (Reducing Nonperforming Assets)

Not all business investments are about growth, mergers and acquisitions, or hostile takeovers. There are times when some businesses will focus intently on ensuring that their focus and primary investment areas are directed toward earning and increasing their bottom line. This typically happens to organizations that have reached market saturation, and/or organizations that are looking to refocus their efforts on a new strategy. In a book written by Geoffrey A. Moore — *Dealing with Darwin: How Great Companies Innovate at Every Phase of Their Evolution* (Penguin, 2008) — Moore discusses how dinosaurs became extinct because they essentially got too big. As the climate changed around them they were not able to adapt quickly enough and therefore died out. They were then replaced with smaller more agile creatures. In this same way, Moore warns large businesses that they too will die off if they don't refocus their efforts on core parts of their business and look to shed non-essential or more commoditized capabilities to other more experienced providers.

Essentially, the question is, "What advantage does commoditized IT capabilities bring you in your business environment?" If the answer is nothing or minimal, it might make sense to start thinking about offloading certain capabilities from your infrastructure. If there are still constraints which are impeding your ability to go "all-in" to public cloud, then this might be a situation to consider a hybrid cloud. This option enables you to move non-essential or nonstrategic elements of your IT environment to the public cloud and still keep on-premises a small footprint of those IT services needed to serve critical but limited personnel or capabilities (for example, a hybrid cloud instance of Office 365 connected to a small on-premises exchange farm for executive personnel).

There are still long-term sustainability challenges to this model, but it does solve the short-term problem; and as your organization becomes more comfortable with public cloud solutions, you can begin shifting more of that footprint to the public cloud and decommission that Exchange instance altogether. In doing so, you will free up cash flow, reduce capital expenses, and redirect the talent that was previously managing or maintaining a messaging environment to provide greater value-added activities to the businesses, such as architecting and designing new or optimized IT services, which do provide market differentiating and competitive advantages in your industry or business segment.

THE GOOD OLD DAYS

An advertising company that we were working with had a fairly interesting business strategy. Year over year their top line revenue was increasing, but their bottom line (or operating revenue) was remaining flat. This within itself is a fairly common issue facing business all over the world. What they noticed was that even though they were doing much more business than ever before their operational and capital expenses were increasing at an alarming rate. The time in the company when they achieved the greatest ratio of profitability was the year 2007. This global company with a high-profile list of clientele was still growing heavily through mergers and acquisitions. As a diversified business this was nothing out of the ordinary, and they planned to continue down this path full bore.

Their strategy included continuing to pursue select acquisitions of complementary companies, expanding their existing business relationship into new markets and with new clients, improving operations and rebalancing their workforce, and increasing their emphasis on enhancing their strategic position. Their main objective for the 2013 fiscal year was to improve earnings before interest, tax, and amortization (operational revenue) to 2007 levels. They were willing to invest, and invest heavily, to achieve this goal. They also identified a parallel objective of reducing nonperforming assets (NPA) from their inventory. This can include just about any assets, including brick-and-mortar buildings, operating businesses, and even a datacenter or two. It is no surprise that IT assets typically are the worst-performing investments for a business (from a pure capital expense view). The intent of these objectives hinged on increasing profitability and efficiency, and decreasing operating and capital expenses.

These objectives spawned a few initiatives, including a business-led activity to consolidate and centralize their IT environment as well as pursuing consolidation in back-office functions. As you can imagine, the senior executives responsible for datacenter operations and infrastructure for each of the operational businesses looked at datacenter consolidation efforts throughout their IT environment. In addition to focusing on what IT capabilities could be consolidated, they also looked at what services they could offload to public service providers. A few of the services included CRM, messaging, collaboration, and their development and test environment. When provided in-house, these IT capabilities cost the business a small fortune, not only in capital expenditures (capex) but also in operational expense (opex). Shifting to a model of converting capex to opex for these services enabled them to significantly decrease their on-premises physical IT environment. The benefits for IT included a smaller footprint to manage, reduced licensing costs, as well as reduced staff to run and operate these IT services. (Note that reduced IT staff did not mean eliminating employees. Instead, they shifted the personnel who operated these services to other activities that were either more customer-facing or related to long-term IT projects.)

Easing Mergers and Acquisitions

In their excellent book *Enterprise Architecture As Strategy: Creating a Foundation for Business Execution* (Harvard Business Review Press, 2006), Jeanne Ross, Peter Weill, and David Robertson describe several business operating models and how each one enables an organization to grow with different challenges and\or constraints. One such business model that grows heavily through mergers and acquisitions is the *diversified business model*. Many holding companies align themselves to this model (think Berkshire Hathaway). The crux of the diversified business model is the idea that the business units which make up the organization typically do not share the same customers or need to cross-sell products or services. Each business line acts fairly autonomously. From a business process perspective, this enables each business line to operate independently and gives the organization the flexibility to grow through mergers and acquisitions fairly easily. Diversified businesses also have the most to gain from a shared IT services perspective; however, this introduces a bit of a challenge.

Integrating and standardizing on a common IT platform or capability does become a fairly exhaustive effort, and it sometimes increases the cost (and complexity) of migrating a new business into the enterprise. What hybrid cloud can do here is essentially act as a bridge between the new business that is coming on board and the existing shared services IT environment. This is done through providing some elements of the shared IT services environment through traditional means and hosting the data or bulk of services within a service provider's environment.

SPIN-UP AND SPIN-DOWN

One such organization that faced issues around the effort and time it took to integrate businesses through their mergers and acquisition activities was a global real-estate management company. It employed a fairly simple business operating model, but that didn't mean that it wasn't effective. One of its main strategies for the year was to purchase properties with high barriers to entry — in this case, expensive properties that required a fair amount of work before they could be used — invest in them to bring them back to "spec," and then sell them off once they were updated. Essentially, they were flipping entire properties, but for utility companies, dams, coal and mining plants, and so on.

The challenge they faced wasn't from a business perspective (they have actually become fairly efficient at buying and selling properties). The challenge was that when these new properties were purchased, the IT department would have to spend an exorbitant amount of time to integrate the newly purchased business into the enterprise shared IT services environment. Although the businesses operated fairly independently, it was essential that the newly purchased business and the existing corporate environment be able to collaborate, coordinate, and share documentation with each other securely and reliably. The IT department would start projects to migrate the new business into the central IT department, but some of these projects took so long that by the time they were finished the business would be sold, and then they would have to start the divestiture process.

It seemed as if the IT department was continuously performing this migration and divestiture activity. Nor did it help that the business planned to kick these M&As and divestitures into high gear during the current fiscal year. Essentially, IT became a bottleneck for a very strategic business function and strategy. The Microsoft Account team suggested to the business a different way of approaching this problem — essentially a mixture of Office 365 (Microsoft's SaaS solutions for messaging and collaboration) and a local deployment of Active Directory Federation Services (ADFS). Whenever a new company was purchased, instead of migrating the entire environment over to the shared IT service, it would be migrated to a dedicated instance of Office 365. Behind the scenes, the newly created instance of Office 365 would be federated with the instance of Office 365 to which the enterprise environment had migrated. This enabled very quick integration of the purchased company with the rest of the enterprise environment. When the property was sold, the lines that connected ADFS would simply be "cut" and the property would then be spun off — greatly reducing the effort previously associated with M&As and divestitures at this business.

SUMMARY

The examples we are sharing here are not the only benefits that business will gain through leveraging hybrid cloud; however, what's important to note is that the traditional thinking around "how" to leverage hybrid cloud is not always correct. It is often *not* the most cost-effective means of deploying or consuming a service (at least not initially), especially when you work in total cost of ownership over the short term (3 years). The acquisition, operating and risk mitigation cost will surely outweigh what is currently spent on IT services. Instead, we feel that understanding the financial and non-financial benefits (market differentiation and increased agility) when justifying hybrid cloud solutions is really key to understanding if a hybrid cloud will be important to your business. In Chapter 3 we will walk through a few methodologies to help you understand and identify those benefits, and which areas of your business will benefit most from hybrid cloud solutions.

3 Project Planning

As we begin this chapter we would like to remind you that from this point forward, performing your due diligence here benefits you by ensuring that the solution you develop will be what your organization needs, and that the benefits that you are looking to achieve through a hybrid cloud solution are realized. Many projects begin with the best of intentions; however, due to shifting priorities, shrinking budgets, and various other causes, they never make it through to completion. What we have assembled here is a concise set of steps, which we feel will put you on the right track towards building and (more importantly) consuming your hybrid cloud solution. We know you've heard it all concerning project planning and management. We also know that you are most likely a seasoned IT veteran with plenty of IT projects under your belt. But whether you are an experienced professional or are just starting your IT career, we highly recommend covering all the sections in this chapter.

We begin by having you pull out the needs of the business and document whatever benefits you think your solution is going to achieve (either financial or non-financial).

We then have you take a pragmatic approach to mapping the needs of your business with possible technical solutions that look to provide the capabilities you need to execute against your business goals and objectives. This is all done through an exercise called benefits realization.

We even help you put together a business case that you can present to C-level executives to gain sponsorship and approval for this initiative.

As an end goal (once your sponsorship is received) we will then help you formulate a vision and scope document that will serve as the first artifact associated with building your hybrid cloud solution.

ENVISIONING AND SCOPING

The first step in beginning your journey to a hybrid cloud solution is to understand which potential business benefits you would like to gain. You carry out this exercise through something called *envisioning*. Envisioning begins by understanding your organization's business objectives and soliciting the business requirements for the initiative. This leads to understanding the technical requirements of the solution, which then leads to the planning phase. Before we get too far ahead of ourselves, however, we would like to point out that envisioning can take place at multiple times during a project. For example, when you are first trying to determine whether moving to a hybrid cloud solution will make sense for your business, a business case is typically made. Envisioning a solution during this stage of a project typically entails understanding the different aspects of the project and its potential and projected costs. After a cost vs. benefits analysis is performed and the IT project is given the green light, those same initial business objectives used to build a business case for the initiative can often carry over to the project execution phase. Note, however, that a much more rigorous business requirements gathering exercise must be performed to accurately define the success criteria for the project and to ensure, from a technical perspective, that a solution's traceability maps directly to business goals and requirements. Figure 3-1 illustrates the five main phases of the envisioning process.

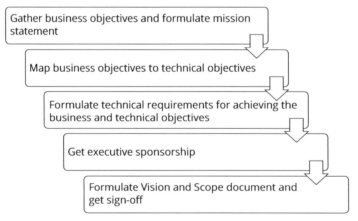

FIGURE 3-1

Gathering Business Objectives

A recurring theme of this book is the importance of beginning an IT initiative by understanding the business goals and objectives that the IT initiative will help enable. The reason why we stress this is because by focusing on the business goals and outcomes, you can objectively consider what technical solutions can help you achieve those goals. It is always tempting to gloss over the business objective of an initiative and jump right into the technical aspect of the solution (the fun stuff). What you lose by jumping to the technical solution habitually is taking an unbiased look at the different solutions available that will assist in realizing our business benefit.

With the different hybrid cloud solutions available today, you can try to break that cycle; rather than default to a specific technology or solution, you can take a much more objective approach and find solutions that best match your business goals. Additionally, because you are just interested in consuming a service, you should take a much closer look to the service description, service-level agreement, and operational-level agreements offered by service providers. This also gives you the opportunity to really focus on your core business, enabling you to get out of the IT business and leave it to those who either specialize in those areas or have created processes and operational procedures that enable the stable and reliable operations of those managed services.

Focusing on just technology can be a tough habit to break. Oddly enough, however, thinking less about technology and more around enabling business capabilities can help individuals take their IT career to the next level. Anyone can learn about a technology stack's features and functions, but not everyone understands how a set of technology features help drive a business toward its goals and strategic objectives.

In this chapter, we will do our best to help you solicit these requirements and business objectives, and create a mapping that demonstrates how hybrid cloud solutions can actually enable your organization to achieve its long-term strategy and objectives. Every organization that goes through this process produces a different result, but it is always good for you to redo this exercise periodically in a systematic way to ensure that your organization's business objectives haven't changed and that course correction is not needed.

NOTE *Not everyone reading this book is a CIO (chief information officer), so we can't assume that you are in a position where you will be making strategic business decision or responsible for any line items on your organizations IT Budget. What we do hope, however, is that even at a high level you have a basic understanding of the business goals and objectives of your organization. Having such an understanding may seem obvious to most people; however, we certainly assure you for an overwhelming majority it is not.*

Identifying Your Organization's Core Function

You begin the process by focusing on the core function of the organization. Although this may seem like a trivial exercise, it ensures that all the stakeholders of a project are on the same page. Who is a stakeholder, you may ask? Well, aside from the usual suspects (CIO, IT director, IT professionals, etc.), a stakeholder can also be a resource outside of the organization. As you solicit the specialists and generalists who are to assist you in your initiatives and endeavors, it is a good practice to relay to all parties involved with a project the purpose and direction of the organization. After all, external resources have just as much interest in ensuring that an initiative is successful if they wish to be called back for future projects. To identify the core functions of your organization, answer the following questions:

➤ What is the focus for my organization?

➤ What services\products do we provide?

➤ How large is our organization?

➤ What is our market share within the industry we operate?

➤ What is our primary means of revenue?

Depending on your role in the organization, you may or may not have access to some of this information. Worry not, because we will provide you with a few resources that, depending on your business segment and industry vertical, will enable you to make some assumptions about the organization's broad business objectives.

Identifying Business Drivers

Once you have a fairly good grasp on your organization's functions, you should then try to determine what some of the drivers are and what investment objectives and benefits the business is trying to achieve. In the case of drivers, the business may not want to add any additional capabilities to the organization but rather streamline processes or reduce operational and capital expenditures to increase their bottom line. One thing to call out here that we feel is fairly important is that one often hears that all a business cares about is money, and that if money isn't directly involved in an initiative in some way then the company won't be interested in it. Although money is the goal for many organizations (but not all — such as nonprofit organizations, for example), we would like to stress that organizations begin initiatives for myriad reasons that don't directly affect either their bottom line or increasing revenue (at least not directly).

For example, rebranding a product or reshaping an organization's public image may have more to do with a campaign to reorganize a business or merge several independent units together (common in mergers and acquisitions). In light of these sorts of initiatives, keep in mind that in order to achieve its objectives, the organization must commit to a strategy, formulate a plan, and execute it. How does this tie into identifying business drivers? Well, for starters, it is always important to understand the current initiatives and campaigns that are underway. Not doing so may cause conflicting projects, and it sometimes causes projects to even compete with one another (this happens more than you might imagine). The result is often wasted investments, inefficient or misaligned processes, and business units within organizations that feel that they are either independent or somehow superior to other business units (we wouldn't believe this either if we didn't see it with our own eyes).

GETTING EVERYONE ON THE SAME PAGE

While working for a bank that was going through a fairly large organization-wide consolidation project, we conducted a workshop that brought together for the first time several business units and IT groups. During the workshop we were attempting to map the process of provisioning a virtual machine. On the surface this may seem like a fairly straightforward task (and for the most part, it is). In this case, however, they also wanted to see what it would take to streamline (or orchestrate) the process through automation. It turned out that because the organization didn't have a standardized service catalog, any number of OS and hardware configurations could be provisioned.

After a request was made it was sent to the networking team, where an IP address was assigned. Next, a request was sent to an infrastructure resource, which provisioned a virtual machine instance, but the OS was not installed. A separate OS install admin was notified and the OS and subsequent applications were then installed. Another request was then generated to install the tools and monitoring agents on the system. This process continued until there were 21 different and independent steps, and sometime different smaller units or groups were responsible for the actions. On average, the entire process would take anywhere from three to four weeks to complete.

The reason why this process was so fragmented was because each IT group felt that its function was the most important step in the request, and that only the subject matter experts who were assigned the task should be permitted to perform the work. As you can imagine, if a business unit that is waiting for the virtual machine to be provisioned can't perform its business functions, consider the impact that would have on testing a new line-of-business application or scaling out a collaboration site. The IT department's inability to rapidly provision resources was costing the bank potentially millions in revenue due to inefficient processes — all because each IT group viewed itself as an independent body.

If only the IT groups had stepped back for one moment from their normal daily functions and considered how they supported the bank's business, they would have been much more inclined to work together collectively to ensure that the IT department's function at the end of the day was to serve the purposes of the business — and to take whatever steps they could to accomplish a timely delivery of resources.

So, what do we suggest to remedy or prevent situations like the ones mentioned? There isn't any shortcut or easy way around this. We suggest three things: collaborate, communicate, and coordinate. Increasing the collaboration between business units (for example, a joint initiative that serves a common purpose) will naturally open up lines of communication within an organization. As business decision makers, we suggest coordinating initiatives between business units to avoid conflicting or competing initiatives; and if at all possible, assign different aspects of a project among multiple business units. You can start down this path by answering the following questions.

- What current initiatives or campaigns are underway within the organization?

- What are some of the challenges and pain points for my organization?

- Who sets the business objectives in my organization?

- Are all of the resources within the organization aware of the top three campaigns and business objectives of my organization?

- Is there currently an up-to-date benefits dependency network maintained for my organization?

Note that one place to look for business drivers is within an annual report or a Letter to the Shareholders. If you belong to a publically traded company, you might be surprised to find how much information is actually located within it, especially in the Management Discussion and Analysis (MD&A) section. Surprisingly, however, few people take the time to read these documents (10Ks, quarterly earnings statements, etc.). As a business solutions architect, Jamal reads the annual report of every client prior to meeting with them. This gives him great insight into the inner workings of the business, along with annual revenue figures and the strategic business direction of the company.

Here are a few examples of common business drivers:

- Grow the business with existing clients.

- Expand the existing business to new markets.

- Pursue selective acquisitions.

- Enhance strategic position.

- Improve operations and rebalance the workforce.

Identifying Investment Objectives

A natural follow-up activity to understanding business drivers is to understand the investment objectives of the business. Investment objectives are self-explanatory — they are investments the business is willing to make to achieve its business drivers and strategic goals. They vary according to the business, but some common investments include the following:

- Improve Earnings Before Income Tax, Deductions, and Amortization (EBITDA) margins.

- Reduce nonperforming assets.

- Recruit the best talent.

- Collaborate and integrate business units.

- Invest where the business possesses competitive advantages.

- Acquire assets on a value basis with a goal of maximizing capital return.

As you can see from the preceding examples, each investment objective should support a higher-level business driver. If it does not, then typically that investment will not be justified. For example, an organization that has the business driver "focus on optimizing the core business in existing markets" will most likely not have an investment objective to "invest in expanding in new and emerging Markets."

Note that it is often difficult to convince a fairly large business to alter its business strategy once it has been set — for most publically traded companies this occurs near the end of the organization's fiscal year. The strategy is also typically set by the board of executives and supporting chief executive officers. Therefore, it is important to understand the current business strategy and to fashion solutions that support the organization's already set or proposed direction. Regardless of whether the business is profitable or not, most publically traded companies will set aside business investment funds to achieve their business goals.

Once you understand the investment objectives of a business, you can put together a compelling business case (more on that later) that attempts to justify IT investments, which are typically very large or require funding outside of the set IT budget. Note also that in order to fully realize the benefits of a hybrid cloud solution, an organization must also change — either through process, functions, or responsibility. Also, sometimes even more important than justifying the cost, understanding and justifying the business change will require executive sponsorship (you are effectively altering the way the business operates, and that takes time and management support).

Identifying Business Benefits

Many of those in the IT world always think about justifying IT investments though means such as net present value, internal rate of return, or return on investment. Although these are elements that are typically part of understanding the impact of large IT investments from a purely financial point of view, they don't really paint a complete picture, as they fail to address the non-financial benefits that IT investments can bring to fruition. Both financial and nonfinancial benefits (NFBs) should be considered when making a decision about IT investments. Taking only a purely financial view can have several unwanted results, including the following:

- ➤ Financial benefits are overstated/overestimated.
- ➤ Follow-up or fulfillment of financial benefits are unrealized.
- ➤ Financial benefits are not verifiable because actual costs are unknown or difficult to obtain.

Does this mean that IT business cases have been doing it wrong all these years? No, that is not what we are saying. What we suggest instead is that in addition to financial benefits, which can be realistically discerned, it is suggested to also state NFBs, which can be categorized as follows:

- ➤ Observable
- ➤ Measurable
- ➤ Quantifiable

All benefits start off as observable. The Cranfield School of Business states that if a benefit is not observable, then it doesn't exist. The Cranfield School of Business states this as the definition of an observable benefit:

> *By use of agreed criteria, specific individuals/groups will decide, based upon their experience or judgment, to what extent the benefit has been realized.*

Typically, this requires a stakeholder who will sign off on whether the benefit was realized. Because the stakeholder's experience or judgment is subjective, this can be the easiest type of IT investment to justify. This doesn't mean that because it is not a direct financial benefit it is not valuable to the business. Take, for example, an organization that wants to cross-sell or integrate product offerings to differentiate itself in the marketplace. If the operating businesses within the organization are currently independent from one another and typically do not work together, which is preventing the business from attaining its strategic business goals, then investing in an enterprise-wide collaboration solution (for example, Office 365) would give the business an observable benefit of increasing collaboration within the enterprise. Of course, you would need sponsorship from as high a level in the business as possible to ensure that resources leveraged the collaboration solution, but with this solution in place the business *should* be able to go to market quicker and remove the barriers to interacting and working together. To insinuate that this collaboration solution will help the business increase its top-line revenue would be a bit far-reaching from our perspective.

Say, however, that you did want to ensure you had measurable benefits. What would that look like? Well, for starters, measurable benefits are defined as follows:

> *Performance is currently being measured or an appropriate measure could be implemented. But it is not possible to estimate by how much performance will improve when changes are completed.*

Simply put, you know what the baseline is today (or you can easily figure it out); however, you cannot quantifiably project or predict the amount of benefit or improvement that will be realized by the solution. This can be due to a multitude of reasons, but the most common include:

➤ Data does not exist which conclusively demonstrates by how much similar organizations realized benefits.

➤ This is the first time a solution of this nature is being implemented.

➤ The business has a unique scenario\situation which makes it difficult to estimate the benefits.

➤ The business has not decided how or in what capacity it will utilize the solution.

Whatever the reason benefits cannot be estimated happens to be, what is important is that once the solution has been implemented, you can measure what benefits were realized in order to verify that there were, in fact, benefits to the solution. Implementing a gauge to determine how long it takes to perform certain tasks, even from the perspective of an existing line of business application that is providing a service (e-mail or a messaging system, for example), can suffice in order to create a baseline. Another means to measure a baseline is through surveys. You use these simple approaches to measure benefits and create a baseline because these same methods can then be used to measure what benefits were realized once the solution has been deployed.

The next order of benefit includes quantifiable benefits. As you can imagine, as you build and collect more dimensions of the benefits (first observing and then measuring current performance), you move to the next stage. Quantifiable benefits are defined as follows:

> *Sufficient evidence exists to forecast how much improvement/benefit should result from the changes.*

NOTE *You can find all these definitions in "Managing the Realization of Business Benefits from IT Investments" by Professor Joe Peppard, Professor John Ward, and Professor Elizabeth Daniel at* http://www.som.cranfield.ac.uk/som/ dinamic-content/research/documents/peppardwarddaniel07.pdf

---

Using the same benefit discussed earlier (increased collaboration) you can measure what can assist you in creating a baseline through the following metrics:

➤ Number of meetings with multiple business unit resources

➤ Ability to coordinate meetings and view of enterprise calendars

➤ Ability to see online presence of personnel in the enterprise

If you can get a baseline of the preceding areas, you then require evidence, either through internal testing (a proof of concept) or by relying on external testing or research (Gartner, IDC, or even from vendors), of what increase in performance or change in baseline will occur. If through a proof of concept or pilot it is shown that business units that had access to these capabilities had more frequent meetings with one another (from once a month to six times a month); gained access to enterprise calendaring (did not have the ability to do this before, so this is a net new capability that eases the pain and decreases the time of scheduling meetings); and are now able to see the online presence of individuals, which allows different business units to reach out to one another in real time (this could have the effect of reducing time spent on problem resolution, for example), you can claim or project the increase in benefit. In order for the benefit to be quantifiable, it must be measurable in two parts (prior to implementation and after the solution is deployed). Also, the projected benefit must also be stated, and evidence of those projections must also be provided.

The last stage of benefits realization is, of course, financial. Before getting too deep in this area (we will take a look at this again later in this chapter), we would like to point out a commonly made mistake: overstating financial benefits. Don't exaggerate, don't guess, and certainly don't assume. As you can imagine, this happens fairly often in financial-only business cases; and the dangers include losing credibility with business decision makers, the inability to validate financial benefits, and being held responsible when financial benefits are not achieved. Imagine building a business case that promised a growth in earnings or a decrease in operational expenses only to find out that those benefits did not (or could not) be realized. We have seen many business cases based on financial-only benefits approved by senior executives, after which everyone cheers in excitement and feels a sense of accomplishment. We assure you, getting an approval for a business case is only the beginning of your journey in deploying a solution and ensuring that the solution achieves the expected benefits. Don't paint yourself into a corner; if you cannot ensure that the financial benefit can be realized in a measurable, quantifiable fashion, don't make promises you can't keep.

What should you do instead in regard to creating financial benefits? For starters, ensure that you choose scenarios that you can either control directly or have a clear line of sight into achieving. What can some of these financial benefits include? Here are a few examples (from an IT perspective):

➤ Reduced server footprint (reduced capital expenditure)

➤ Reduced operating expenses (heating, cooling, or even renting space)

➤ Reduced licensing costs

Each of these financial benefits (again, from an IT perspective) should be able to be realized. The reduction in server footprint can be assigned an owner to ensure that after a solution is put into place, the legacy hardware is decommissioned. This will also have an impact on operating expenses related to hardware maintenance (such as cooling or renting space in a datacenter). The same holds true for a decrease in licensing costs, as you know the current costs and can project future costs based on the solution that is developed and as vendors are consolidated. This information can then be fed into net present value, internal rate of return, break-even points, and return on investment analysis (which is typically a combination of everything above) represented as a percentage over a given amount of time.

You'll notice we are not talking about decreasing operating expenses in terms of human operating cost. We omitted these areas because reducing staff, or rebalancing the workforce (as it is called in some places), is typically something that a business decision maker must agree to and believe is warranted. Additionally, there aren't many IT resources that will wholeheartedly advocate the reduction of their role or that of their peers. In terms of the cloud (since that is the focus of this book), we suggest leaving the reduction of human resources out of a business case. The reason is because hybrid cloud solutions typically do not require fewer resources to run but they require a different type of resource — this holds true for all the cloud operating models (public, private, and hybrid). If you do include staff modifications in a business case, we suggest including retraining or adjusting their focus instead (and yes this does have its own cost). We'll cover this and more in the "Building the Business Case" section later in the chapter.

MAPPING TECHNICAL SOLUTIONS TO BUSINESS OBJECTIVES (BUILDING BUSINESS REQUIREMENTS)

This is an opportunity for a business to understand its pain points and exactly what strategic direction it wants to execute, and then find a technical solution and road map to achieve its objectives. Because an organization usually has multiple objectives, finding the two or three that support the main drivers for the business is key. Typically, you weigh the importance of business objectives against the following characteristics:

- Value
- Ability to execute (feasibility)
- Strategic importance

Once you have identified the areas of the business or pain points you would like to address, capture those pain points and areas of chance and validate them with a business decision maker. This saves a lot of time, as it ensures that you are working to solve the right type of problem. If the business doesn't feel pain or isn't interested in investing in certain areas, changing their minds will be fairly difficult (remember that most publicly traded companies spend months figuring out their business strategy for the next fiscal year). Determine what the business is already trying to achieve and assist them in getting there.

FORMULATING TECHNICAL REQUIREMENTS

Now, as they say, on to the fun stuff. Although we have spent a considerable amount of time speaking to the business aspect and implications of moving to a hybrid cloud solution, many readers are probably interested mainly in understanding the technical challenges. If the proper steps were taken to understand your business goals and objectives, you can now map the technical initiatives that are either currently underway or being decided upon to those areas. In this section we will take a look at the current technical landscape of your environment and then begin creating a strategy to appropriately position the environment and organization to properly consume these cloud services.

NOTE *The technical aspect of preparing an organization to consume a hybrid cloud solution is probably the simplest of the tasks necessary to make this transition. There are nontechnical challenges that must be addressed as well. For example, if an IaaS solution is to be leveraged, the IT staff of the organization will require training on the portal solution through which it will provision virtual machines, new processes must be put into place that will affect the use of this new capability, and a contract vehicle must be put into place that enables the organization to pay an outside vendor for virtual machines. We cover these aspects in subsequent chapters.*

Discovery and Assessment

In order to assess the current datacenter, it's useful to consider what the organization's current IT environment consists of: various hardware platforms, hypervisors, operating systems, applications, systems management solutions, and network and storage hardware. You should perform this assessment regardless of which cloud service model you are leveraging. The reason for this is because performing an assessment of the entire current datacenter(s) gives you a complete view of where you are starting from and potentially uncovers issues that you may not have been aware of.

A thorough datacenter assessment (where you are today) can be fairly time consuming. It is suggested that you use a tool such as the Microsoft Assessment and Planning (MAP) Toolkit along with an existing systems management solution (such as System Center Configuration Manager) to gain an adequate view of your organization's current IT environment.

To gauge your current IT environment, ask the following:

- How many datacenters are managed?
- Are they managed by a single IT services department or several?
- How many server operating systems are maintained within the environment?
- What is the distribution of operating systems within the datacenters (e.g., percentage of Windows vs. Linux)?
- What are the main applications supported by these servers (database servers, web servers, line-of-business, messaging, collaboration, etc.)?
- What systems management solutions are used within the environment?
- What client operating systems are supported?
- What hypervisors are used within the environment?

If you are a larger organization, then you may want to break out the assessment into a separate phase and perform a much more thorough assessment exercise. During the assessment phase, there is no such thing as having too much information. In the real world, however, we do have to deal with budgets and constraints, so if the assessment portion is taking on a life of its own, be sure to either constrain or limit the time you are spending on this. We suggest spending no more than one week (40 hours' worth of effort) on average for a small to medium-size business. This will consist of understanding the current physical environment, applications being utilized, and the processes that govern the use of those applications. For example, if the entire organization leverages Microsoft Exchange Server and Outlook 2007 as the primarily mail client for messaging capabilities, be sure to capture that. Also be sure to capture any business processes that are currently attached to that messaging system as well. For example, our clients send us an e-mail to place an order for a product. The ordering technician then forwards that e-mail to the fulfillment team, which preps the order for delivery. This process continues until the order is completed (you get the idea). It is absolutely necessary to understand how the messaging environment is being used to support business processes.

This analysis not only gives you insight into how an on-premises application is being leveraged, it also gives you the opportunity to prepare for how moving those business processes to leverage hybrid cloud solutions will potentially be impacted if the hybrid cloud solution experiences issues or even in the event of a disaster. Another purpose of performing this exercise is to understand how to transition or migrate the processes or capabilities to the hybrid cloud solution. It will most likely not be as easy as "flipping a switch." In most cases, there will be a period of time during which both on-premise and off-premise solutions will be online. We call that period the *transition phase*. Try to capture as much of this knowledge as possible.

What Is the Desired End State?

Now you are going to jump forward a bit to try to understand (again aligning to your business goals and objectives) the end state of the IT environment you would like to achieve. For example, if enabling an *organizational-wide collaboration solution that unifies the business under a common platform* is the desired end state, then you know that you will most likely be moving your messaging, and potentially communication, platforms off-premise. That in itself can have some fairly lofty business and organizational implications. You must ask yourself the following:

- ➤ How will our support processes change?
- ➤ How do we provision new users?
- ➤ How do we deprovision users?
- ➤ What does disaster recovery look like in the cloud?
- ➤ What business continuity capabilities are offered in this model?
- ➤ How do we migrate our existing users to this solution?

Before you can answer these questions you must understand the state of a successful environment. In other words, what does success look like? On the surface, it seems an easy enough question to answer; however, as you start to really think about it, you quickly see how deep the rabbit hole goes. This is not so much answering a questionnaire, but more a setting of technical objectives. For example, consider some of the following technical objectives for moving to an off-premise messaging and communication platform:

- ➤ Users both internal and external to the business network environment must be able to access the hybrid cloud solution.
- ➤ The solution must support multi-site business continuity capabilities.
- ➤ User provisioning and deprovisioning must be automated and controlled through assigned help desk personnel.
- ➤ Information resources' usage must be easily accessible and attainable.

This list could go on and on. Can you see how much fun this can be? The best part about this is that the burden of meeting the technical requirements is on the service provider! Now, is it realistic to state that every service provider (or even one for that matter) will be able to meet all your technical objectives? The answer is no; therefore, you must also create a list of "tradeoffs" you are willing to make. This is a very important exercise as it puts into perspective for you the requirements that matter most and gives you an objective way to "stack rank" the features that will give you what you need to function as a business and those that you are willing to let go in order to come to a reasonable solution.

PRIORITIZING YOUR OBJECTIVES

Now that you know your organization's business objectives, it's time to prioritize them. In order to do this properly, you should leverage a system that categorizes the objectives into the following buckets:

M — Must

S — Should

C — Could

W — Won't

By categorizing your objectives, you will be able to intelligently make trade-off decisions based on the price, maturity, and features offered by service providers. Additionally, by prioritizing your objectives, you can try to rationalize the features and functionality of service offerings in order to match the capabilities most important to the business against those offered in the market. If you find yourself in the position where everything is a priority, consider the following maxim:

> *If everything is a priority, then nothing is.*

Don't kid yourself when it comes to prioritizing objectives. Often, this seemingly simple act is not performed, and attempting to build a solution against an array of objectives that have equal weight can have a disrupting effect on an organization and its ability to execute on point initiatives.

A tried-and-true way to approach categorizing business objectives is assigning each one of them a weight based on the following characteristics:

➤ Value

➤ Cost

➤ Risk

➤ Ease of implementation

➤ Dependency on other objectives

The business objectives with the highest weight should be executed first, of course, because those will garner the most immediate, and most likely the most impactful, changes to the business.

BUILDING THE SOLUTION

After you have nailed down the technical objectives that you want to achieve, you can start exploring the set of public service offerings available and gauging the level of effort that will be required for this initiative. As stated earlier, making this transition will be more than a technical initiative; it will affect the organization's IT and business processes as well. With this in mind, you should understand that unlike some IT initiatives, this one should be treated as a campaign that requires enterprise-wide effort. Encouraging all aspects of the business to contribute to this cause can also be used as a conduit to attain resources' involvement, buy-in, and support.

We have had hundreds of conversations with C-level executives, and one of the main concerns we hear about over and over again is their lack of confidence regarding how their IT departments are executing initiatives — that is, whether these departments have the best interests of the business in mind. One may ask how it is possible for an organization's IT environment to have anything but the best interests of the business at heart; but over time many IT departments develop capabilities that they are now comfortable delivering. As business needs change, IT departments must also change to accommodate new capabilities and benefits. As you can imagine, having to keep up with changing business needs keeps the IT department in a constant state of flux. Because IT departments are comprised of people, and (gasp) people are resistant to constant change, once the IT department sets up a new technology or capability, their natural inclination is to maintain that technology for as long as possible. They will resist programs and initiatives that cause them to alter their current configuration or capabilities because over time this can be a fairly tiring exercise. Additionally, change typically also requires funding, and many IT organizations today are dealing with shrinking budgets, an increasing number of "prioritized" IT projects, and fast approaching deadlines. This "predicament" that IT finds itself in can seem overwhelming.

We have come to realize that the defining moment in our IT careers happened when we were able to objectively look at what goals a business was looking to achieve and then decide upon the technical solutions that met the requirements of the business. This can be a very difficult exercise to practice (as it was for us the first few times we performed it). The reason why this was so difficult for us was because we always defaulted to a specific toolset or technology that we were comfortable with (and why shouldn't we since it doesn't make sense to explore or consider solutions that we are unfamiliar with). When we stepped away from the technology we were comfortable with and instead analyzed the business and technical requirements for the initiative, we were able to broaden the number of solutions, which we could leverage by tenfold. Additionally, it allowed us to make proper trade-offs and benefit dependencies.

To map technical solutions to business needs, you must take into account the past, current, and future plans for the business; and you should consider the direct and indirect impact of choosing one technology over another. This exercise is often not performed, resulting in point solutions that have no direct relationship with either other projects and initiatives or the overall business strategy and objectives. The outcome is typically a poorly run, inefficient, and overly complicated IT environment. This doesn't lend itself to a very customer-focused IT department or enable the rapid delivery of services to end users. If this sounds a lot like your IT environment, don't despair. This is fairly common in many enterprises, and exercises like the ones we suggest in prioritizing business objectives can help your organization make the shift to a more efficient and agile IT group.

Organizational Changes

The last and most important aspect of moving to a hybrid cloud solution is identifying the organizational changes that will be required in order to consume the solution. This section illustrates some of these potential changes according to service model, and note that moving to a hybrid cloud solution doesn't necessarily mean the reduction of IT staff or resources. In some instances they can even increase, although ideally you can reassign existing staff to either different or additional responsibilities. In any of the scenarios, some or all aspects of an organization's IT and business unit will be impacted in some way. You can use the following to map some of these changes. Note that only some example responsibilities have been captured; be sure to include as many tasks, activities, and functions that constitute the responsibilities of the different IT roles for your organization.

IaaS

Help Desk\Support Staff

Existing role/responsibility:

➤ Accept and log support calls.

➤ Triage and resolve all possible calls.

➤ Categorize, document, and escalate calls that cannot be resolved.

➤ Manage the incident completion and customer experience/satisfaction.

New role/responsibility:

➤

➤

➤

➤

IT Professional

Existing role/responsibility:

> ➤ Build, install, and configure bare metal systems with operating systems.

> ➤ Troubleshoot hardware issues.

> ➤ Manage SAN environment.

> ➤ Manage network environment.

> ➤ Manage operating systems.

New role/responsibility:

> ➤

> ➤

> ➤

> ➤

> ➤

Application Owner\Developer

Existing role/responsibility:

> ➤ Request the provisioning of operating systems.

> ➤ Manage, build, and maintain applications and workloads.

New role/responsibility:

> ➤

> ➤

PaaS

Help Desk\Support Staff

Existing role/responsibility;

> ➤ Accept and log support calls.

> ➤ Triage and resolve all possible calls.

> ➤ Categorize, document, and escalate calls that cannot be resolved.

> ➤ Manage the incident completion and customer experience/satisfaction.

New role/responsibility:

> ➤
>
> ➤
>
> ➤
>
> ➤

IT Professional

Existing role/responsibility:

> ➤ Build, install, and configure bare metal systems with operating systems.
>
> ➤ Troubleshoot hardware issues.
>
> ➤ Manage SAN environment.
>
> ➤ Manage network environment.

New role/responsibility:

> ➤
>
> ➤
>
> ➤
>
> ➤

Application Owner\Developer

Existing role/responsibility:

> ➤ Request the provisioning of operating systems.
>
> ➤ Manage, build, and maintain applications and workloads.

New role/responsibility:

> ➤
>
> ➤

SaaS

Help Desk\Support Staff

Existing role/responsibility:

> ➤ Accept and log support calls.
>
> ➤ Triage and resolve all possible calls.

➤ Categorize, document, and escalate calls that cannot be resolved.

➤ Manage the incident completion and customer experience/satisfaction.

New role/responsibility:

➤

➤

➤

➤

IT Professional

Existing role/responsibility:

➤ Build, install, and configure bare metal systems with operating systems.

➤ Troubleshoot hardware issues.

➤ Manage SAN environment.

➤ Manage network environment.

New role/responsibility:

➤

➤

➤

➤

Application Owner\Developer

Existing role/responsibility:

➤ Request the provisioning of operating systems.

➤ Manage, build, and maintain applications and workloads.

New role/responsibility:

➤

➤

Deployment Planning

At this point, you are on the right path; you know what you want to achieve; you know what the end state should look like; and, for the most part, you can now start sharing your vision across your organization. So, who should your first stop be: Mr. or Mrs. Executive? Chances are good that if you have made it this far, you have had some level of interaction with a CIO, CTO, CFO, or even a CEO. If so, you are almost halfway there. If you have not had a direct line to that executive, see the next section about how to gain executive-level sponsorship for an initiative.

Additionally, it will require some restructuring of the organization (either increasing or decreasing head count) based on the cloud model being leveraged. We have seen many initiatives fall by the wayside when hard decisions were made because:

- ➤ Cloud initiatives didn't have the visibility they needed.
- ➤ The initiatives became too costly.
- ➤ The architects didn't understand the impact that moving to such a solution would have on their business.

NOTE *In 2007, we were engaged with a fairly large project that arose out of the need to deploy a modernized systems management solution. Everyone who was part of the project understood why it was important because it would impact the way in which this organization managed, deployed, and patched servers and clients throughout the enterprise. Additionally, there were several dependencies related to managing and patching the latest operating systems; therefore, failing to deploy this new management solution would prevent the organization from achieving the infrastructure modernization objective. This was apparent to everyone working on the project, but the reasoning behind it and the potential impact to the business were never relayed to the key business decision makers.*

One day, word came down that some budget cuts would have to be made to get the organization's profit and loss statements back in the black. Among the many projects that the organization was embarking on, guess which project had its funds frozen for a quarter? You guessed it — the systems management modernization project. Without going into a lot of detail about how much money the organization ultimately lost over this decision, suffice it to say that it was substantial, and the company ended up paying almost three times the cost of the project to renew service contracts on legacy hardware and software systems.

Ensuring that the proper business case is made when starting a project not only ensures that the right solution is chosen, it also protects against the project being cut, abandoned, or deprioritized in the event of unforeseen or unfortunate circumstances. Always build a business case and always look to gain executive sponsorship, especially when it pertains to projects that will most likely involve organization-wide impact, change, or adoption to be successful.

Gaining Executive-Level Sponsorship

We are going to switch gears for a moment and talk a little about strategy. When most IT organizations are looking for executive-level sponsorship, they seek to demonstrate how an initiative would impact a business financially. That's because at the end of the day, most organizations are concerned about their bottom line and are always looking for ways to increase their margins. Some organizations, however, are more concerned about delivering specific capabilities and benefits to their business and are willing to make an investment in an initiative if the benefits seem justified.

Leveraging Benefits Dependency Networks

In all of our cumulative experience as solution architects, no tool has been as useful to us as Cranfield's Benefits Dependency Network (BDN). For readers unfamiliar with the BDN, you can take a moment to read about it in "Managing the Realization of Business Benefits from IT Investments" by Professor Joe Peppard, Professor John Ward, and Professor Elizabeth Daniel:

```
http://www.som.cranfield.ac.uk/som/dinamic-content/research/documents/
peppardwarddaniel07.pdf
```

In a nutshell, the BDN provides a way to map business drivers to investment objectives, business benefits, and business change, enabling changes, which include IT projects and technologies. The inherent value of leveraging a BDN enables an organization to create a direct line of sight between business drivers and potentially the technology that enables those drivers. This can then be used to build business cases, which are often needed to fund programs that help with the deployment of the specific technology.

Often the most difficult step in building a BDN is understanding or soliciting the specific business drivers of an organization. If you are a CIO reading this book (or any other business decision maker for that matter), hopefully we have helped you flush those drivers out already. If you are a resource who reports to a CIO and you don't have direct access to these drivers, there are a number of ways to get access to them. If the organization you are working with is a publicly traded company, then you are in luck, as most publicly traded companies publish business drivers through annual reports and can be found on the company website in the Investor Relations section. Many nonprofits (such as government organizations) also provide this information as well. If this source is unavailable, try to set up a time to solicit this information from key business decision makers and their direct reports. Even in privately owned companies, some type of documentation is typically released to indicate the direction of the business from a strategic perspective.

Since you have gone through the process of understanding all these elements already (including the investment objectives, business benefits, and organizational change needed to achieve those benefits), you can place them into the model shown in Figure 3-2.

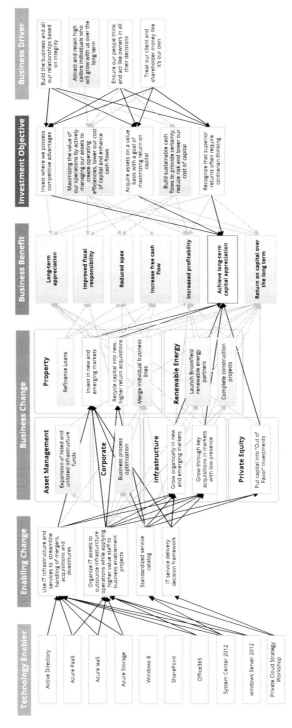

FIGURE 3-2

As you can see, the Benefits Dependency Network helps to demonstrate how the different business-related and technical solutions are interconnected within the business environment. Additionally, it forces you to incorporate business change in an IT project to ensure that you actually realize a specific benefit you are intending to achieve. This enables you to not only understand the strategy of the business but also potentially shape your IT strategy to match what the business wants to achieve. The applications of the BDN are many, but you will use it here to ensure that the IT investments you want to make are mapped to appropriate business drivers and investment objectives.

Building the Business Case

You've spent quite a bit of time in understanding the business drivers, investment objectives, and benefits your organizations is looking to achieve. Building a business case then should be a fairly straightforward exercise. You must now "connect the dots." As a side note, we have always wondered why more people don't do this. Unfortunately, integrating all the plans, goals, and ideas into a cohesive business case is not an exercise that is performed very often. For the purposes of this book however, you are going to do just that. You can go about this in one of two ways. Again, depending on the size of your organization, you can choose to attach this to an existing IT strategy or campaign (e.g., "reducing operational and capital expenses" or "decreasing the time to market for goods and services") or you can start your own campaign. We would like to warn readers, however, that beginning a business campaign from scratch can add weeks, if not months, to the time line of an IT project (or any initiative for that matter). In either case, it is often necessary to formulate your own business case to justify an investment for any number of initiatives. In building a business case, you should identify nonfinancial benefits along with financial benefits to ensure that you are considering all the dimensions of the solution. This has the added advantage of preventing you from overestimating or overstating benefits to business decision makers. Only state benefits that you know you can measure and see through to realization. If you are not the benefit owner, ensure that you get sponsorship from a stakeholder who can see the benefit through to realization.

Define Business Drivers and Investment Objectives

Appropriately define the current state of either the business or the industry (for example, "the business has been experiencing a decline in revenue of 8 percent yearly for the past two years"). It may also be useful to compare and contrast what other organizations within the industry are experiencing or acting upon. A simple statement defining the drivers (current opportunities and issues facing the organization) and the investment objectives (what proposed investments seek to achieve for the organization) should suffice. This is also where you can state pain that the business is experiencing in conjunction with indicating the current state of the environment. Here is an example of an opening statement for a fictitious software company, Contoso:

As Contoso looks toward the future it sees itself transforming "into a Global Solutions company" states Midas Wale (Chairman and CEO). Contoso also intends to deliver integrated solutions for customers and drive shareholder value while focusing efforts around higher-margin solutions and growing core areas of the business. These drivers have been identified as areas of focus by Contoso because of transforming market conditions especially in the areas of social networking, software-based solutions, and cloud technologies. Contoso is committed to ushering in a new era of solutions that not only leverage its existing investments made within the enterprise business but also integrate multiple technologies and resources within the consumer business as well.

Contoso will execute against these business drivers through pursuing new markets (specifically areas in developing countries) and diversifying revenues across both the enterprise and the consumer space. Within the enterprise business, Contoso is continuing to build out its asset management, ERP, and business intelligence systems and offerings. The consumer business will also purchase additional niche businesses across both developed and underdeveloped markets. Within the enterprise business there will be an increased investment within the global IT services strategy, as well as investments made in order to cater to healthcare, education, and energy management segments. Contoso will also look to invest in improving its ability to be a strategic partner for large businesses and government and wholesale customers.

Propose the Solution

This can be accomplished in several ways, but we suggest shaping your proposal as options. You may ask why this is even necessary given that the intended initiative should be the only thing captured here, but consider that busy business decision makers are asked to make difficult choices every day. What they don't have is the luxury of an ample amount of time to research different options when making a decision. That is a burden that must be shouldered by the resources creating the business case. Think of it in the same way as a start-up company needing a business plan for investors to evaluate. Therefore, we suggest that proposals contain two to three options from which a business decision maker should choose. Does this mean extra effort for the resources building the business case? Yes, it does. Accept it, embrace it, and move on. Offering multiple options within a business case also shows decision makers that various avenues were thought through and that the case is thorough. For the purposes of this book and for the sake of simplicity, the following example reflects the proposal for a single solution; however, remember to include similar elements for all the options:

A collaboration solution that consists of both public cloud and private cloud capabilities (forming a hybrid cloud) will allow Contoso to improve its bottom line, streamline product development and processes, improve customer service, and broaden its global reach. An area of focus for the business is to build new solutions that leverage investment from both the enterprise and consumer businesses. Currently, the enterprise and consumer business units operate independently from one another, not in an integrated or standardized manner. In order to increase productivity between the operating businesses, a single collaboration solution is recommended to achieve this outcome. This collaboration solution will also enable the organization to improve customer service by allowing service desks to reach out to internal resources for troubleshooting and engage directly with customers through VOIP functionality effectively and reliably.

As vendor consolidation efforts are already underway, Contoso will also be able to shed vendor contracts and licensing agreements, which today provide redundant capabilities and functionality from a software perspective and also decommission up to 100 physical servers from within its datacenter, resulting in not only a decrease in operational expenses but also capital expenses. In order to properly account for security and data sovereignty concerns, a hybrid cloud messaging solution is proposed, which will provide messaging and collaboration capabilities to key Contoso executives through an on-premise private cloud, and a public cloud messaging and collaboration solution (Office365) for all other employees in the organization.

Determine the Explicit Value of Each Benefit

The preceding example outlines a few benefits that the solution will provide. As we are sure you noticed, both financial and nonfinancial benefits are included. After you define the benefit, ensure that you provide a means to measure it. Flip back to the different types of benefits that exist and how you can measure them. Lastly, provide a justification for the benefit and identify a benefit owner if it is required. The following demonstrates how you could present this information for the Contoso example.

Benefit — Improved Bottom Line:

- ➤ **Measure** — 12 percent decrease in IT operational costs deployed and managed by the enterprise and consumer businesses

- ➤ **Justification** — Contoso's operational IT budget combined for the enterprise and consumer business is $45m. Through vendor consolidation there will be a savings of approximately $6m/year. Through the off-loading and consolidation of collaboration technologies, the server footprint for this capability will decrease by 90 percent. Additionally, Contoso will also save approximately $2m over 3 years of cost avoidance related to server hardware and operational expenses.

Benefit — Streamlined Products and Processes:

- ➤ **Measure** — 30 percent decrease in time for releasing products to market

- ➤ **Justification** — Currently, the consumer and enterprise business operate independently of one another and the capabilities enabled through SharePoint, Lync, and Exchange provide Contoso with the capability to work across organizational boundaries and collaborate productively with one another. Independent research has shown that collaboration solutions such as these reduce friction in terms of collaboration, and provide the capability to streamline processes across the Contoso business.

Benefit — Improved Customer Service:

➤ **Measure** — 20 percent increase in customer satisfaction scores

➤ **Justification** — As Contoso reaches out to an ever-growing number of customers, the ability to track down and triage issues becomes a differentiator between itself and Contoso's competitors. Additionally, through collaboration solutions that connect various business groups and operational teams, service and support staff can effectively and efficiently field and resolve customer issues, complaints, and concerns.

Benefit — Broadened Global Reach:

➤ **Measure** — 75 percent increase in reaching target addressable market

➤ **Justification** — With investments being made in new and emerging markets, Contoso will be able to leverage local resources to ensure that products and services intended for these regions are relevant and appropriate for their respective economic climates.

It may also be necessary to speak to specific numbers like ROI, internal rate of return, or net present value. We suggest putting these elements in the appendix or providing a separate spreadsheet with these calculations. Most large organizations have methods and formulas that you, as an IT department, can leverage. Reach out to the CFO or finance department and ask them how they calculate the mentioned figures. Typically, they can calculate this for you; however, they require information such as hardware, software, and training costs to do the calculations. Unfortunately, some IT shops try to calculate these figures on their own even when there is an entire department that does these sorts of calculations on a daily basis. Additionally, some figures (such as discount rate) can be different for each organization. A spreadsheet used for this purpose is typically named "Risk Adjusted Cash Flow Statement" or something similar.

Identify Costs, Risks, and Mitigation Plans

Typically, two types of costs are incorporated into a business case: direct and indirect. Direct costs represent hardware and software, and operational and administrative costs. Essentially, these costs are anything that you can attribute directly to the solution itself and that are not shared by other solutions or technologies. Indirect costs include costs such as end user operations or downtime. Check with the business to see how it typically breaks down direct and indirect costs. Keep in mind that it is typically different for every organization. The total cost of ownership is what you are trying to represent here, therefore you want to pick a time frame that is in line with the expectations of the business. Three to five years is usually a time frame that businesses would like to see in terms of total cost of ownership of the solution (this also ties in to ROI calculations as well). Figure 3-3 provides an example of total cost of ownership (TCO) for a solution over a three-year period (with year 0 being the acquisition date).

Cost Chart of Accounts	Year 0 (Acquisition)	Year 1 (Deployment)	Year 2 (Operations)	Year 3 (Operations)
Direct Costs				
Hardware and software	$300,000	$20,000	$10,000	$10,000
Operations		$10,000	$10,000	$10,000
Administration		$5,000	$5,000	$5,000
Total direct costs	$300,000	$35,000	$25,000	$25,000
Indirect Costs				
End user operations		$5,000	$5,000	$5,000
Downtime		$1,000	$1,000	$1,000
Total indirect costs		$6,000	$6,000	$6,000
Annual Total Cost of Ownership (TCO)	$300,000	$41,000	$31,000	$31,000

FIGURE 3-3

You may be wondering whether a comparative TCO analysis would reveal that your on-premise solution can provide similar capabilities for a lower cost. This is a bit of a touchy subject for a lot of vendors, but we are not going to sugarcoat anything. The truth is that if you add up all direct and indirect costs associated with consuming a cloud solution (specifically hybrid cloud), the costs are often greater than the costs for an on-premise solution for the short term (1 to 3 years). That is why we always stress that moving to a hybrid cloud solution for short-term financial benefits is usually a mistake, as it can take from 4 to 6 years to realize such benefits. Does that mean you shouldn't do it? Absolutely not. This is why we continuously stress weighing non-financial benefits in the decision-making process of moving to a hybrid cloud solution. Although it may be more expensive in the short term, the non-financial benefits can often outweigh short-term financial costs, especially when those benefits enable the organization to be more competitive or differentiate itself from competitors. Again, be very specific about direct and indirect costs, and do not force a financial figure on a benefit that is difficult to realize or justify, such as "increased collaboration could help the organization earn $3m in increased revenue." If a financial benefit were called out for this collaboration solution, cost avoidance of travel would be a much better and easier financial benefit to justify and realize. Is it possible to attach a number to any financial benefit? Sure, with enough time, access to resources, and effort it can be done. The point is to weigh the effort vs. what you get in return, and to ensure the accuracy of the data in making that decision.

Now, on to risk. A number of elements will factor into a risk assessment, but what you are actually seeking is a *mitigation plan*. Mitigation plans to address risk usually add cost to financial figures (hence the term *risk-adjusted cash flow statement*). Typically, three types of risks are accounted for:

➤ Technical

➤ Financial

➤ Organizational

Each risk has a probability, justification, and mitigation plan. Based on the probability of the risk, the cost will also fluctuate. Having an understanding of what the mitigation plan is or what the cost of training is should be included within the TCO of the solution. The following provides an example of a simple risk analysis for Contoso.

Technical:

➤ **Risks** — The complexity of the system's functionality; the number of system interfaces and systems being replaced

➤ **Probability** — Medium/high

➤ **Justification** — The systems being replaced are from various vendors and are currently being used sporadically throughout Contoso. Understanding the current infrastructure will require additional analysis and effort in relation to most enterprise environments.

➤ **Mitigation** — We suggest leveraging Microsoft Consulting Services (MCS) to architect, design, test, and assist in deploying the solution for Contoso. MCS has a proven track record of mitigating risk, an industry-leading development methodology, and highly skilled resources who are very experienced in large-scale cloud deployments.

Financial:

➤ **Risks** — Investment costs; evidence of benefits; business criticality of areas affected by the system

➤ **Probability** — Low

➤ **Justification** — The investment costs for Contoso in comparison to other vendors is fairly small. The evidence of benefits will require appropriate follow-through to ensure benefits realization.

➤ **Mitigation** — We suggest that Microsoft and Contoso jointly agree upon benefit owners and metrics to ensure that benefits are realized as stated within the business case.

Organizational:

➤ **Risks** — Cultural

➤ **Probability** — Medium\high

➤ **Justification** — As new services are deployed into the organization, Contoso will see a shift in the processes and procedures associated with delivering services to itself and customers.

➤ **Mitigation** — Ensure that this initiative has the support of an executive and that the vision of the program is shared broadly throughout the organization.

NOTE *For individuals who are building business cases for external organizations (e.g., consultants, contractors, and vendors), it is often necessary to have available specific information about the organization's financials (pay for resources, revenue, market cap, etc.). Some of this data can be gathered from public forums, but other information is a little more difficult to come by. For example, the pay of resources, operational expenses, capital expenses, or IT budget may be more closely guarded information. If the organization you are working with is reluctant to share that information with you, attempt to explain that building a business case that is relevant and worth the consideration of business decision makers often requires this information. If the organization is still reluctant to share it, do what we have suggested earlier: default to industry standards. For example, resource salaries, cost of hardware, and even IT budget by industry vertical is information that is easily attainable through analyst firms such as Gartner, IDC, and BizMiner. If you are able to gain the sensitive financial information, always assure the organization that you will keep the information private. Treat it as confidential and take great care about who has access to it.*

Augmenting/Modifying Business Processes

This section has been broken out because it requires some special attention. Many organizations move to hybrid cloud solutions and then look for ways that their business can leverage these new capabilities. Although this may have worked for on-premises IT projects, an organization should firmly understand the impact that moving a specific capability or function will have on its business and organization. For example, in the case where an organization is moving its customer relationship management system to a hybrid cloud solution, it must understand what business functionality is being either lost or gained by moving to that solution. If this exercise is not performed, then the result might be potentially unrealized ROI that the business will not be able to take advantage of from the new capabilities. Obviously, functionality that is not leveraged provides no value to an organization. Subsequently, understanding how outages will impact the organization's business now that the customer relationship management solution is hosted off-premises is also a valuable exercise to perform.

Most business processes can be mapped using a number of common IT applications (for example, PowerPoint, Visio, and even Word), or you can use specialized applications. Regardless of the method you choose, the goal of this exercise is to understand the logic or process by which common business functions are completed. This exercise maps these processes to the new capabilities provided by the hybrid cloud solution, which enables developing a migration or transitional strategy to move a current process to a new one utilizing the capabilities provided by a new offering or solution. Special care is required here because this is often where most projects struggle to gain traction.

So, what can be done here? We suggest the following approach for adopting new processes within a business. The project owner should begin by identifying the benefit that the new process will bring to the individual or business unit affected by the change. A benefit or incentive must be provided to these resources because without a positive motivating factor (gaining buy-in), the individual or business unit will most likely find a reason or excuse to revert to the processes that they are already comfortable with.

Here is a list of some common benefits that moving to a hybrid cloud solution can provide to IT professionals, business units, and individual contributors of an organization.

Business Units:

➤ Decrease the amount of time needed to provision business applications and workloads (increase agility; decrease time to market).

➤ Streamline and automate standard business processes.

➤ Optimize business processes based on latest-generation technology.

➤ Increase resiliency of business-critical workloads and applications.

IT Professionals:

➤ Shifting common/repetitive IT administrative tasks to the cloud enables individuals to contribute to activities that are directly beneficial to the business.

➤ IT admins can focus on customer relationships and look to improve their experience of leveraging technical solutions.

➤ Being promoted to manage end-to-end technical solutions, not just focused on specialized technical areas

➤ Moving to or contributing to core business functions

End Users:

➤ Access business data anywhere.

➤ Increased uptime and service availability due to service provider expertise in the products and operational excellence

➤ Recoverability of business data and information

➤ Leveraging business continuity built into solution offerings

In order to gain their buy-in, each of these "stakeholders" must have a benefit that is specified for them. This is especially important at the business level to gain project sponsorship to fund an initiative, at the IT admin level to garner support in the migration or execution of the initiative, and at the individual contributor level to ease the transitional or process changes that will no doubt occur in leveraging a cloud service offering.

In building the strategy to augment the business processes, be sure to create an open and transparent plan that is shared across stakeholders. Some organizations even try to solicit ideas or strategies from different stakeholders regarding changes to these processes. This can be a very solid approach in also gaining buy-in from stakeholders because it makes them feel like they are contributing to the overall initiative instead of having dictated to them the changes that will be occurring within their environment.

Formulating the Vision and Scope Document

If you have gotten this far (and focused on leveraging an external or public hybrid cloud solution), congratulations! You have completed some of the more difficult parts of the process. Now you need to identify each step explicitly, understand the order in which they must be executed, and assign them to the appropriate resources. In this section we'll give you an overview of the outcome of the process: writing and articulating your understanding of the overall effort required to perform this transition.

What you want to do now is put everything you have learned up to this point about your motives, objectives, and projected outcome into a document that articulates these concisely. Essentially, the goal of a Vision and Scope document is to get everyone on the same page and to keep them on the same page as the initiative moves forward. It's a statement of what you want to do, why you want to do it, and how you plan to execute it. This document usually serves as a gate for the project to move forward, aligning all the departments that will need to be involved and then landing on the CIO's desk for sign-off. The following sections lay out the major sections of such a document with brief explanations. Keep in mind that this is just an example; your unique vision and scope should reflect as much detail as needed for the size and complexity of both the solution and the organization. It could be 2 pages or 20.

Executive Summary

If interested parties were to read only this section of the Vision and Scope document, they should come away with an accurate high-level summary of why you are embarking on this initiative and how you plan to get there.

What is the problem you're trying to solve? Example: The organization has experienced multiple iterations of growth and restructuring, resulting in a fragmented IT environment. This fragmentation slows its ability to respond to requests and often results in quality issues. The following specific problems have resulted:

1. Operational complexity has significant cost implications.

2. Agility is severely impacted by having multiple redundant systems that serve the same purpose.

3. Several groups have separated into silos and are unwilling to cooperate and collaborate with other teams.

What specific business benefits will be realized? Word this in a way that speaks to your audience. If they care about numbers, give them the numbers. If they want progression, paint a picture of a healthy, cutting-edge business able to progress. You get the idea!

Lastly, explain how the long-term road map of technology supports this vision.

Possible Sections

Problem Statement

Business Opportunity

Technology Road Map

Project Vision and Scope

This section may be lengthy or short and sweet depending on your audience. Do you need to align many departments to execute the project successfully? Better be verbose. No? Keep it terse. You want to ensure that you clearly describe your vision of what a successful implementation will look like and what the specific benefits will include from a functionality perspective. What business requirements are being satisfied and how are they being fulfilled? This means demonstrating a solid understanding of what users require from the system. Who are the users? What are their needs? How is this going to fulfill those needs and how will it adapt to changing needs? Lastly, translate all that into the nuts and bolts of the technology scope: how it will be released and introduced to the users, what defines how it will be accepted as successful, and what operational requirements it drives.

Possible Sections

Vision Statement

Benefits Analysis

Business Objectives and Requirements

User Requirements

Operational Requirements

System Requirements

Scope of Project

System Release Strategy

Acceptance Criteria

Operational Criteria

Solution Design

This section should not try to be a replacement for a functional specification or design document, but rather an overview of the architectural principles, design methodology, and specific technologies that will need detailed design and implementation. Even if an area is not fully understood yet, as many may not be, call them out as critical design areas and explain how that planning and analysis will take place. Equally as important is documenting the constraints that will impact the design process. For example, DNS may be a critical dependency that will need some work performed, but you probably don't want to do a full redesign of your DNS systems. Therefore, just document the requirements of the DNS system and indicate that a major redesign effort is out of scope; and that workarounds or alternatives may be necessary.

Possible Sections

Design Strategy

Technology Design Area #1

Technology Design Area #2

Technology Design Area #3

Constraints

Project Management Strategy

Entire books have been written on project management, and you don't want to reinvent the wheel here. What you should include is the project management overall plan and specific strategy that will be employed to ensure success. Project management is often the linchpin that can make or break your initiative. Diagram the project team. Who will be responsible for what? If you don't have all the people needed, just document the roles and leave the names unassigned. Try to be honest and objective.

The scheduling estimation can be difficult at this stage. Usually it's a good approach to start with a work breakdown structure (WBS) that time-boxes major phases of the project and their dependencies. For example, phase 1 might be three weeks of planning and design work, and phase 2 cannot begin until that is completed. Attempt to get the major work efforts identified and milestones on paper as a baseline for your detailed project plan. The detailed project planning will occur after Vision and Scope sign-off, filling in the detailed tasks, dependencies, who will perform them, and when they need to be completed.

Risk identification and any mitigations for them you can spell out are very important. Try to perform the right amount of analysis. Don't overdo it or underdo it. As you move forward you can always add details about the risks and what can be done about them.

Communication is absolutely key. Try to provide a basic diagram of who needs to be informed of what aspects of the project along the way. Will you have weekly project status meetings with the stakeholders? Do you need to do periodic executive reporting? How will you escalate risks as they become more real? Who makes the tough decisions when issues arise? Over-communicating is always a safer bet that you can correct much more easily than under-communication. Under-communication is where things can go awry very fast.

Does the staff responsible for executing the project have the skills they need? Outline here how that will be addressed.

Finally, when the system goes live, what will the impact be to the end users? Document any training IT needs to provide to successfully utilize the new technology and processes.

Possible Sections

> Project Team
>
> Project Schedule Estimates
>
> Initial Project Risks
>
> Project Communications and Escalations
>
> Staff Preparedness/Training
>
> End User Training (if applicable)

SUMMARY

No doubt in this chapter you have covered quite a bit of material. One thing that we hope sticks out about this chapter is the emphasis placed on organizational change and the planning that should go into a cloud solution. If it is not already clear, a cloud solution will redefine the way in which your organization will function (either at the business or IT layer — or sometimes both), and anticipating what those changes might be and preparing your organizations for them really is the key to a successful cloud solution deployment.

We started by talking through the business objectives for your organizations and ensuring the cloud solution you are building does in fact meet the needs of your business. We did this by analyzing investment objectives and the specific benefits that your business is trying to achieve (remember it is not always about financial benefits). Quantifying benefits is also another key area, which should drive the go\no-go criteria for a cloud solution (do the financial and non-financial benefits outweigh the cost and risk of implementing the solution?). Mapping the technical solution to business requirements is really just an exercise to understand what business capabilities the cloud solution will enable and to understand the underlying or supporting technical capabilities that will support the business. After gathering this information you can build a business case to get executive buy-in. Once you are approved, this chapter walked through building the first tangible artifact for the project: the Vision and Scope document.

Try your hardest to not skip these steps covered in this chapter. Although this may not be the most rewarding phase of building and deploying your cloud solution, it will save you from building the wrong solution and will increase your chances of having a successful hybrid cloud deployment.

4 What You Need to Know About Windows Azure As a Platform

Up to this point we have been talking about strategy — the direction you head long term. Now we are going to support this long-term strategy with the concrete cloud technology platform that should help you to determine the right tools and services available for your selection from the myriad of cloud vendors and service providers. Of course, we are not starting out this journey, we are well into it, and so in this chapter and in the remainder of the book, we are going to focus on the Microsoft Windows Azure platform, which is one of the core components of the broader Microsoft vision for the new era — the Cloud OS. We will also talk about how it can help you understand what core work must be done in order to build sound, reliable, and high-performing hybrid cloud architectures.

To understand what Windows Azure offers, it's useful to group its services into distinct categories. Figure 4-1 shows one way to do this.

This chapter walks through the technologies shown in the figure, describing what each offers and how you might use it when building hybrid cloud architectures.

EXECUTION MODELS

We'll begin by taking a step back and looking at existing applications today. Fundamentally, we need to talk about the differences between traditional on-premises, line-of-business application solutions and the underlying execution environment these solutions require that bring about the cloud transformation phase. Consider Figure 4-2, which shows the traditional reference model.

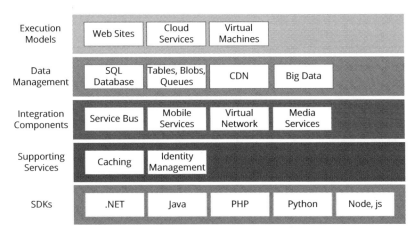

FIGURE 4-1

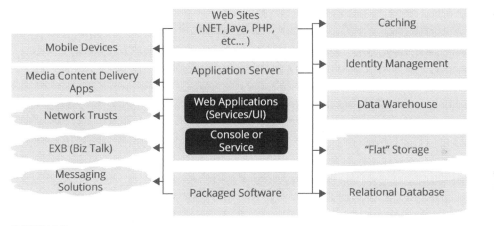

FIGURE 4-2

Building for the cloud platform means designing for cloud-optimized architectures, and because cloud platforms are a little different from traditional on-premises server platforms, that results in a new developmental paradigm. In the following sections we will use the sample of the on-premises multi-tier reference architecture, presented in Figure 4-2, to illustrate how this traditional on-premises architecture can be transformed into a *hybrid cloud* reference architecture and how the Windows Azure platform can help you achieve it. We'll begin with the most familiar cloud application model, websites.

Websites

For 15 years we have been able to take advantage of low-cost website hosting options. These options leverage a high-density model whereby websites share physical resources but exist in their own silos. For a premium, we can even leverage a dedicated model that gives us exclusive access to our hosting environment.

Typical characteristics of website applications include the following:

➤ Inexpensive and leverages a high-density hosting model

➤ Simple administration, ease of deployment

➤ Available in both shared and dedicated environments

With flexible hosting and deployment options that support multiple languages and are supported by common open-source frameworks, this model helped bring the Internet within the reach of even the most novice of technologists.

Web apps have specific and simpler needs in terms of execution; and at the same time, for a web app you can go higher up the stack, focusing on just your business logic and HTML. Therefore, it takes significantly less effort and brings higher benefits when deploying web applications in the public cloud.

Windows Azure has introduced its Web Sites service, giving users this common experience while bringing it forward into the world of cloud computing. Taking advantage of the automation available via the *Windows Azure Fabric*, simple websites are no longer bound to a single machine and can be automatically recovered if there is a failure. Additionally, due to the capacity made available by cloud scaling services, these sites can be scaled up to meet your growing demands.

This execution model offers a managed web environment using Internet Information Services (IIS). You can move an existing IIS website into Windows Azure Web Sites unchanged, or you can create a new one directly in the cloud. Once a website is running, you can add or remove instances dynamically, relying on Web Sites to load-balance requests across them. *Web Sites* gives you access to all of the other Windows Azure services like caching, Service Bus, SQL Database, and Storage.

In addition, Windows Azure Web Sites offers both a shared option, whereby your website runs in a virtual machine with other sites, and an option for a site to run in its own VM.

Windows Azure Web Sites is intended to be useful for both developers and web design agencies. For development, it supports .NET, PHP, and Node.js, along with SQL Database and MySQL for relational storage. It also provides built-in support for several popular applications, including WordPress, Joomla, and Drupal. The goal is to provide a low-cost, scalable, and broadly useful platform for creating websites and web applications in the public cloud.

Windows Azure Web Sites is available in three tiers:

➤ **Free** — This tier enables you to host up to 10 websites and gives you up to 150 GB of outbound data transfer (bandwidth) per month in a multi-tenant, high-density hosting model.

➤ **Shared** — The Free tier does have some limitations that can affect high-traffic websites, so as your business grows you may need to leverage the Shared tier, which increases the resources available to your website for a small monthly charge per site (comparable to other shared web hosting plans).

➤ **Reserved** — If the Shared tier is still not sufficient, you can opt to move to a Reserved mode, which enables you to host up to 100 websites on a dedicated virtual machine. As your needs increase further, this option can be scaled out to up to 10 VMs.

All these tiers share the same deployment model and leverage the Windows Azure Fabric to help ensure that your sites remain available in the event of hardware failures.

So, it's time to update our reference architecture by replacing the traditional websites on-premises hosting solution with the cloud deployment of Windows Azure Web Sites, as highlighted in Figure 4-3.

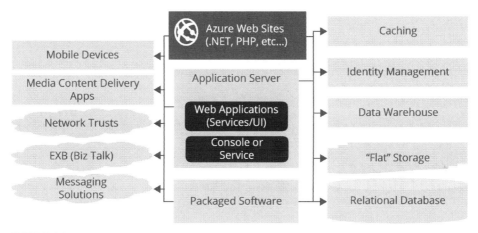

FIGURE 4-3

Cloud Services

Windows Azure Web Sites are a great solution for you if you don't have multiple layers to deploy and you just need an IIS container to run your code. Or, if you are porting an existing website, then Web Sites is most likely the first stop for you as well. Just picking up your existing bits and dropping them into a Windows Azure Web Sites environment should be a fairly easy path to follow.

And while Windows Azure Web Sites offers a relative easy and cost-effective transition of your web applications to the cloud, there are times when you need more flexibility and a little bit more control over the hosting environment, while still allowing Windows Azure to take care of managing the underlying OS and the application platform to build your applications on.

Windows Azure Web Sites enables many interesting deployment scenarios for your web applications, but there are some constraints. For example, you don't have administrative access to the underlying infrastructure, which means that you can't install arbitrary software.

Windows Azure Virtual Machines (reviewed later in this chapter) gives you a lot of flexibility, including administrative access, and you certainly can use it to build a very scalable hybrid application, but you'll have to handle many aspects of reliability and administration yourself. What you would like is an option that not only gives you the control you need, but also handles most of the work required for reliability and administration. For example, you can tweak the standard image with startup tasks, configure what network traffic is allowed, and so on. Or you may need to deploy multi-tier layers of your web applications while leaving you an option to logically, and physically, abstract these layers for better scalability, performance, and interoperability.

This is exactly what's provided by *Windows Azure Cloud Services*. This technology is designed expressly to support scalable, reliable, and low-admin applications, which is why we are going to apply it in place of the web application tier in our evolving hybrid cloud reference architecture diagram, as shown in Figure 4-4.

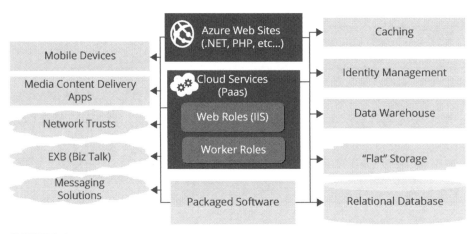

FIGURE 4-4

To use Windows Azure Cloud Services, you create an application using the technology you choose, such as C#, Java, PHP, Python, Node.js, or something else. Your code then executes in VMs (referred to as *instances*) running a version of Windows Server in the cloud environment. These VM instances are coming in different sizes to accommodate different deployment and application scenarios. You can find a table that describes the available sizes and core characteristics for a virtual machine running in Windows Azure at `http://msdn.microsoft`
`.com/en-us/library/windowsazure/dn197896.aspx`.

So, how is it different from hosting VMs in a private cloud environment? For one thing, Windows Azure itself manages them, doing things like installing operating system patches and automatically rolling out new patched images. (This implies that your application shouldn't maintain state in web or worker role instances; it should instead be kept in one of the Windows Azure data management options described later in this chapter.) Windows Azure also monitors the VMs, restarting any that fail.

As Figure 4-4 shows, you have two roles to choose from when you create an instance, both based on Windows Server 64-bit OS. The main difference between the web role and the worker role is that an instance of a web role runs IIS, whereas an instance of a worker role does not. Both are managed in the same way, however, and it's common for an application to use both. For example, a web role instance might accept requests from users that are routed in a round-robin fashion between available web role instances — thanks to the *Windows Azure Load Balancer* deployed on each external endpoint of any Windows Azure Cloud Service — and then pass them to a worker role instance for processing; while in order to accommodate highly intense workloads, some cloud service implementation solutions also involve use of Windows Azure Queue (described later), which Queues all web role requests for asynchronously processing them on worker role instances at the controlled and varied pace.

The primary shift in moving from an on-premises application to Windows Azure Cloud Services is related to how applications scale. The traditional method of building larger applications relies on a mix of scale-out (stateless web and application servers) and scale-up (buy a bigger multi-core/large memory system, database server, build a bigger data center, and so on). In the cloud, scale-up is not a realistic option; the only path to achieving truly scalable applications is by explicit design for scale-out.

To scale your application out or down on Windows Azure, you can request that Windows Azure create more instances of either role or shut down existing instances. To accomplish this effectively, by the virtue of the design, the Cloud Services VMs are stateless. This enables the Windows Azure Fabric to quickly provision new machines if you decide you need additional capacity or to move a virtual machine to another location of the datacenter if there is a hardware or software-related issue impacting availability.

Virtual Machines

Oftentimes, and this is especially true of existing line-of-business applications today, there are applications that need full access to the underlying operating system services, or applications with tight dependencies across the services they need and the underlying scale/resilience architecture of those services. These back-end services are often available in the form of packaged software solutions, sometimes from third-party vendors, and they are rarely available for customization, let alone source code modifications. This category of applications typically has the following characteristics:

- ➤ Have more complex heterogeneous environments
- ➤ Require significant compute and memory resources
- ➤ Require stateful transactions often translated in availability of persistent storage and disks
- ➤ Require greater control of application setup and management

The capability to create a virtual machine on demand, whether from a standard image or from one you supply, can be very useful. Adding the capability to pay for this VM by the hour is even more useful. This approach, commonly known as IaaS (and described in Chapter 1) is what Windows Azure Virtual Machines provides.

To create a VM, you specify which virtual hard disk (VHD) to use and the VM's size. Windows Azure Virtual Machines offers a gallery of standard VHDs. These include Microsoft-provided options, such as Windows Server 2008 R2, Windows Server 2012, SQL Server 2012, and BizTalk Server 2013, along with Linux images provided by Microsoft partners. You're free to upload and create VMs from your own VHDs as well.

Wherever the image comes from, you can persistently store any changes made while a VM is running. The next time you create a VM from that VHD, things pick up where you left off. It's also possible to copy the changed VHD from Windows Azure, and then run it locally; and just like Windows Azure Cloud Services VM instances, you're charged by the hour for each Windows Azure VM.

Windows Azure VMs can be used in many different ways. You might use them to create an inexpensive development and test platform that you can shut down when you have finished using it. You might also create and run applications that use whatever languages and libraries you like. Those applications can use any of the data-management options that Windows Azure provides, and you can also choose to use SQL Server or another database management system (RDBMS) running in one or more VMs.

Another option is to use Windows Azure VMs in a hybrid cloud architecture as an extension of your on-premises datacenter, running SharePoint or other applications. To support this, it's possible to create Windows domains in the cloud by running Active Directory in Windows Azure VMs. Figure 4-5 illustrates the sample SharePoint farm architecture hosted in Windows Azure VMs.

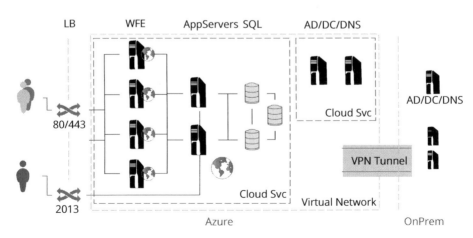

FIGURE 4-5

This quite general approach to cloud computing can be used to address many different problems. What you do is up to you.

Choosing the Right Execution Model

Each of the three Windows Azure execution models has its own role to play. Windows Azure Virtual Machines provides a general-purpose computing environment; Windows Azure Web Sites offers low-cost web hosting; and Windows Azure Cloud Services are the best choice for creating scalable, reliable applications with low administration costs. In addition, as mentioned earlier, you can use these technologies separately or combine them as needed to create the right foundation for your hybrid cloud application. The approach you choose depends on what problems you're trying to solve. Go to `http://msdn.microsoft.com/en-us/library/windowsazure/jj218759.aspx` to read about the benefits each makes available to you.

DATA MANAGEMENT

The late, great American stand-up comedian George Carlin had a routine in which he talked about how humans seem to spend their lives accumulating "stuff." Once they have gathered enough stuff, they have to find places to store all of it. If Carlin were to update that routine today, he could make the same observation about computer information. It seems that everyone with a computer spends a lot of time acquiring data and then trying to find a way to store it. For some computer owners, especially for large enterprise businesses, finding enough storage space to hold all the data they have acquired is a real challenge. Data storage and management in the cloud? Seems like no-brainer, right?

Applications need data, and different kinds of applications need different kinds of data. Therefore, Windows Azure provides four different ways to store and manage data.

Each of the four options addresses a different need:

- ➤ **SQL Database** — Relational storage
- ➤ **Tables** — Fast access to potentially large amounts of simple typed data
- ➤ **Blobs** — Unstructured binary storage
- ➤ **SQL Server** — Running your own database in the cloud

In all four cases, data is automatically replicated across three different computers in a Windows Azure datacenter to provide high availability. You can also specify that data should be copied to another Windows Azure datacenter in the same region but at least 500 miles away. This copying, called *geo-replication*, happens within a few minutes of an update to the storage, and it's useful for disaster recovery. It's also worth pointing out that all four options can be accessed either by Windows Azure applications or by applications running elsewhere, such as your on-premises datacenter, your laptop, or your phone.

SQL Database

For many people, running RDBMS in a VM is the first option that comes to mind for managing structured data in the cloud. It's important to realize that the capability to run SQL Server or another RDBMS in a VM created with Windows Azure Virtual Machines isn't limited to relational systems: You're also free to run NoSQL technologies such as MongoDB and Cassandra. It's not the only choice, though, nor is it always the best choice. Running your own database system is straightforward — it replicates what you are used to in your own datacenters — but it also requires handling the administration of that RDBMS. In some cases, managing data using a Platform-as-a-Service (PaaS) approach makes more sense. Windows Azure provides a PaaS technology called *SQL Database* that enables you to do this for relational data. The SQL Database, formerly known as SQL Azure Database, is a cloud-based relational database platform built on SQL Server technologies. SQL Database will seem very familiar to developers and administrators because data is stored in SQL Database just like it is stored in SQL Server, by using Transact-SQL. Conceptually similar to SQL Server, a SQL Database however does not support all features available in SQL Server. The full list of the non-supported features and limitations that exist today in SQL Database are documented at http://msdn.microsoft.com/en-us/library/windowsazure/ee336245.aspx.

Figure 4-6 shows how SQL Database can be used in the reference architecture for our evolving hybrid cloud application.

SQL Database provides all the key features of a relational database management system (RDBMS), including atomic transactions, concurrent data access by multiple users with data integrity, ANSI SQL queries, and a familiar programming model. Like SQL Server, SQL Database can be accessed using Entity Framework, ADO.NET, JDBC, and other familiar data access technologies. It also supports most of the T-SQL language, along with SQL Server tools such as SQL Server Management Studio. For anybody familiar with SQL Server (or another relational database), using SQL Database is straightforward.

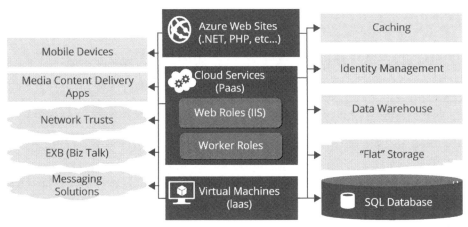

FIGURE 4-6

But SQL Database isn't just a RDBMS in the cloud — it is a PaaS service. You still control your data and who can access it, but Windows Azure takes care of the administrative grunt work, such as managing the hardware infrastructure and automatically keeping the database and operating system software up to date. SQL Database also provides a federation option with support for fan-out queries, which distributes data across multiple servers. This is useful for applications that work with large amounts of data or need to spread data access requests across multiple servers for better performance.

If you're creating a hybrid cloud application that needs relational storage, SQL Database can be a good option. Applications and services running outside the cloud can also use this storage. For instance, data stored in SQL Database can be accessed from different public and private cloud client systems, including on-premises server applications and client applications running on desktops, laptops, tablets, and phones; and because it provides built-in high availability through replication, using SQL Database can help minimize downtime.

Storage: Tables, Blobs, and Queues

Windows Azure Storage is a scalable cloud storage system that has been used in production systems long ago before Windows Azure platform went live. In fact, it has been in production since November 2008. It is used by Microsoft internal applications such as social networking search; serving video, music, and game content; managing medical records, and more. But since the Windows Azure era started in February 2010, the Windows Azure Storage is used by thousands of customers outside Microsoft, with over 4 trillion objects stored and counting, processing an average of 270,000 requests per second, and registering peaks of 880,000 requests per second.

Windows Azure Storage provides cloud storage in the form of Blobs (user files), Tables (structured storage), and Queues (message delivery). A common usage hybrid cloud pattern we see with Windows Azure Storage is when the raw data is uploaded and stored in Blobs, the data carrying the message providing the overall workflow for processing is transmitted via Queues, and intermediate service state and final results are being kept in Azure Tables or Blobs.

An excellent example of this pattern is built in Microsoft Bing, an ingestion engine service providing near real-time Facebook and Twitter searchable content within 15 seconds of a Facebook or Twitter user's posting or status update. The data volume being processed by this ingestion engine for Facebook and Twitter is getting close to 1000 TB (1 Petabyte)!

In the process of building and constantly improving Windows Azure Storage, feedback from both internal and external customers drove many design decisions. There have been many key design features implemented in Windows Azure Storage since its first release, but the one, relatively recent (about a year ago) design change — deployment of a flat network across all of the Windows Azure data centers to create Flat Network Storage — has dramatically resulted in bandwidth network connectivity improvements, and allowed Microsoft to introduce and support durable network attached disks used by Windows Azure VMs. This single network redesign has improved the overall storage node network speed ten times, from 1 Gbps to 10 Gbps.

Tables

Relational data is useful in many situations, but it's not always the right choice. Suppose you want to create a Windows Azure application that needs fast access to typed data, maybe a lot of it, but it doesn't need to perform complex SQL queries on this data. For example, imagine you're creating a consumer application that needs to store customer profile information for each user. Your app is going to be very popular, so you need to allow for a lot of data, but you won't do much with this data beyond storing it and then retrieving it in simple ways. This is exactly the kind of scenario for which Windows Azure Tables makes sense.

But don't be confused by the name: Windows Azure Tables do not provide relational storage. In fact, it's an example of a NoSQL approach called a *key/value store* — and like NoSQL, Windows Azure Tables lets an application store properties of various types, such as strings, integers, and dates. An application can then retrieve a group of properties by providing a unique key for that group. While complex operations such as joins aren't supported, tables offer fast access to typed data.

To use Windows Azure Tables, you first create a Windows Azure Storage account. As part of this, you specify the Windows Azure datacenter that will store the tables you create using this account. Wherever it lives, each table you create belongs to some container in your storage account. To access a table, an application provides a URL with the following form:

    http://<StorageAccount>.table.core.windows.net/<TableName>

<StorageAccount> is a unique identifier assigned when a new storage account is created, while <TableName> is the name of a specific table containing your data.

Each table is divided into some number of partitions, each of which can be stored on a separate machine. This is a form of sharing, as with SQL Federation. Both Windows Azure applications and applications running elsewhere can access a table using either the RESTful OData protocol or the Windows Azure Storage Client Library (SCL).

To identify a particular entity within a table, an application provides the key associated with the single entity, such as a table row in SQL Database that may contain as many as 255 properties. The key has two parts: a *partition key* that identifies a specific partition and a *row key* that identifies an entity within that partition.

This structure allows for big tables — a single table can contain up to 200 terabytes of data — and fast access to the data they contain. And matching their simplicity, Windows Azure Tables are usually less expensive to use than SQL Database's relational storage. Which leads to a common question that we often are asked when talking to our customers: "Why wouldn't I always want to use Windows Azure Tables over SQL Database?" That's a good question whose answer depends on your application and data needs.

This typically leads to the storage comparison discussion while weighing the pros and cons each data storage technology brings and how they may impact the specific application. For example, Windows Azure Tables has no support for transactional updates that span tables or even partitions in a single table. A set of updates to a table can only be grouped into an atomic transaction if all the entities involved are in the same partition. Nor is there a way to query a table based on the value of its properties, or support for joins across multiple tables. And unlike relational databases, tables have no support for stored procedures.

On the other hand, Windows Azure Tables is a good choice for applications that need fast, cheap access to large amounts of loosely structured data. Fast access is important in this situation, and the application probably doesn't need the full power of SQL. Giving up this functionality to gain speed and size can sometimes make sense, so Table Storage is just the right solution for some problems.

Blobs

Another option for data management, Windows Azure Blobs is designed to store unstructured binary data.

Like tables, each Blob is associated with a Windows Azure Storage account. Blobs are also named much like tables, with a URL of the following form:

```
http://<StorageAccount>.Blob.core.windows.net/<Container>/<BlobName>
```

<StorageAccount> is a unique identifier assigned when a new storage account is created, while *<Container>* and *<BlobName>* are the names of a specific container and Blob within that container, respectively.

Also like tables, Blobs provide inexpensive storage, and a single Blob can be as large as one terabyte. An application that stores video, for example, or backup data or other binary information can use Blobs for simple, cheap storage.

To guard against hardware failures and improve availability, every Blob is replicated across three computers in a Windows Azure datacenter — and as we mentioned in the beginning of this chapter, if you choose to use geo-replication for your Blob storage, a Blob's data will be copied to another Windows Azure datacenter, providing a total of six copies.

Queues

Queuing has a relatively primitive application scenario: One application places a message in a Queue, and another application eventually reads that message from the Queue. If your application needs only this straightforward service, Windows Azure Queues might be the best choice.

One common use of Queues today is to enable a web role instance to communicate with a worker role instance within the same Cloud Services application. For example, suppose you create a Windows Azure application for video sharing. The application consists of PHP code running in a web role that lets users upload and watch videos, together with a worker role implemented in C# that translates uploaded video into various formats. When a web role instance gets a new video from a user, it can store the video in a Blob, and then send a message to a worker role via a Queue, telling it where to find this new video. A worker role instance — it doesn't matter which one — will then read the message from the Queue and carry out the required video translations in the background. Structuring an application in this way allows asynchronous processing, and it makes the application easier to scale, as the number of web role instances and worker role instances can be varied independently.

Windows Azure Queues provide an intermediary (brokered) messaging service between publishers and subscribers. Queues support multiple concurrent publishers and subscribers, but do not natively expose higher-order messaging primitives such as publish-subscribe or topic-based routing. They are typically used to distribute work items (such as messages, documents, tasks, etc.) to a set of worker role instances (or between multiple hosted services, etc.).

CDN

Data in Blobs can also be made available via the *Windows Azure Content Delivery Network* (*CDN*). By caching copies of Blob data at 24 (the actual count was correct at the time of writing this book) geographically distributed Edge Network nodes around the world, the CDN can speed up access to information that's accessed repeatedly. The goal of a CDN is to serve content to end users with high availability and high performance.

By utilizing a network of servers located around the world, Windows Azure CDNs consist of a unique network infrastructure that ensures all your data — videos, pictures, websites static pages — is available quickly and at all times. These servers are placed at globally significant points that experience the most traffic, with each containing an identical copy of cacheable data from the Windows Azure storage account linked to CDN. For example, when end users request a piece of data from a website, they are redirected to the server containing the information that is geographically closest to them, reducing time lags and latency while also increasing download speeds. With multiple servers located around the world, CDNs can deal with large amounts of data requests from several different regions, with each continent usually having its own network points of presence. Furthermore, with dynamic load balancing technologies, CDNs allow requests to be rerouted to the next nearest server in times of high traffic and when the closest server to an end user is at full load. The architecture of CDNs also means that they are highly scalable, with customers being able to add permanent additional capacity quickly and easily as their website grows.

Managing and analyzing data in the cloud is just as important as it is anywhere else — and because the main topic of our book is hybrid cloud, it is worth stressing the importance of making the right decision about where to place your data, how this data will be accessed, and what services exist to help you with data management and analysis. Figure 4-7 reflects the data management options that are available for you in Windows Azure as it pertains to our hybrid cloud reference architecture.

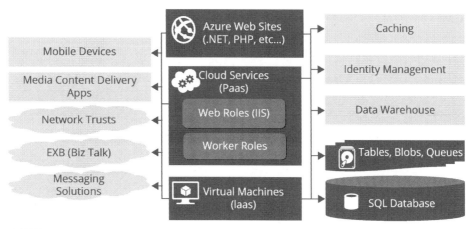

FIGURE 4-7

Big Data

When people talk about big data platforms, they're typically referring to an appliance that is purpose-built for large, complex data volumes. Big data platforms often involve commodity hardware and open-source software, making adoption easy and data analysis whip-fast. Incumbent technologies such as data warehouses or master data management hubs aren't optimized for this type of processing. As companies research emerging technologies, what they really want to know is not only how they work, but also how they fit into increasingly unwieldy technology infrastructures.

For many years, the bulk of data analysis has been done on relational data stored in a data warehouse built with a relational RDBMS. With SQL Server, for instance, it's common to use tools such as SQL Server Analysis Services to do this. This kind of business analytics is still important, and it will be for a long time to come; but what if the data you want to analyze is so big that relational databases just can't handle it? And suppose the data isn't relational? Your data might take many forms: information from sensors or RFID tags, log files in server farms, clickstream data produced by web applications, images from medical diagnostic devices, and more. This data might also be really big, too big to be used effectively with a traditional data warehouse. In cases like this, you have what's known as a big data problem. Big data problems, rare just a few years ago, have now become quite common.

The dominant technology today for analyzing big data is Hadoop. An Apache open-source project, this technology runs on a cluster of physical servers or VMs, spreading the data it works on across those machines and processing it in parallel. The more machines Hadoop has to use, the faster it can complete whatever work it is doing.

This kind of problem is a natural fit for the public cloud. Rather than maintain an army of on-premises servers that might sit idle much of the time, running Hadoop in the cloud enables you to create (and pay for) VMs only when you need them. Even better, more and more of the big data that you want to analyze with Hadoop is created in the cloud, saving you the trouble of moving it around. To help you exploit these synergies, Microsoft provides a Hadoop service on Windows Azure called *Windows Azure HDInsight Service.*

A Hadoop application, commonly called a *job*, uses a programming model known as *MapReduce.* For more information about MapReduce, please follow this link: `http://www.windowsazure` `.com/en-us/manage/services/hdinsight/using-mapreduce-with-hdinsight/#header-1`.

On Windows Azure, the data a MapReduce job works on is typically kept in Blob storage. In Hadoop, however, MapReduce jobs expect data to be stored in the *Hadoop Distributed File System* (*HDFS*). HDFS is similar to Blob Storage in some ways; for example, it replicates data across multiple physical servers. Rather than duplicate this functionality, Windows Azure HDInsight instead exposes Blob Storage through the HDFS API, as the figure shows. While the logic in a MapReduce job thinks it is accessing ordinary HDFS files, the job is in fact working with data streamed to it from Blobs. And to support the case where multiple jobs are run over the same data, Windows Azure HDInsight also allows copying data from Blobs into full HDFS running in the VMs.

To use Hadoop on Windows Azure, you first ask this cloud platform to create a Hadoop cluster, specifying the number of VMs you need. Setting up a Hadoop cluster yourself is a nontrivial task, so letting Windows Azure do it for you makes sense. When you're done using the cluster, you shut it down. There's no need to pay for compute resources that you aren't using.

As Figure 4-8 suggests, the Windows Azure HDInsight Service fits perfectly into our reference architecture, landing in the place of Data Warehouse, which is commonly used for big data storage and management. We see the promise of big data and the foresight of investing in the technologies that process and provision it. Big data will not only help to keep our customers from defecting, it could save our planet from overheating. The promise of big data analytics is as expansive as our imaginations.

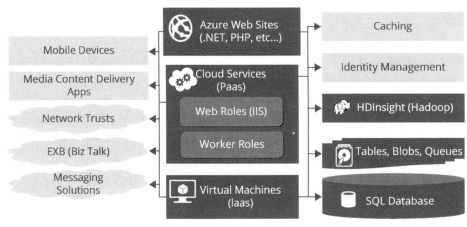

FIGURE 4-8

MESSAGING AND INTEGRATION COMPONENTS

No matter what it's doing, code frequently needs to interact with other code. In some situations, all that's needed is basic Queued messaging. In other cases, more complex business-to-business (B2B) messaging transactions are required. This is especially true for hybrid cloud applications. The grand canonical example for messaging B2B transactions is a bank account transfer. You debit one account and credit another. These two operations need to succeed or fail together because otherwise you are either creating or destroying money (which is illegal, by the way). Sounds simple, doesn't it? The catch is that it's not as simple as it sounds.

Getting money from one bank account to another bank account is a fairly complicated affair that touches a ton of other processes. More important, it's not a synchronous fail-together/succeed-together scenario. Instead, principles of accounting apply (surprise!). When a transfer is initiated, let's say through online banking, the transfer is recorded in the form of a message sent for submission into the accounting system, and the debit is recorded in the message originating account as a "pending" transaction that affects the displayed balance. From the user's perspective, the transaction is "done," but truthfully nothing has happened, yet. Eventually, the accounting system will get the message and start performing the transfer, which typically causes a cascade of operations, many of them yielding further messages, including booking into clearing accounts and notifying the other bank of the transfer.

The point here is that distributed messaging should never tolerate any kind of "doubt" about the state of any operation. All participants must be able to have a high degree of confidence in their knowledge about the success or failure of their respective action. No shots into the dark. There's no maybe. Succeed or fail.

That said, "fail" is a well-known state that often happens in distributed systems. In many cases "fail" isn't something that a bit of patience can't fix, which means that teaching the system some patience and tenacity is probably a good idea instead of giving up too easily. Therefore, if an operation fails because it runs into a database deadlock or the database is offline, or the network is down, or the local machine's network adapter just got electrocuted, none of that is necessarily a reason to fail the operation. It's a reason to write an alert into a log and call for help for someone to fix the environment condition.

Windows Azure provides a few different ways to avoid or remedy these "failures."

Service Bus

Whether applications run in the cloud, in your datacenter, on a mobile device, or somewhere else, they need to interact. The goal of Windows Azure Service Bus is to enable applications running pretty much anywhere to exchange data.

Service Bus provides a queuing service. This service isn't identical to the Windows Azure Queues just described, however. While both queuing technologies exist concurrently, Windows Azure Queues were introduced first, as a dedicated queue storage mechanism built on top of the

Windows Azure Storage services. Service Bus Queues, introduced with the latest release of the Service Bus, are built on top of the broader "brokered messaging" infrastructure designed to integrate applications or application components that may span multiple communication protocols, data contracts, trust domains, and/or network environments.

For example, unlike Windows Azure Queues, Service Bus provides a publish-and-subscribe mechanism. An application can send messages to a topic, while other applications can create subscriptions to this topic. This allows one-to-many communication among a set of applications, enabling the same message to be read by multiple recipients.

And queuing isn't the only option: Service Bus also allows direct communication, providing a secure way to interact through firewalls. This service supports direct one-way messaging, request/response messaging, and peer-to-peer messaging. The pattern associated with this kind of messaging solution is referred to as *relayed* messaging. In the relayed messaging pattern, an on-premises or cloud-based service connects to the relay service through an outbound port and creates a bi-directional socket for communication tied to a particular rendezvous address. The client does not have to know where the service resides, and the on-premises service does not need any inbound ports open on the firewall. Relayed messaging provides many benefits, but it requires the server and client to both be online at the same time in order to send and receive messages.

The second messaging solution, introduced in the latest version of the Service Bus, enables *brokered* messaging capabilities. The brokered messaging scheme can also be thought of as asynchronous or "temporally decoupled" messaging. Producers (senders) and consumers (receivers) do not have to be online at the same time. The messaging infrastructure reliably stores messages until the consuming party is ready to receive them. This allows the components of the distributed application to be disconnected, either voluntarily — for example, for maintenance — or due to a component crash, without affecting the whole system. Furthermore, the receiving application may only have to come online during certain times of the day, such as an inventory management system that only is required to run at the end of a business day.

The core components of the Service Bus brokered messaging infrastructure are *Queues*, *topics*, and *subscriptions*. These components enable new asynchronous messaging scenarios, such as temporal decoupling, publish-subscribe, load leveling, and load balancing.

Applications that communicate through Service Bus might be Windows Azure applications or software running on some other cloud platform. They can also be applications running outside the cloud, however. For example, consider the hybrid cloud architecture shown in Figure 4-9 for an airline that implements reservation services in computers inside its own datacenter.

The airline needs to expose these services to many clients, including check-in kiosks in airports, reservation agent terminals, and maybe even customers' phones. It might use Service Bus to do this, creating loosely coupled interactions among the various applications.

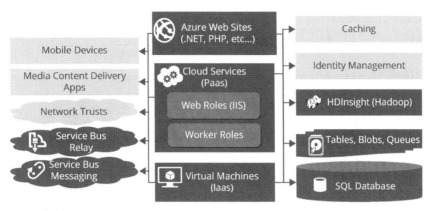

FIGURE 4-9

Virtual Network

Windows Azure runs today in several datacenters spread across the United States, Europe, and Asia. When you run an application or store data, you can select one or more of these datacenters to use. Until now we have considered Windows Azure components as standalone or, as in the case of web and worker role VM instances, within the boundaries of Cloud Services VMs. However, as in your own datacenter and as in most of the hybrid cloud scenarios, you may also need to "stich" various applications together in what is called a *virtual private network (VPN)*, networks that span the boundaries of the cloud and on-premises datacenters as well as individual remote connections from a single or many on-premises machines to the networks or machines running in the cloud.

Windows Azure Virtual Network enables you to create secure site-to-site connectivity (S2S) linking one or more on-premises network subnets to a network subnet (defined by the VNET configuration) that could, for example, encompass both Windows Azure execution models: Cloud Services Web/Worker roles and Windows Azure VMs. Additionally, a new feature, called point to site (P2S) (it was added in April 2013, which effectively replaced the previously known Azure Connect point-to-point service) can now connect on-premises desktops and servers to a specified Windows Azure VNET from remote locations.

One useful way to use Windows Azure VNET in a hybrid cloud is when you treat a public cloud as an extension of your own datacenter. Because you can create VMs on demand, and then remove them (and stop paying) when they're no longer needed, you can have computing power only when you want it. And because you can deploy VMs running Windows Server, SQL Server, SharePoint, Active Directory, BizTalk Server, Linux, and other familiar on-premises products, this approach can work with the applications you already have.

To make this really useful, though, your users ought to be able to treat these applications as if they were running in your own datacenter. This is exactly what Windows Azure VNET allows. Using a VPN gateway device, an administrator can set up a VPN between your local network and a defined group of VMs running in Windows Azure. Because you assign your own IP v4 addresses to the cloud VMs, they appear to be on your own network. Users in your organization can access the applications those VMs contain as if they were running locally.

Configuring a Windows Azure Virtual Network

You can configure a virtual network in one of three ways:

➤ By using the Windows Azure Management Portal wizard

➤ By executing a PowerShell custom script

➤ By importing a network configuration file (.netcfg)

Each method of configuring a virtual network results in the configuration of a network configuration file. The network configuration file contains all the configuration information for your virtual network.

Using the Windows Azure Management Portal Wizard

When you use the Windows Azure Management Portal (https://manage.windowsazure.com) wizard to configure your virtual network, you are presented with three options (see Figure 4-10):

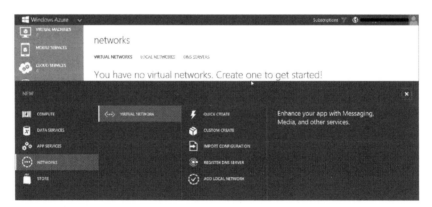

FIGURE 4-10

➤ Quick Create

➤ Custom Create

➤ Import Configuration

Either option will allow you to create the virtual network and specify commonly used network configuration settings, such as network address space and subnets, DNS servers, and affinity groups.

Say you want to extend your datacenter by adding additional capacity to your on-premises SQL Server (this pattern sometimes is called "cloud bursting"). Your on-premises application uses this SQL Server for various CRUD operations, while SQL connection is established via Windows

Authentication mode. In order to protect your SQL Server in the cloud, you need to allow your extended SQL Server VM to support Windows Authentication as well. This can be achieved by extending your on-premises network via Windows Azure VNET, deploying a copy of your on-premises SQL Server into one of the Windows Azure VMs that will be linked into this new virtual network, and then joining a SQL Server VM to the Active Directory Domain Controller located on-premises. Figure 4-11 illustrates this scenario.

Figure 4-12 shows one of the steps in the Custom Create wizard workflow of the Windows Azure Management Portal.

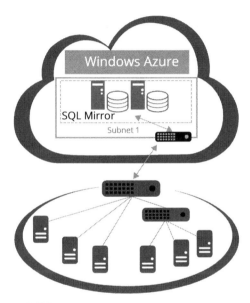

FIGURE 4-11

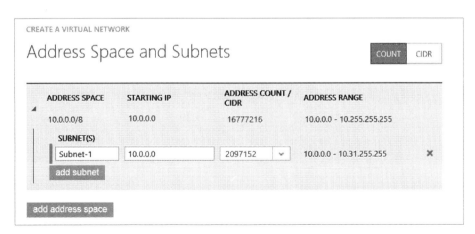

FIGURE 4-12

Executing a PowerShell Custom Script

With the release of Windows Azure IaaS into general availability, the Windows Azure
PowerShell team has provided an even more powerful automation experience for deploying
virtual machines in the cloud than ever before. The following code excerpt illustrates the same
task of creating a virtual private network using a PowerShell script:

```
# Affinity Group parameters
$AGLocation = "East US"
$AGDesc = "My Affinity Group"
$AGName = "MYAG"

#See if the affinity group already exists
$aff = Get-AzureAffinityGroup -Name $AGName | Select Name

if ($aff.Name.Contains($AGName))
{
      #Already exist, skip this step
      Write-Host "The Affinity Group ""$AGName"" already exists. Skipping this step..."
}
else
{
      #Does not exist, let's create it
      Write-Host "The Affinity Group ""$AGName"" does not exist. Creating a new one..."
      # Create a new affinity Group
      New-AzureAffinityGroup -Location $AGLocation -Description $AGDesc -Name $AGName
}

#Set the current storage account
$store = Get-AzureStorageAccount -StorageAccountName $storageAccount | Select
StorageAccountName
if ($store.StorageAccountName.Contains($storageAccount))
{
      Write-Host "The storage account ""$storageAccount"" already exists. Setting it
up..."
      Set-AzureSubscription -SubscriptionName $sub -CurrentStorageAccount $storageAccount
}
else
{
      #Create Storage account for VNet assets
      Write-Host "Creating a new storage account ""$storageAccount""..."
      # The storage account name must be unique to Windows Azure and
      # must be between 3 and 24 characters in length and
      # use lowercase letters and numbers only.
      New-AzureStorageAccount -StorageAccountName $storageAccount -Label $label
-AffinityGroup $AGName
}


# Clear current settings
```

```
Remove-AzureVNetConfig -ErrorAction SilentlyContinue

# Apply new network
$configPath = (Split-Path -Path $MyInvocation.MyCommand.Definition -Parent) + "\MyVNET.xml"
Set-AzureVNetConfig -ConfigurationPath $configPath

# Check results
Get-AzureVNetConfig | Select -ExpandProperty XMLConfiguration -AffinityGroup $ag -VNetName
$vnetname -VMs $dc
```

NOTE *When Windows Azure VMs are placed in the logical "containers" called* affinity
groups, *the Windows Azure Fabric Controller during the provisioning stage will deploy
them in the same cluster, making them as close as possible, while reducing the latency, and
increasing the performance and high availability, as two VMs in the same affinity group
will not be put down at the same time for maintenance tasks such as OS upgrades and
security patches.*

People tend to make mistakes. It's in our nature. Human errors are impossible to avoid
… unless there is an automation process that can be repeatedly executed without human
interactions. Using PowerShell scripts to automatically configure Azure virtual networks not
only dramatically simplifies the tasks of IT admins, but also makes these tasks less error-prone,
therefore, producing better and quicker final results.

Importing a Network Configuration File

The MyVNET.xml file referenced in the preceding script points to the network configuration file
that can be either downloaded from the Windows Azure Management Portal after you created
your first virtual network or created in any XML editor from scratch. The following code
excerpt demonstrates a sample configuration file:

```
<NetworkConfiguration xmlns:xsi="http://www.w3.org/2001/XMLSchema-instance"
xmlns:xsd="http://www.w3.org/2001/XMLSchema" xmlns="http://schemas.microsoft.com/
ServiceHosting/2011/07/NetworkConfiguration">
  <VirtualNetworkConfiguration>
    <Dns>
      <DnsServers>
        <DnsServer name="myDNS" IPAddress="10.1.10.4" />
      </DnsServers>
    </Dns>
    <VirtualNetworkSites>
      <VirtualNetworkSite name="MyVNET" AffinityGroup="MYAG">
        <AddressSpace>
          <AddressPrefix>10.1.0.0/16</AddressPrefix>
        </AddressSpace>
        <Subnets>
          <Subnet name="AD-Subnet">
```

```
              <AddressPrefix>10.1.10.10/24</AddressPrefix>
          </Subnet>
          <Subnet name="PaaS-Subnet">
              <AddressPrefix>10.1.1.0/24</AddressPrefix>
          </Subnet>
          <Subnet name="IaaS-Subnet">
              <AddressPrefix>10.1.2.0/24</AddressPrefix>
          </Subnet>
        </Subnets>
        <DnsServersRef>
          <DnsServerRef name="myDNS" />
        </DnsServersRef>
      </VirtualNetworkSite>
    </VirtualNetworkSites>
  </VirtualNetworkConfiguration>
</NetworkConfiguration>
```

Using the features of Windows Azure Virtual Network, you can create dedicated private virtual networks in the cloud as well as branch-office and cross-premises solutions.

The fundamental requirements for deploying your on-premises software applications on Windows Azure Virtual Private Networks differ very little from deploying them in VMs (and, to some extent, physical machines) on-premises. For example, in the case of Windows Server AD DS, if the Domain Controllers (DCs) that you deploy on Windows Azure VMs are replicas in an existing on-premises corporate domain/forest, then the Windows Azure deployment can largely be treated in the same way as you might treat any other additional Windows Server Active Directory site. That is, you can safely use Windows Azure Virtual Networks in the hybrid cloud reference architecture diagram in place of on-premises Network Trusts component, as shown in Figure 4-13.

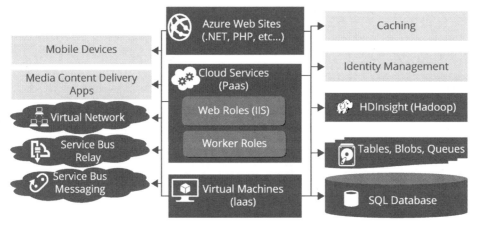

FIGURE 4-13

Traffic Manager

An application with users scattered around the world, however, is more likely to run in multiple datacenters, maybe even all of them. In this second situation, you face a problem: How do you intelligently assign users to application instances? Most of the time, you probably want users to access the datacenter closest to them, as it will likely give them the best response time. But what if that copy of the application is overloaded or unavailable? In this case, it would be nice to route their request automatically to another datacenter. This is exactly what's done by Windows Azure Traffic Manager.

The owner of an application defines rules that specify how requests from users should be routed to datacenters, and then relies on Traffic Manager to carry out these rules. For example, users might normally be routed to the closest Windows Azure datacenter, but be sent to another one when the response time from their default datacenter exceeds a certain threshold. For globally distributed applications with many users, having a built-in service to handle problems like these is useful.

BizTalk Services

Integrating an on-premises process with processes running in Windows Azure opens up a wide range of opportunities that enable customers to extend their on-premises solutions into the Cloud environment. However, given the fact that these processes operate in their own "space," but at the same time need to interact with other on-premises or cloud applications, there is a need to bridge the message and transport protocol mismatch between these disparate applications. *Windows Azure BizTalk Services* provides Business-to-Business (B2B) and Enterprise Application Integration (EAI) capabilities for bridging cloud and on-premises applications enabling new messaging integration capabilities within the next generation of hybrid integration solutions. It includes built-in support for managing EDI relationships between partners, as well as EAI bridges with on-premises assets — including built-in support for integrating with on-premises SAP, SQL Server, Oracle, and Siebel systems. You can also optionally integrate Windows Azure BizTalk Services with on-premises BizTalk Server deployments — enabling powerful hybrid enterprise solutions.

BizTalk Services run on a secure, dedicated per tenant, environment that you can provision on demand in a matter of minutes. It does not require any upfront license, and supports a pay-only for what you use billing model.

Media Services

Video makes up a large part of Internet traffic today, and that percentage will be even larger tomorrow. Yet providing video on the web isn't simple. There are many variables, such as the encoding algorithm and the display resolution of the user's screen. Video also tends to have bursts in demand, like a Saturday night spike when a lot of people decide they would like to watch an online movie.

Given video's popularity, it's a safe bet that many new applications will be created to take advantage of that technology. Yet all of them will need to solve some of the same problems, and making each one solve those problems on its own makes no sense. A better approach is to create a platform that provides common solutions for many applications to use — and building this platform in the cloud has some clear advantages. It can be broadly available on a pay-as-you-go basis, and it can handle the variability in demand that video applications often face.

Windows Azure Media Services address this problem. It provides a set of cloud components that make life easier for people creating and running applications using video and other media. Windows Azure Media Services form an extensible cloud-based media platform that enables developers to build solutions for consuming, encoding, processing, managing, and delivering media content, while protecting the media assets using encryption, digital right management, or both. Media Services are built on the infrastructure of Windows Azure (to provide media processing and asset storage), and IIS Media Services (to provide content delivery). Figure 4-14 illustrates this technology combined with on-premises and other network-based resources into a hybrid cloud media solution.

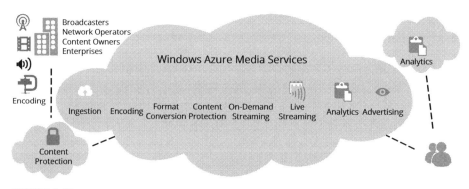

FIGURE 4-14

As the figure shows, Media Services provides a set of components for applications that work with video and other media. For example, it includes a media ingest component to upload video into Media Services (where it's stored in Windows Azure Blob Storage), an encoding component that supports various video and audio formats, a content protection component that provides digital rights management, a component for inserting ads into a video stream, components for streaming, and more. Microsoft partners can also provide components for the platform, which Microsoft can then distribute and bill for on their behalf.

Applications that use this platform can run on Windows Azure or elsewhere. For example, in a hybrid cloud scenario a desktop application for a video production house might enable users to upload video to Media Services and then process it in various ways. Alternatively, a cloud-based content management service running on Windows Azure might rely on Media Services to process and distribute video. Wherever it runs and whatever it does, each application chooses which components it needs to use, accessing them through RESTful interfaces.

To distribute what it produces, an application can use the Windows Azure CDN, other vendor CDNs, or just send bits directly to users. However it gets there, video created using Media Services can be consumed by various client systems, including Windows 7 and Windows 8, HTML 5 supporting browsers, iOS, Android, Windows Phone, Flash, Silverlight, and a new standard for adaptive streaming over HTTP: DASH. DASH (Dynamic Adaptive Stream over HTTP) has the potential to replace existing proprietary technologies such as Microsoft Smooth Streaming, Adobe Dynamic Streaming, and Apple HTTP Live Streaming (HLS). A unified standard would be a boon to content publishers, who could produce one set of files that play on all DASH-compatible devices.

Another interesting opportunity is to combine the capabilities of Windows Azure Media Services with the new SharePoint 2013 app model. Combining the multimedia capabilities that Windows Azure Media Services provide with the power of content management and search capabilities that SharePoint 2013 offers creates a completely new market of modern media applications. The goal of Windows Azure Media Services is to make it easier to create modern media applications.

Mobile Services

Gartner reports that mobile device enablement is a driving factor for cloud adoption, but supporting the growing ecosystem of mobile solutions becomes problematic and many organizations face challenges with exposing internal solutions to potentially thousands, or tens of thousands of mobile devices being run by unknown parties. Additionally, these solutions usually require specialized knowledge of the services that are required by mobile devices (such as push notification).

Windows Azure Mobile Services makes it incredibly easy to connect a scalable cloud back end to your client and mobile applications. It enables you to easily store structured data in the cloud that can span both devices and users, integrate it with user authentication, as well as send out updates to clients via push notifications.

Windows Azure Mobile Services provides the following back-end capabilities in Windows Azure to support your apps:

> Simple provisioning and management of tables for storing app data

> Integration with notification services to deliver push notifications to your app

> Integration with well-known identity providers for authentication

> Granular control for authorizing access to tables

> Supports scripts to inject business logic into data access operations

> Integration with other cloud services

➤ Supports the capability to scale a mobile service instance

➤ Ability to create and expose Custom APIs from your Mobile Service back end

➤ Service monitoring and logging

When you develop hybrid cloud applications, it is very important to design your applications so they can quickly reach users across myriad platforms and devices without having to maintain multiple code bases. Windows Azure Mobile Services' support for Windows 8, Windows Phone, iOS, Android, and HTML5 client applications dovetails with the overarching Mobile Services drive for simplicity.

Using Windows Azure Mobile Services in your hybrid cloud architectures makes the task of storing data in the cloud incredibly easy. When you create a Windows Azure Mobile Service, Windows Azure automatically associates it with a SQL Database in the cloud. The Windows Azure Mobile Service back end then provides built-in support for enabling remote apps to securely store and retrieve data from it (via secure REST endpoints utilizing a JSON-based OData format), without you having to write or deploy any custom server code. The custom APIs also provide the ability to work with data sources other than SQL Databases (Azure Table Services or MongoDB); broker calls to 3rd party APIs; integrate with Windows Azure Queues or Service Bus; work with custom non-JSON payloads; route client requests to services back on-premises (e.g. with the Windows Azure BizTalk Services); or simply implement functionality that doesn't correspond to a database operation. Built-in management support is provided within the Windows Azure portal for creating new tables, browsing data, setting indexes, and controlling access permissions.

Our hybrid cloud reference architecture can vastly benefit from inclusion of both Windows Azure Media Services and Windows Azure Mobile Services (ironically, both having the same abbreviation, WAMS) into an updated diagram, as shown in Figure 4-15.

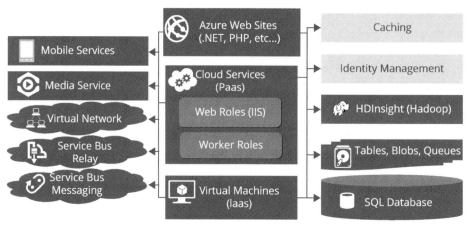

FIGURE 4-15

SUPPORTING SERVICES

Expanding a business into new regions of the world with branch offices is a great idea from a business perspective, but it often presents challenges to network architects and implementers. Connecting each branch office to a central location requires some sort of physical or logical connection, with bandwidth that is typically orders of magnitude smaller than local area connections. Low bandwidth combined with the trend toward centralizing organization data often yields branch office links that are congested, resulting in poor performance for applications. Moreover, many types of wide area network (WAN) links are expensive and can incur substantial startup and monthly costs.

To better utilize an existing WAN link or to prevent incurring the costs associated with increasing the bandwidth of your WAN link, you can use a variety of WAN optimization techniques. Some of these techniques require additional equipment. One prominent WAN optimization technique is caching; data obtained across the WAN link is cached at the branch office. A computer in the branch office that requests data already requested by another computer will retrieve the data from a branch office cache, rather than pull it across the WAN link.

Another WAN optimization technique is bringing identity management to the cloud. As enterprise IT transitions to a new hybrid cloud configuration, controlling who is granted access to which applications becomes increasingly important. This presents CIOs and their teams with a whole new set of identity management challenges. Authenticating users to your cloud environment requires multiple round-trips between your cloud application and the security identity store on-premises (whether it is Active Directory, LDAP, or another user credentials management store). In addition, users must keep track of multiple URLs, user names, and passwords to access their applications. The next two sections describe how Windows Azure can support achieving these two prominent WAN optimization techniques.

Caching

Applications tend to access the same data repeatedly. One way to improve performance is to keep a copy of that data closer to the application, minimizing the time needed to retrieve it. Caching provides several benefits to application developers. It increases performance by temporarily storing information from other back-end sources. High performance is achieved by maintaining this cache in-memory across multiple cache servers.

Accessing data stored in any of Windows Azure's data management services — SQL Database, Tables, or Blobs — is quite fast. Yet accessing data stored in memory is even faster. Therefore, keeping an in-memory copy of frequently accessed data can improve application performance. You can use Windows Azure Caching service to do this.

A Cloud Services application can store data in this cache, then retrieve it directly without needing to access persistent storage. As Figure 4-16 shows, the cache can be maintained inside your application's VMs (*co-located cache*) or be provided by VMs dedicated solely to caching (*dedicated cache*). In either case, the cache can be distributed, with the data it contains spread across multiple VMs in a Windows Azure datacenter.

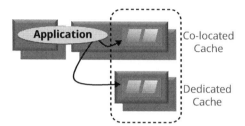

FIGURE 4-16

In the dedicated topology, you define a worker role that is dedicated to caching. This means that all of the worker role's available memory is used for the caching and operating overhead. In a co-located topology, you use a percentage of available memory on application roles for caching. For example, you could assign 20 percent of the physical memory for caching on each web role instance. In both cases, you only pay for the compute services required for the running role instances.

An application that repeatedly reads a product catalog might benefit from using this kind of caching, for example, as the data it needs will be available more quickly. The technology also supports locking, enabling it to be used with read/write as well as read-only data.

As Figure 4-17 depicts, leveraging Windows Azure Caching in your hybrid cloud reference architecture can help to optimize the overall performance of your hybrid applications, as well as reduce costs and increase the scalability of other storage services, such as SQL Database or Azure storage. Hybrid cloud applications can use caching for the common scenario of session state and output caching. As user load increases the cache helps applications be more responsive, enabling your applications to scale.

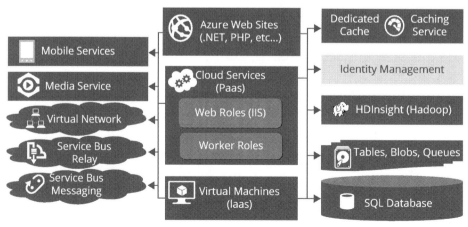

FIGURE 4-17

Identity Management

Having a strong enterprise identity strategy is a key component of enabling new applications and infrastructure in the cloud. Working with identity is part of any hybrid cloud application. For example, knowing who a user is enables an application to determine how it should interact with that user. To help you do this, Microsoft provides Windows Azure Active Directory. Windows Azure Active Directory is the world's largest cloud-based, enterprise-quality, Internet-scale identity and access management solution. Currently, more than 2.9 million businesses, government bodies, and schools are already enjoying the benefits of Windows Azure Active Directory, using it to manage access to Office 365, Dynamics CRM online, Windows Intune, and Windows Azure. You will learn more about identity management in the cloud, and how it helps to bridge both private cloud and public cloud together, in Chapter 5.

Like most directory services, Windows Azure Active Directory stores information about users and the organizations to which they belong. It enables users to log in, and then supplies them with tokens they can present to applications to prove their identity. It also enables synchronizing user information with Windows Server Active Directory running on-premises in your local network, as shown on Figure 4-18.

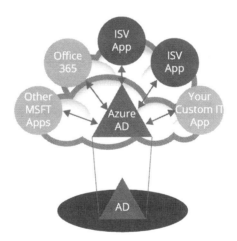

FIGURE 4-18

Windows Azure AD is a cloud-based identity management service built to support global scale, reliability, and availability for your customers, and the basic directory is included without additional cost. This cloud-based directory makes it easy to do the following:

➤   Manage employee access to cloud-based, line-of-business apps, Microsoft cloud services such as Office 365, and third-party SAAS applications.

➤   Deliver a single sign-on experience for hybrid cloud applications, eliminating the need for multiple usernames and passwords and limiting help desk calls and password resets.

➤ Revoke access to cloud-based business applications when an employee leaves the company or changes jobs.

➤ Manage federation and access to cloud-facing services for partners and customers.

While the mechanisms and data formats used by Windows Azure Active Directory aren't identical to those used in Windows Server Active Directory, the functions it performs are quite similar.

It's important to understand that Windows Azure Active Directory is designed primarily for use by cloud applications. It can be used by applications running on Windows Azure, for example, or on other cloud platforms. It's also used by Microsoft's own cloud applications, such as those in Office 365. If you want to extend your datacenter into the cloud using Windows Azure Virtual Machines and Windows Azure Virtual Network, however, Windows Azure Active Directory isn't the right choice. Instead, you'll want to run Windows Server Active Directory in cloud VMs, as described earlier.

To enable applications to access the information it contains, Windows Azure Active Directory provides a RESTful API called *Windows Azure Active Directory Graph.*

Windows Azure Active Directory Graph

Windows Azure AD Graph provides programmatic access to Windows Azure Active Directory (AD) through REST API endpoints. Using Windows Azure AD Graph, developers can perform create, read, update, and delete (CRUD) operations on Windows Azure AD objects such as users and groups. In the on-premises world, you would usually programmatically access Windows Server Active Directory by using ADSI or ADO.NET libraries. In the cloud, you programmatically access Windows Azure AD using Windows Azure AD Graph.

Windows Azure AD Graph enables two key hybrid cloud scenarios:

➤ **Line-of-business applications (LOB)** — In this scenario, you are an enterprise developer and your organization purchased a subscription that includes Windows Azure AD (for example, Office 365 or Windows Intune). The Office 365 functionality mainly fulfills your organization's needs, but some are not met by the service. As an enterprise developer, you need to extend the functionality of Office 365. This may require access to Windows Azure AD objects. You use Windows Azure AD Graph to accomplish this scenario.

➤ **Creating reusable features that require Windows Azure AD access** — In this scenario, you are an independent software vendor (ISV) that specializes in creating and selling reusable features that extend the functionality of cloud applications. As an ISV you want to offer to your customers reusable features that require access to Windows Azure AD objects. You use the REST API to accomplish this scenario.

Windows Azure AD Graph enables applications running on any platform access to directory objects and the relationships among them. For example, an authorized application might use this API to learn about a user, the groups to which the user belongs, and other information. Applications can also see relationships between users — their social graph — enabling them to work more intelligently with the connections among people.

Windows Azure AD Access Control

In order to execute any of the operations available through Windows Azure Graph, the client needs to be authenticated first. Windows Azure AD Graph relies on Windows Azure Active Directory Access Control for authentication. Windows Azure AD Access Control federates with Windows Azure Active Directory and serves as a Security Token Service (STS) for client requests.

Windows Azure Active Directory Access Control makes it easier for an application to accept identity information from Facebook, Google, Microsoft account (formerly Windows Live ID), and other popular identity providers. Rather than require the application to understand the diverse data formats and protocols used by each of these providers, Access Control translates all of them into a single common format represented by Simple Web Token (SWT). It also enables an application to accept logins from one or more Active Directory domains. For example, a vendor providing a SaaS application might use Windows Azure Active Directory Access Control to give all their users a single sign-on to the application.

Directory services are a core underpinning of hybrid cloud applications. It shouldn't be surprising that they find a place on our hybrid cloud reference architecture among other important services offered by the Windows Azure platform, as shown in Figure 4-19.

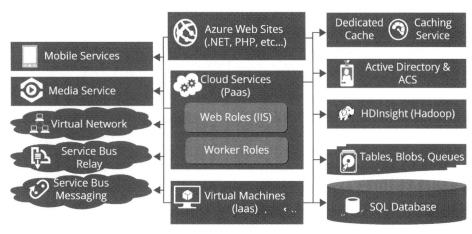

FIGURE 4-19

For companies that already run Windows Server Active Directory on-premises, Windows Azure AD is a natural extension for enabling existing identities in the cloud. Based on open standards, including SAML, OData, and WS-FED, Windows Azure AD works with any modern browsers running on a PC, tablet, or mobile device and can be easily integrated into hybrid cloud applications running on a multitude of platforms from Microsoft and third parties.

SOFTWARE DEVELOPMENT KITS

Over five years ago, when the first pre-release version of Windows Azure was released, it supported only .NET development. Today, however, you can create Windows Azure applications in pretty much any language. Microsoft currently provides language-specific software development kits (SDKs) for .NET, Java, PHP, Node.js, Python, and Ruby. There's also a general Windows Azure SDK that provides basic support for any language, such as C++.

These SDKs help you build, deploy, and manage Windows Azure applications. They're available from either `http://www.windowsazure.com/en-us/downloads/` or directly from the NuGet Gallery (`http://nuget.org/packages?q=windowsazureofficial`), and they can be used with Visual Studio and Eclipse. Windows Azure also offers command-line tools that developers can use with any editor or development environment, including tools for deploying applications to Windows Azure from Linux and iOS systems.

Along with helping you build Windows Azure applications, these SDKs also provide client libraries to help you create software running outside the cloud that uses Windows Azure services. For example, you might build an application running at a hoster that relies on Windows Azure Blobs, or create a tool that deploys Windows Azure applications through the Windows Azure management interface.

SUMMARY

Windows Azure delivers an enterprise-grade cloud platform for today's most demanding enterprise applications. With Windows Azure, you can build brand-new applications architected for cloud scale, extend existing applications to the cloud, or provide hybrid cloud "burst" capacity to handle uneven or unexpected loads. For example, you can build new applications with the cloud in mind, or use Service Bus to extend existing applications through hybrid solutions across private infrastructure running in your datacenter and Windows Azure. Figure 4-20 shows the final version of the hybrid cloud architecture we began with at the beginning of this chapter, now including all the Windows Azure components we have covered.

As we close our discussion about how the Windows Azure platform can help you in designing and building your hybrid cloud applications, keep in mind that understanding the life cycle of your workload will help you choose the desired Windows Azure service component that you'd like to deliver.

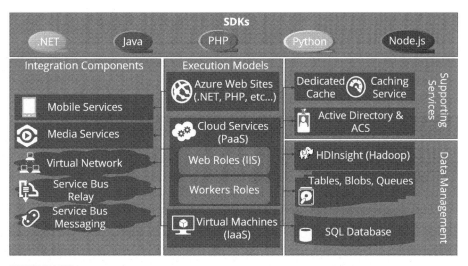

FIGURE 4-20

A number of Windows Azure components can be leveraged to provide the desired scalability, elasticity, and resiliency. These have varying costs and may also affect multiple layers. At an application level, utilizing all of these isn't feasible for most projects due to cost and implementation time. By decomposing your application to the workload level, you gain the benefit of making these investments at a more targeted level.

Even at the workload level, you may not choose to implement every component. What you choose to implement or not is determined by your requirements. Regardless of the Windows Azure components you do choose, you should make an informed choice after considering all the options.

5

Private Cloud Components and Services That Help to Build Hybrid Clouds

IN THIS CHAPTER:

➤ Examining the layers of a private cloud that enable successful hybrid cloud adoption

➤ Introducing the System Center as the linchpin of successful hybrid cloud management

➤ Networking, identify management, and other technical considerations

You've made significant progress up to this point. You should have a solid understanding of cloud computing and the hybrid cloud model; its significance to the business and how to build a business case; the critical aspects of project envisioning and scoping; and a technical drill-down of the main Azure components and services. Hopefully, along the way we've built up some trust with you. You know that we're here to tell you the whole truth, and the truth is that adopting a cloud computing model of any kind can be a significant disruption to nearly every aspect of the existing IT environment, including the people and processes — and that is really at the heart of this chapter.

This chapter assumes that you're invested in or are considering investing in the cloud not just as a technology purchase but as a new way of life. The truth is that if you're going to mature your IT infrastructure, management, and operations and mitigate the disruption the cloud brings, you will need to embrace at least some aspects of what it means to be a cloud service provider. This chapter begins with a brief explanation of what a private cloud looks like and then goes into detail about the cloud management platform, a critical component of the hybrid cloud architecture that enables you to provision, manage, and operate both your on-premises and Azure-based resources with a single set of tools. You'll also learn about networking and identity management considerations that enable this extension of your toolset to the public cloud.

NOTE *In Chapter 1, we covered the key service models, characteristics, trends, and considerations for cloud computing and the basic definition of a private cloud. With that understanding in mind, we want to reemphasize the highly customizable nature of a private cloud. When constructing your on-premises cloud, it's critically important to focus on those aspects that line up directly with your previously identified business objectives. Building your own cloud infrastructure and adopting service provider operational practices is neither cheap nor easy. You need to be able to justify these investments during the project, and be able to report milestones along the way that are aligned with the business's stated objectives. This not only allows your project to proceed with the proper sponsorship and funding, but also makes management happy, which is always a good thing.*

You can use the Microsoft Cloud Analysis Tool (found at `http://www.microsoft.com/optimization/tools/overview.mspx`*) to determine the characteristics you need and to give your solution architecture and design proper focus. Because this is not a private cloud book, we cover only briefly what a reference architecture looks like for a private cloud. At Microsoft, we look at the private cloud architecture very holistically. For a complete view of all aspects of a private cloud architecture, please see the Private Cloud Reference Model at* `http://go.microsoft.com/?linkid=9784986` *or within the Private Cloud Solutions Hub on TechNet at* `http://www.technet.com/cloud/private-cloud`*.*

THE CLOUD MANAGEMENT PLATFORM

Let's start by considering Figure 5-1, which depicts the logical functional layers of a private cloud. This focuses on System Center as the foundation for your cloud management platform and helps you understand the high-level functions provided by this model. System Center is Microsoft's integrated management platform, which has deep and broad capabilities spanning the datacenter, clouds, user devices, and more. Herein we will focus primarily on the capabilities essential to hybrid cloud management.

At the bottom are the on-premises fabric and at the top are public cloud services. The on-premises fabric basically consists of your pooled computing resources: compute, storage, and network, typically including a virtualization layer that does the majority of the resource pooling. The middle layer is the cloud management platform, which, among other things, provides the following:

- ➤ Self-service
- ➤ Service delivery
- ➤ Process orchestration
- ➤ Management and operations
- ➤ Automation

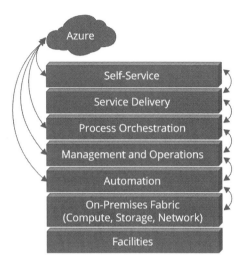

FIGURE 5-1

Each category in the previous list is enabled by a number of technologies; and in some cases multiple options are available to achieve the higher-level goal, depending on the business need (see Figure 5-2). The following sections describe each technology and how to make those decisions. These are the key integration points to connect the cloud management platform to Azure and other cloud providers. Figure 5-2 takes the previous model to a much deeper level of understanding by expanding the high-level functions into specific System Center capabilities.

Self-Service

The goal here is not to provide self-service access and back-end automation for everything IT does or can do, but only for those items that enable the business value you identified. Therefore, customization capabilities are key. Equally as important is building out a service catalog that breaks down the barrier between business owners (IT consumers) and the IT resources they need. This is why public cloud services are so attractive! Most organizations are faced with a decision at this inflection point in the IT industry evolution of client/server to cloud computing: either provide a frictionless mechanism for providing access to IT resources or risk the business bypassing IT to use cloud providers who do. Therefore, you need a self-service mechanism that provides this functionality and also gives IT control over where those resources are sourced, either in-house or via a public cloud. IT essentially begins to also become a service broker, albeit not always the service provider.

You have a couple of options for providing a self-service portal within System Center. First is the Service Manager Portal, which provides the capability to surface service requests to end users.

Service Function	System Center Capability	System Center Technology Enabler
Self-Service	Self-Service Portal(s)	Service Manager Portal
		App Controller
Service Delivery	Service Catalog	Request Offerings and Service Offerings
	Service Management	CMDB (Configuration Management Database)
	Incident and Problem Management	CI Connectors (Configuration Item Connectors)
		User Roles
		Virtual Machine Manager Objects (Clouds, Hypervisors, Storage, and Network classifications)
		Operations Manager Objects
		Operations Manager Alerts
		Reporting
Process Orchestration	Orchestrator Runbooks	Integration Packs
		Activities
		PowerShell
		External APIs
		Representational State Transfer (REST)-based web service
Management and Operations	Virtual Machine Manager	Fabric Management (Hypervisor, Storage, and Network Integration)
	Operations Manager	Performance, Availability, and Health Management
		Resource Optimization
		Capacity Management
		Maintenance
		Reporting
Automation	System Center Integration	Native Connectors
		External Connectors
		Management Packs
		PowerShell
		WMI
		SMI-S and SMP

FIGURE 5-2

These service requests are tied to Orchestrator runbooks, which in turn trigger the actual management systems to provide the services. The service request is where you define user roles, which determine who can see and fill out the service request form via the self-service portal. In addition, the service request determines the workflow of the request: any approvals needed for request fulfillment, configuration parameters for the request, and the Orchestrator runbook that will take these inputs and perform the action using the lower-level management systems.

The simplest example of this is a service request for a single virtual machine (VM). In this scenario the service request would take input parameters such as name, sizing characteristics such as processors and memory, network access, and so on, and the cloud or resource pool where the VM will run. These parameters are passed to the Orchestrator runbook, which sends the VM provisioning request to the appropriate management system, either Virtual Machine Manager (VMM), which controls the on-premises fabric, or Windows Azure.

This simple concept of tying self-service to a service management system that talks to the lower-level systems is quite powerful. You can actually build out a self-service portal that lights up your service catalog and also ties in existing IT processes such as change management.

In the second scenario, you do not need the service management layer in the mix. In this case, you'll want to use App Controller. App Controller talks directly to both Virtual Machine Manager and Azure; no service request or orchestration engine is involved. The self-service portal is a web front-end to your on-premises and Azure-based virtual machine resources. This portal would be most suitable for IT professionals so that they may quickly and easily provision services based on standard templates, without having to involve the infrastructure administrators.

The difference between these two methods of providing self-service is service management. Do you need the self-service activities to adhere to your service management framework (ITIL, MOF, DevOps)? Do you want to grow and mature your service catalog over time to include more IT services, such as password resets, collaboration requests, and so on? Will you need to integrate and extend the service-request process to trigger non-Microsoft management systems, such as other ticketing and monitoring systems? If the answer to these questions is yes, you want a self-service system that is driven by your service delivery tool and has orchestration capabilities. System Center 2012 SP1 Service Manager and Orchestrator are key components in these scenarios. If you answered no, App Controller is a good choice, providing self-service for provisioning and managing virtual machines. You can also leverage a combination of the two portals to get the best of both worlds.

There has also been a recent entry into the self-service portal scene at Microsoft known as the Windows Azure Pack. This adds another, third choice for providing self-service. For the context of this book, however, it doesn't require a lot of detailed explanation because at this time it does not communicate with Windows Azure. Instead, this package is designed to bring some key elements of Windows Azure to your on-premises, private cloud environments based on Windows Server and System Center. The target audience for the Windows Azure Pack seems to be both enterprises building private clouds and service providers who re-sell IT services publically. While the package makes the slick, Silverlight-based Azure portal available to the public, it also brings some other interesting functionality including:

➤ **Management Portal** – The self-service portal that consumers of the cloud authenticate to and use to provision and manage their services.

➤ **Service Management API** – An OData Rest API that the Management Portal leverages. This API is also available for building your own or integrating with an existing portal and/or programming automation for the underlying fabric.

➤ **Web Sites service** – A multi-tenant web hosting service supporting many popular development languages and template web applications. This would be vital functionality for service providers.

➤ **Virtual Machines service** – Everything you would expect for supporting self-service virtual machine provisioning and management plus a gallery of both stand-alone and multi-tier VM templates.

➤ **Service Bus** – Similar to the Windows Azure Service Bus topic covered in Chapter 4, this provides an asynchronous messaging service for a variety of scenarios.

Again, the Windows Azure Pack self-service portal does not work with both on-premises and Windows Azure environments so it's not a valid choice for true hybrid cloud, but does bring some powerful functionality for private clouds and service provider environments.

Service Delivery

Service Delivery is a broad topic indeed. Many elements of the Service Delivery layer are impacted by shifting toward a hybrid cloud computing model, and it is those we discuss here. The subcategories of Service Delivery that are most affected include the following:

➤ Service catalog and service mapping

➤ Change management

➤ Auditing and compliance

➤ Incident and problem management

➤ Financial management

➤ Demand management

➤ Service life-cycle management

Most enterprise IT environments have long since embarked upon implementing processes based on a service management framework such as ITIL. This has often been a big step in aligning IT with the business and for improving operational maturity. In some cases, the processes have been refined over time and are working well. If so, you don't want cloud computing to disrupt these, but rather leverage and enhance them.

In other cases the processes are based on antiquated methodologies that may not lend themselves well to adopting new ways of delivering IT services. In this scenario you can use the cloud initiative to try out some new methods and perhaps supplement or replace the existing system.

At Microsoft, we typically embark upon a cloud computing project with a workshop specifically focused on answering the preceding questions, called a *Solution Alignment Workshop*. This entails meeting with key stakeholders and process owners to understand the existing organization, processes, and tools, and to identify what needs to be changed, supplemented, integrated with, or replaced. This includes the service catalog, the configuration management databases (CMDB), the change management system and processes, auditing and compliance requirements, and so on.

System Center Service Manager SP1 is the primary component in this layer of the architecture. This component of System Center provides all the previously mentioned capabilities and, when combined with Orchestrator, becomes the brain of the cloud management platform. Service Manager includes configuration item (CI) connectors that automatically and dynamically populate the configuration management database (CMDB), shown in Figure 5-3, from sources such as Active Directory, Orchestrator, Operations Manager, and Virtual Machine Manager. This enables the service requests you create to contain objects from throughout the other cloud management systems.

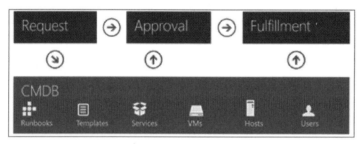

FIGURE 5-3

This is a powerful feature that enables you to do such things as assign a business unit (Active Directory Security Group) within your organization to a resource pool (Virtual Machine Manager Cloud) that has a specific SLA tied to it, and allow specific VMM templates to be provisioned to the cloud. The service request may then initiate a change request, which either requires approvals or is auto-approved. All change requests are automatically logged, thereby giving you a record of all self-service activities.

Once provisioning is completed, you of course still care about what happens to the service over time. The resources are automatically discovered and monitored by Operations Manager, and any performance, health, or other alerts you have configured in Operations Manager can auto-create incidents back in Service Manager. However, they are not just isolated incidents; they are tied to the service. Therefore, you instantly have a map from the auto-created incidents to the provisioned service and change management history, answering the most common question asked when problems arise - what was last changed? From a consumption perspective, you might have created an inherent problem by introducing self-service, as you have made it very easy to provision resources. We all know enterprise IT equipment isn't free, and in the enterprise space this is especially important because the business model may not include IT systems as the commodity being monetized. For example, for a pizza company, IT is a critical mechanism, but at the end of the day the cost of IT cuts into the profits of the pizza. This is where demand management and financial management are critical. You need to pay attention to the principle of incentivizing the desired resource consumption behavior, and you do this by providing cost transparency and even perhaps charging business units for the resources they consume. Therefore, you need to inform the consumers of IT of the service's cost — both at provisioning time and at intervals (monthly, quarterly, etc.).

Finally, the life cycle of an IT service is often a difficult thing to manage. How do you know when the operating systems, applications, and so on need to be upgraded to maintain support by the vendor? How do you know that the IT service provisioned two years ago is still in use today? This is also an area that might be either already well defined and needs to be extended or integrated with, or perhaps a problem that needs to be addressed.

Process Orchestration

You can think of orchestration as the glue of the solution. This layer is what brings the higher and lower level systems of the solution together. Orchestration is the ability to tie together multiple disparate automation routines into a holistic workflow incorporating technologies and business processes from different systems and teams within the organization. This is best illustrated by an example. Maintaining patches and updates throughout the datacenter has become difficult, to put it nicely. Even with some scripting and automation, many manual steps and multiple teams are involved in an enterprise environment. Information Security has the responsibility of setting policy and auditing the compliance of system updates. IT administrators are tasked with testing and deploying updates while maintaining the availability of systems. Meanwhile, operations-focused groups require changes to go through an approval process (usually a Change Advisory Board, or CAB). Finally, the business units that own the applications need to be informed of changes and then perform their final acceptance testing. From end to end, this can be a very labor-intensive and error-prone process, causing operational complexity and even outages. Orchestration enables you to build a workflow that accounts for each step in this process and complete automation of the entire patching process itself.

Management and Operations

Managing and operating your cloud system can be yet another very broad topic. This section highlights the critical points for the service provider model specifically and how those are impacted by adding public cloud resources to your architecture.

First and foremost, a tightly integrated cloud management platform significantly eases the burden in these areas. Whatever elements comprise your cloud, both on-premises and Azure, need to be automatically discovered and monitored by the management and operations systems. You cannot be surprised by a new element added to the fabric because it was not being monitored and reported on. Within System Center, you have this integration. Once integrated and configured, any new objects added to the fabric and any services deployed to the fabric are automatically discovered and monitored by Operations Manager. With your on-premises resources, Virtual Machine Manager is the primary management tool, actually controlling the fabric and enabling you to define end-user access to those resources. You do this by formulating the VMM library objects that may be used. These are items such as virtual disks, hardware profiles, operating system profiles, logical networks, VM templates, and Service templates. You then define and scope one or more VMM clouds. A VMM cloud enables you to aggregate these resources and scope the cloud to administrators and end users. You also define capabilities for the cloud, such as the hypervisors allowed and capacity limitations for the fabric resources. For example, you might have 100 TB of storage available in total, but want a particular cloud to only be able to consume up to 15 TB. You can configure similar limitations on virtual processors, memory, and so on.

On the Azure side, you don't, of course, have control over the fabric itself, as Microsoft manages all that for you. Instead, you configure only the items above the virtualization layer: virtual machine templates, storage, networks, data, and applications.

Both your on-premises cloud and the Azure subscriptions are very dynamic by nature. So what happens when someone adds capacity to the datacenter private cloud fabric or Azure subscription? What about new templates and other objects? In addition, of course, when services are provisioned to these systems, you need to discover, monitor, and report on those as well.

The System Center Management Pack for Windows Azure Fabric (found at `http://www .microsoft.com/en-us/download/details.aspx?id=38414`) addresses these concerns. When changes occur within your Azure subscription, the Management Pack automatically discovers these objects. You can then decide what is monitored and how those events are addressed. Via the Operations Manager and Service Manager integration, you can then automatically have incidents created with relationships to these objects. This is a highly configurable and customizable management setup that enables you to tune the management system to appropriately fit into your operational model. We'll dig into some of these integration points in a moment.

The last management and operational area to highlight is using Windows Azure to extend your on-premises storage capacity into the cloud, and using the cloud storage as a backup and disaster recovery technique. One way to extend your on-premises storage capacity into Windows Azure is via a recent acquisition made by Microsoft of a company called StorSimple. StorSimple offers physical hardware storage devices that have a built-in automated storage algorithm that includes Windows Azure as a storage tier. Essentially, you have a local storage device with fast local disks and an encrypted connection to Windows Azure. The device knows which storage blocks are accessed most frequently and which can be moved to the cloud for slower access or archival. It's estimated that this technique can reduce enterprise storage costs by 60–80 percent. You can leverage this technique for both scaling storage to the cloud in an automated way for cost reduction as well as using the cloud as a recovery point for disaster recovery.

For backup and disaster recovery, a few mechanisms are available. The StorSimple devices just mentioned is one, but you also have the capability to back up and recover to the cloud both from within the Windows Server 2012 platform as well as with System Center Data Protection Manager 2012 SP1.

Automation

Automation is the layer that resides between the management systems and the underlying resources. All System Center components include a set of PowerShell cmdlets that allow for rich automation of any functions System Center provides. But having automation available in other places is critical as well. For example, Windows Azure ships a set of PowerShell cmdlets that enables you to build and extend your automation routines using this rich scripting language, and with the same people and tools that manage your existing infrastructure. As we have seen in the past few years, it's increasingly important to build out your datacenter using vendors who provide this automation capability. Storage, networks, and servers are all being centrally pooled and controlled in a private cloud, so having this automation built in greatly enhances the cloud capabilities we are able to provide, and eases the burden on staff to learn new ways of integrating these pieces. On the public cloud side, the same philosophy applies.

Figure 5-4 is a visual illustration to help explain the main integration points of the solution and how all the pieces fit together. This can also help you envision how your other existing management, infrastructure, and cloud environments might integrate.

You can see Azure at the top of the figure, on-premises cloud infrastructure below, Active Directory on the left, data warehousing on the right, and System Center in the middle. At the top three boxes, we have our self-service portals and then Service Manager and its configuration management database (CMDB). Below that in the center is Orchestrator, which directs the actions of the remaining management systems, Virtual Machine Manager and Operations Manager. (Configuration Manager and Data Protection Manager are examples of other commonly used components not shown here.)

Now please note the arrows which indicate different types of connectors. You can see the CI (configuration item) Connectors, which dynamically populate and update the CMDB. Notice how Virtual Machine Manager and Operations Manager have bi-directional communication, and both use agent-based management of Hyper-V Hosts. Then, take note of the Orchestrator Integration Packs, which allow automation of all the components. And finally, note the four main integration points with Windows Azure which are detailed further in this chapter.

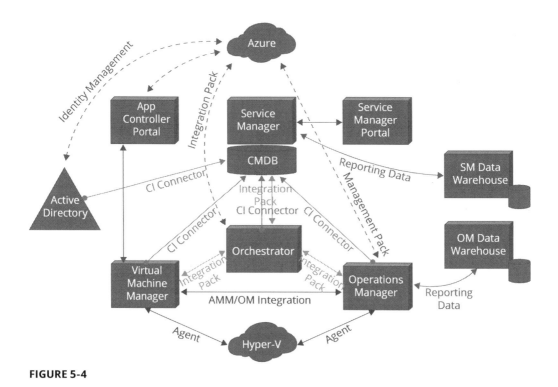

FIGURE 5-4

INTEGRATING SYSTEM CENTER AND WINDOWS AZURE

Now let's dig into the specific techniques and enabling tools for integrating your cloud management platform with Windows Azure. There are currently four primary integration points for the Microsoft hybrid cloud solution:

➤   Self-service with either App Controller, Service Manager Portal, or both

➤   Process orchestration with Orchestrator plus Windows Azure Integration Pack and Windows Azure PowerShell cmdlets

➤   Performance and health monitoring, alerting, and reporting with Operations Manager and the System Center Management Pack for Windows Azure Fabric

➤   Storage tiering and data protection with StorSimple, backup to Azure with Data Protection Manager and natively in Windows Server

Application Self-Service across Clouds

First up is self-service. As previously stated, you have two roads to self-service in System Center: App Controller and Service Manager. App Controller is the self-service portal that talks directly to Azure services and Virtual Machine Manager with no options for Service

Management or Orchestration. It's a simple web portal that surfaces your defined clouds and templates to end users. Typically, the end users best served by this experience are IT professionals or application developers, as the portal is not extensible or able to provide a complete service catalog, which is typically the goal of an enterprise IT self-service portal for end-user consumption.

Installing App Controller is pretty simple. It's recommended that you install on a standalone web server, and it does require SSL authentication. You can use your enterprise certificate services to issue a certificate, or the install wizard will provide you with a self-signed certificate. In the case of a self-signed certificate, be aware that the URL and the certificate friendly name need to match; otherwise, some browsers will not allow access to the website. Also note that using a self-signed certificate generates an error in all browsers because the certificate authority is not known.

After installing App Controller, you simply add your VMM environment and Azure subscription. At this point, depending on the rights of the authenticated user, you can now begin provisioning and controlling both your on-premises and Azure-based virtual environments in one console. You can also go so far as to provide the same VM templates in both clouds by uploading your VHD images to the Azure library. Figure 5-5 shows App Controller with an Azure subscription selected.

FIGURE 5-5

Pretty easy so far, right? The hard part about this situation is regulating what is done, as you have no gates or controls, only a bill you will receive each month for usage! One other interesting scenario (unfortunately, not available at this time) would be the capability to build a hybrid service template whereby different tiers of the application reside in Azure and on-premises. Currently, you would have to provision VMs and services in each location and then connect them, but ideally you would be able to define a template where, for example, the web tier VMs are provisioned in Azure and the middle-tier and data-tier are provisioned on-premises.

On to the more comprehensive and more complex self-service experience: Service Manager. To recap and build on the previously described advantages with this portal, you can do the following:

- ➤ Create a comprehensive service catalog.

- ➤ Tie self-service items to service requests.

- ➤ Group service requests into request offerings (for example, cloud services, VMs or user accounts, password resets).

- ➤ Leverage change requests with manual approvals or auto-approvals and notifications.

- ➤ Trigger Orchestrator runbooks and pass user-input parameters to the runbooks' variables.

What makes all this possible is the Service Manager CMDB. The first step in this configuration is to get the CMDB populated with CIs from all the systems that are leveraged in putting together a service request. This includes Active Directory, which enables you to scope the service requests to a specific set of users; and Orchestrator, which brings in the runbook and its properties, which will be driven by the service request inputs. To get you started, Microsoft publishes for free download an accelerator called the *Cloud Service Process Pack (CSPP).* This add-on is a collection of pre-defined service requests and runbooks that are geared toward the IaaS scenario. This means you aren't starting from scratch. You can easily extend the CSPP provided VM provisioning runbook and service request to trigger Azure Virtual Machine provisioning instead of VMM using the Azure Integration Pack for Orchestrator.

There are many ways you might want to extend or construct your runbook. One way would be to check the business unit of the person requesting it; if they are in department A, provision on-premises in VMM, but if they are in department B, use Azure. Another alternative is to have the service request include an optional selection for Production, Development, or Testing, and provision appropriately according to the hybrid scenario of "develop and test in the public cloud and deploy production on-premises." Within the service request you could also just expose a selection for on-premises or Azure and let the user decide. Figure 5-6 shows a Service Manager service catalog where you can see services requests nested beneath service offerings, or categories.

This is where it becomes important to have defined in advance the business drivers and use cases for adopting public cloud services, as we have illustrated in previous chapters.

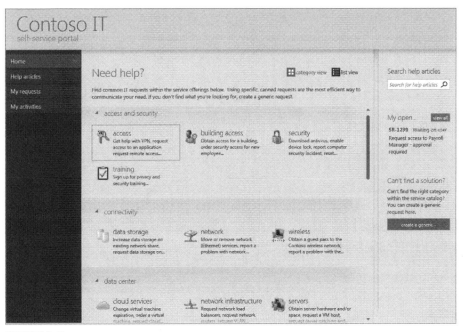

FIGURE 5-6

Cloud Management and Operations

Let's now take a minute to deconstruct the integration points for extending your management and operations tools to Windows Azure. The first thing you want to do is ensure that you have the same level of automated discovery of new objects (virtual networks, storage, VMs, and so on) in the environment for Azure as you do with VMM. Via VMM and Operations Manager integration, Operations Manager will automatically discover and begin monitoring any objects under the management of VMM. Management packs are the packages that give Operations Manager the intelligence to understand what exactly to monitor and how to monitor it. This intelligence consists of the following:

➤ Monitors, which direct an agent to track the state of various parts of a managed component

➤ Rules, which direct an agent to collect performance and discovery data, send alerts and events, and more

➤ Tasks, which define activities that can be executed by either the agent or the console

➤ Knowledge, which provides textual advice to help operators diagnose and fix problems

➤ Views, which offer customized user interfaces for monitoring and managing this component

➤ Reports, which define specialized ways to report on information about this managed component

➤ Object discoveries, which identify objects to be monitored

➤ Run As profiles, which enable you to run different rules, tasks, monitors, or discoveries under different accounts on different computers

As the company that develops Hyper-V, VMM, and Azure, Microsoft has the deep knowledge required to construct the intelligence necessary to build a management pack for all aspects of the hybrid cloud solution.

After installing the System Center Management Pack for Windows Azure Fabric, you will first need to configure it. At the time of writing, Microsoft has just released a preview of an updated version of the Management Pack that greatly simplifies the configuration. In addition to basic configuration, after discovery of your Azure resources is completed, you need to further specify which Azure resources you want to monitor. For details, please see the guide included with the Management Pack at http://www.microsoft.com/en-us/download/details.aspx?id=38414. The below list is an excerpt from this guide.

After configuration, the Management Pack offers the following functionality, as quoted from Walter Myers III in his blog "Walkthrough to Configure System Center Management Pack for Windows Azure Fabric Preview for SCOM 2012 SP1":

➤ Discovers Windows Azure Cloud Services.

➤ Provides the status of each role instance.

➤ Collects and monitors performance information per role instance.

➤ Collects and monitors Windows events per role instance.

➤ Collects and monitors the .NET Framework trace messages from each role instance.

➤ Grooms performance, event, and the .NET Framework trace data from Windows Azure storage.

➤ Changes the number of role instances.

➤ Discovers Windows Azure Virtual Machines.

➤ Provides the status of each role instance of the Virtual Machine.

➤ Discovers Windows Azure Storage.

➤ Monitors the availability and size of each Storage and optionally alerts.

➤ Discovers relationships between discovered Azure resources, to determine which other resources a particular Azure resource uses. This information is then displayed in a topology dashboard.

➤ Monitors management and cloud service certificates, and alerts if the certificates are about to expire.

➤ Includes a new Distributed Application template that enables you to create distributed applications that span Azure as well as on-premises resources, for hybrid monitoring scenarios.

➤ Includes a set of dashboards for the hybrid monitoring scenarios.

> **NOTE** *You can read the rest of this blog at* `http://blogs.msdn.com/b/walterm/` `archive/2013/04/13/first-impressions-on-system-center-management-pack-` `for-windows-azure-fabric-preview-for-scom-2012-sp1.aspx.`

The important part of monitoring Windows Azure as an extension of your overall datacenter management strategy is that your operational processes are well defined in order to properly surface this information to the right team, be it infrastructure or application owner, and that any necessary alerts are routed and tracked appropriately. In essence, you're treating Azure as you would any other new datacenter component. This is the value of the private and public integration.

The other key integration point is within System Center Orchestrator and with the Windows Azure PowerShell cmdlets. PowerShell is a widely adopted scripting language designed to simplify scripting and enhance automation from the perspective of an IT administrator. Nearly every application team at Microsoft ships PowerShell cmdlets in support of this mission. Cmdlets simplify the scripting process by surfacing simple commands to the shell that leverage the underlying .NET CLR and Framework.

Windows Azure ships new cmdlets and functionality approximately every three weeks, so you can be sure you have the latest capabilities exposed through PowerShell. The current capabilities of the Windows Azure PowerShell cmdlets include the following:

➤ **Automation** — Query, manage, and configure Windows Azure resources (VMs, cloud services, websites, storage, queues, databases, etc.) across multiple subscriptions and data centers.

➤ **Provisioning fully composed VMs** — Storage and networking configured, domain joined (PowerShell), PowerShell-enabled for remote management and configuration

➤ **Virtual networking** — Configure and manage virtual network configuration and VPN gateway management.

➤ **Storage** — Upload and download VHDs from your Windows Azure storage accounts to your on-premises servers. Copy VHDs between storage accounts and subscriptions.

We believe that the best way to leverage PowerShell and the available cmdlets is in conjunction with System Center Orchestrator. As previously mentioned, Orchestrator also has available an Integration Pack for Windows Azure. This pack includes a set of activities that enable even more simplified automation of Azure objects, and you can include integration of your other processes and management systems within the workflow. The cool thing about Orchestrator is that you can actually use both scripting and Integration Packs together for very robust and comprehensive automation. Therefore, if the Integration Pack doesn't include all the activities you need for your automation routine, you can add a script that will also be a seamless part of the workflow. For a complete list of Azure Integration Pack Activities, please see `http:// technet.microsoft.com/en-us/library/jj721977.aspx`.

To illustrate this, Figure 5-7 shows a simple runbook that is triggered from a Service Manager service request. It looks up the department and, depending on what value is returned, will provision the VM either on-premises or in Windows Azure.

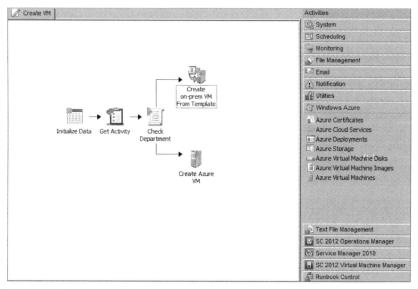

FIGURE 5-7

There are many more things to consider in an automation and orchestration framework, but hopefully, this has sparked some ideas about what is possible.

NETWORKING

Wow, we've covered a lot of ground. At this point we feel it's important to set the scope of this networking topic. Networking and identity management (covered in the next section of the chapter) are areas where there's a lot of nuance. The purpose of this book is to educate you on the *what* and the *why*: what the important aspects of hybrid cloud are, and why it matters to you. That being said, in this section it is tempting to get into the *how*, but that would require a level of depth that would more than double the page count of this book. So we're going to explain some fundamental concepts without the details about implementing the said technology or design. That's okay, however; there's a plethora of documentation on the how aspect. We want you to first have a clear understanding of what it is you can do and be able to make clear decisions on why you should do one thing over another.

That being said, the most common use-case, and the one we focus on in this section, is extending your corporate network into Windows Azure for the purposes of running VMs and applications therein. In Windows Azure, VMs are simple enough to create, but naturally you want them to be able to communicate on the network. In a hybrid cloud scenario, you also want your Azure-based VMs to talk to your on-premises VMs, as well as other infrastructure services, such as network services (Active Directory, DNS, etc.) and the aforementioned management systems.

The first thing to note about creating a VM is that it can belong to an affinity group. An affinity group basically tells Windows Azure Fabric Controller, "Hey, these VMs belong together. Please place them close to each other within the fabric so that they can have low-latency network communication." Microsoft's datacenters are quite vast, so without setting an affinity group, two VMs may end up being provisioned far apart from each other. More will be discussed about affinity groups in later chapters.

Virtual Networks

After creating VMs, you need to do some networking configuration. Windows Azure allows you to create *virtual networks*, logical networks that consist of IP address spaces, subnets, DNS settings, and gateways.

An IP address space contains one or more subnets and must be a private range: 10.0.0.0, 172.16.0.0, or 192.168.0.0. This is a range of IP addresses that will be automatically assigned to your VMs. Within the subnet you can specify how many IP addresses you will need — from 8 all the way up to more than 16 million.

NOTE *Although IP addresses are dynamically assigned to your VMs, they are persistent for the life of that VM, so you can treat them like static IP addresses. A VM will always have that IP address assigned to it until it's deleted.*

Next up is DNS, and in a hybrid environment you have some choices to make. Windows Azure will provide DNS servers for you, but they will have no knowledge of your private DNS infrastructure back at your datacenter. Therefore, most likely you will want to do one of two things: Either run your own DNS server within an Azure VM or, via Azure VPN, use DNS servers already in place at your datacenter. One thing to consider is what will happen if there's a loss of network connectivity between your datacenter and Azure. If you're not running your own DNS in an Azure VM, your other Azure VMs, which are dependent on it, will shortly become quite confused and not be able to resolve names. That being said, however, you probably don't want a completely new and independent DNS environment for your Azure VMs! You want all the magic of hybrid cloud, so you'll want to consider creating DNS servers in existing DNS zones you are already running — and that is absolutely possible. It's made possible via a virtual private network (VPN) tunnel between your Azure virtual network and your corporate network.

Using a VPN within your virtual network allows your Internet-facing router gateway to create a secure connection to Azure via an Azure gateway IP provided for your Azure virtual network. This is known as a site-to-site VPN tunnel. Via this secure VPN tunnel, all your VMs on the Azure virtual network can communicate with devices on your corporate network. Think of this as you would think of a branch office or remote office.

You do have another option for connecting Azure Virtual Networks to your on-premises systems — point-to-site VPN. This is actually a small service you would install on your on-premises systems that allows a point-to-site VPN between them and your Azure Virtual Networks. This may be suitable if, for example, you are just creating a single hybrid application and only need connectivity between Azure and a few specific servers on your local network. There is a good article, with tables to help you understand the different scenarios and design choices for these network considerations, at `http://msdn.microsoft.com/en-us/library/windowsazure/jj156007.aspx`.

To summarize the pertinent considerations for virtual networks you need to determine the following:

➤ **IP addressing scheme** — Subnets and network masking

➤ **DNS configuration** — Bring your own DNS *or* use Azure DNS? Run your own DNS in your Azure virtual network or connect back to on-premises DNS?

➤ **VPN configuration** — Local router and gateway public IP and local networks with which you want your Azure VMs to communicate

Don't worry; we know you probably have questions — which router types are supported, which encryption is used, and so on. As mentioned at the beginning of the chapter, these questions comprise the *how* part of this topic, and are a bit out of scope here. But rest assured that once you have determined what you want to do and why, the how to do it part is actually pretty easy and very well documented. Here's a good place to start `http://www.windowsazure.com/en-us/manage/services/networking`.

IDENTITY MANAGEMENT

The next and final part of your journey to formulate a holistic cloud environment using both private and public resources is authentication and authorization. Most enterprise IT environments have long since addressed this vital need in a variety of ways and have matured their services over time to provide a more seamless and secure login experience both for external customers and internal employees. That being said, you want to enhance your existing investments, not fragment them. So, how can you leverage public cloud resources without losing functionality or degrading the login experience? This section focuses primarily on Active Directory options in Windows Azure, although other, non-Microsoft directory and authentication services are available.

> **NOTE** *To clarify: You have something called Windows Azure Active Directory, and you also have the capability to run Active Directory within a Windows Azure VM. These are not the same thing! Since you're now a bit cloud savvy, think of it this way: Windows Azure Active Directory is SaaS, whereas running your own Active Directory environment in Windows Azure VMs is IaaS. Windows Azure Active Directory is a service provided by Azure that enables cloud-based identities. Consider the scenario in which you wish to run a web application entirely in Windows Azure. Your application requires authentication so that visitors to your website can create an account and sign in. Do you want to design and manage a whole directory service for your application? No! You want to just leverage a service that provides secure account creation and authentication that's always available. This is exactly what Microsoft's own cloud services do, such as Office 365.*

However, in enterprise IT environments you already have directory services running. Here's where you have some decisions to make. Your options are as follows:

> ➤ Extend your existing Active Directory by creating domain controllers in Windows Azure VMs.

> ➤ Leverage Windows Azure Active Directory and either synchronize or federate with your existing Active Directory.

There are a few good reasons to extend your existing Active Directory into Windows Azure. It's probably the least painful way to get started with hybrid cloud. You don't have to do additional identity management design work; simply fire up some domain controllers on your virtual network and off you go, just as you would with a branch office site. All the other benefits of a branch office domain controller are included with this scenario, such as disaster recovery, high availability, and keeping authentication network traffic localized.

Conversely, there are a few reasons to start thinking about using the cloud-based identity services going forward. First of all, it was mentioned previously that you will likely start building applications that are 100 percent based in Azure. In this case, you may not want the application to have dependencies on any corporate assets, such as your enterprise Active Directory. In addition, if and when your organization starts leveraging SaaS services (such as Office 365, CRM Online, and so on), this will force the issue because those services must use Windows Azure Active Directory. Therefore, let's explore your options for this route.

First, you can simply synchronize your corporate Active Directory with Azure Active Directory using a feature called Directory Synchronization. This service allows you to make a copy of Active Directory accounts in Azure Active Directory with a limited subset of the full user, group, and contact object's properties. You also have the option of synchronizing the user accounts' passwords as well, so that a single password can be maintained and used in both identity stores. However, at this point users would still be potentially required to sign-on twice: once to the corporate Active Directory, and again when accessing a service that uses Azure Active Directory. For true single sign-on, meaning users sign on to their corporate computer once and access services seamlessly, you need federation. There are multiple supported identity federation providers, including Active Directory Federation Services, Shibboleth Identity Provider, and other third party services.

Active Directory Federation Server (ADFS) can perform a token exchange with Windows Azure Active Directory so that when you authenticate to Azure-based services, your credentials are verified with your corporate account and you are passed through. This is obviously the more complex route, requiring several systems such as ADFS servers. Following are the pros and cons of each approach.

Directory Synchronization

Pros:

➤ Users and groups mastered on-premises

➤ Enables co-existence

➤ Single server deployment

Cons:

➤ No 2FA

➤ Two sets of credentials to manage with differing password policies or manual/third-party password sync or use FIM

➤ No SSO

Directory Synchronization + Federation

Pros:

➤ SSO with corporate credentials

➤ IDs mastered on-premises

➤ Password policy controlled on-premises

- ➤ 2FA solutions possible
- ➤ Enables hybrid scenarios
- ➤ Location isolation
- ➤ Ideal for multiple forests

Cons:

- ➤ Additional servers required

Other options and technologies are available, but these are the main ones most organizations will want to consider.

SUMMARY

This chapter discussed some of the main elements of a private cloud solution and how you can extend your on-premises environments into the public cloud, with some key considerations for enterprise IT. Your cloud management platform is a critical piece of the puzzle and should be one that takes into account your longer term vision for leveraging public cloud resources. Extending your operational processes and management tools to include self-service, monitoring, and orchestration across both public and private environments will enable your organization to realize the business benefits of a hybrid cloud solution while maintaining the maturity and experience you've gained from years of operating your own datacenters. Networking and identity management capabilities are paramount to making hybrid cloud computing a reality that works for you, rather than against you.

6 Hybrid Options in Windows Azure

As you work your way through the various Windows Azure platform and private cloud components and services described in this book, you often need to clarify and validate best practice guidelines for using them in architecting your solutions in hybrid clouds.

Continuing the analogy of buying, renting, or leasing cars started in Chapter 1, imagine that you are at the car dealership and about to purchase a new car. But before putting your signature on a sales contract, you want to ensure that the car you're buying meets your basic needs — providing the transportation means for all your daily and, oftentimes, leisure commutes. For example, if your plans include using this car to drive you, your wife, and two wonderful kids around your town and its vicinities, most likely you would buy at least a full-size sedan or an SUV or a minivan, but rarely (if ever) a two-door sport car, even if you loved it at first sight when you spotted it in the dealership's showroom. Likewise, if you live in a cold-climate state, which for 6 or 7 months a year is covered in snow, in all likelihood you would want to buy a car equipped with a four-wheel drive option, so you could feel comfortable maneuvering your vehicle through winter storms and snowy roads.

Similarly, when considering migration of an existing application to a hybrid cloud, you want to make sure you use appropriate hybrid cloud scenarios and services to match your business drivers and business investments. The typical business driver of hybrid computing is to deliver IT capabilities to a business faster and with greater agility. The business investment is to transform IT to new levels of productivity by piloting non-mission-critical activities to gain greater experience and expertise to formulate future strategy. This chapter discusses relevant considerations for any organization that wants to implement a hybrid cloud strategy.

Outside analogies, strategic approaches, and models for hybrid computing, there is the real world of hybrid computing work already underway. Currently, enterprises are finding ways to handle the complexity that results from increased delivery models and standardization of core IT services. Hybrid computing is generating considerable interest, but the reality is a relatively small mixed implementation of non-mission-critical and line-of-business (LOB) workloads.

Though a hybrid cloud provides flexibility that combines the advantages of private and public clouds to improve services and increase agility while lowering costs, you must evaluate numerous hybrid cloud scenarios in Windows Azure when determining whether to use a private or public cloud for a service or capability. To choose the best option, an organization needs to develop a decision framework and deliver standards and guidelines for each option.

When choosing a particular hybrid option applicable to your business scenario, it is likely that you will have concerns centered on issues such as communication and connectivity. For example, how will cloud-based applications call on-premises services, or send messages to on-premises applications? How will cloud-based applications access data in on-premises data stores? How can you ensure that all instances of the application running in cloud datacenters have data that is up-to-date?

In addition, moving parts of an application to the cloud prompts questions about performance, availability, management, authentication, and security. When elements of your application are now running in a remote location, and are accessible only over the Internet, can they still work successfully as part of the overall application?

It is possible to divide many of the aforementioned challenges and concerns into separate hybrid cloud options. This helps you to identify them more accurately, and discover the scenarios that are available to help you to design a hybrid cloud solution for your business goals. These hybrid options are described in the following sections.

ON-PREMISES SERVICE INTEGRATED WITH CLOUD SERVICE

This scenario includes components of an existing application that are located in the on-premises IT environment and connected to services in an off-premises public cloud. One example of a way to leverage Windows Azure public cloud would be to outsource compute-intensive custom application components to a Windows Azure Platform-as-a-Service (PaaS) while the main application remains on-premises. Typical candidates for such a configuration would be simulations or data analysis that require manipulation of Big Data and provide only the results back to the on-premises application.

The key aspect of this solution is that all data and analysis remain in the public cloud where it can best be aggregated and processed, with the final results being securely stored on-premises. Figure 6-1 illustrates on-premises service integrated with scalable Windows Azure Cloud Service.

Traditionally, to connect your on-premises applications to the off-premises applications (cloud or otherwise), you would begin by "poking" a hole in your firewall and configuring NAT routing so that Internet clients can talk to your services directly. This approach has numerous issues and limitations, not the least of which is the management overhead, security concerns, and configuration challenges.

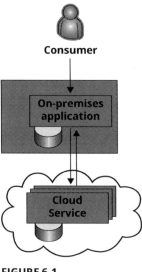

FIGURE 6-1

Therefore, the big question here is this: *How* do you get your on-premises services to talk to your Windows Azure hosted services? You can take either of the following approaches:

➤ Use the Windows Azure Service Bus.

➤ Use the Windows Azure Virtual Networks.

Using Windows Azure Service Bus

If your on-premises solution includes WCF Services, WCF Workflow Services, SOAP Services, or REST services that communicate via HTTP(S) or TCP, you can use the Service Bus to create an externally accessible endpoint in the cloud through which your services can be reached. Clients of your solution, whether they are other Windows Azure-hosted services or Internet clients, simply communicate with that endpoint, and the Windows Azure Service Bus takes care of relaying traffic securely to your service and returning replies to the client.

The key value proposition of leveraging the Service Bus is that it is designed to transparently communicate across firewalls, NAT gateways, or other challenging network boundaries that exist between the client and the on-premises service. You get the following additional benefits:

➤ The actual endpoint address of your services is never made available to clients.

➤ You can move your services around because the clients are bound only to the Service Bus endpoint address, which is a virtual, not a physical, address.

➤ If both the client and the service happen to be on the same LAN and could therefore communicate directly, the Service Bus can set them up with a direct link that removes the hop out to the cloud and back, thereby improving throughput and latency.

Using Windows Azure Virtual Network

Recently released for general availability, Windows Azure Virtual Network is an alternative means for connecting your cloud services to your on-premises services. Windows Azure Virtual Network effectively offers IP-level, secure, VPN-like connections from your Windows Azure hosted roles to your on-premises services. Windows Azure Virtual Network enables you to accomplish the following tasks:

➤ **Create a virtual private network with persistent private IPs** — You can bring your preferred private IPv4 space (10.x, 172.x, 192.x) to Windows Azure using a virtual network. Furthermore, virtual machines within a virtual network will have a stable, private IP address, even across hardware failures.

➤ **Cross-premises connectivity over site-to-site IPsec VPNs** — You can extend your on-premises network to Windows Azure and treat virtual machines in Windows Azure as a part of your organization's hybrid cloud network using a virtual network gateway to broker the IPSec connection. You can use standard VPN hardware devices from Cisco or Juniper to enable this.

➤ **Configure custom DNS servers** — Using a virtual network, you can point your virtual machines to a DNS server on-premises or a DNS server running in Windows Azure on the same virtual network. This also enables running a Windows Server Active Directory Domain Controller on Windows Azure.

➤ **Extended trust and security boundary** — Deploying virtual machines into a virtual network will extend the trust boundary to that virtual network. You can create several virtual machines and cloud services within a single virtual network and have them communicate using the private address space. This enables simple communication between different virtual machines or even virtual machines and web/worker roles in separate cloud services, without having to go through a public IP address. Furthermore, virtual machines outside the virtual network have no way to identify or connect to services hosted within the virtual network, providing an added layer of isolation to your services.

CLOUD SERVICE INTEGRATED WITH ON-PREMISES SERVICE

This option, a scalable cloud service integrated with a local on-premises service and illustrated in Figure 6-2, reflects scenarios in which the scalability and Internet accessibility of the public cloud is leveraged and integrated with on-premises applications.

Examples of this hybrid cloud configuration include the use of Software-as-a-Service (SaaS) offerings, such as Customer Relationship Management (CRM) online, with integration to local applications, such as Enterprise Resource Planning (ERP) systems, unified communication and collaboration services for e-mail, calendaring, and voicemail; and management systems integrated with local directories, vacation request tools, travel and expense services, or any other custom developed service.

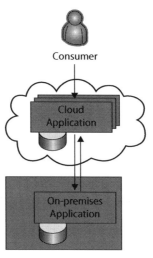

FIGURE 6-2

This option can also be used to move a website to a Windows Azure Web Sites cloud-based service for cost savings and agility, while moving financial transaction processing to a private cloud for payment card industry (PCI) compliance. This approach is a clever way to deal with financial governance, risk management, and compliance (GRC).

On-Premises Application Integrated with Low-Cost Windows Azure Storage

A variation of the previously mentioned hybrid cloud option is the use of on-premises applications enhanced with low-cost storage in Windows Azure, as shown in Figure 6-3.

Such an option might be reasonable for large files such as X-ray images, maps, media content, or websites, because it moves images and videos to Windows Azure cloud storage for improved streaming purposes and a smaller footprint in the on-premises infrastructure.

> **NOTE** *To improve the streaming performance in such scenarios, content delivery networks (CDNs) are typically used for close-to-consumer caching.*

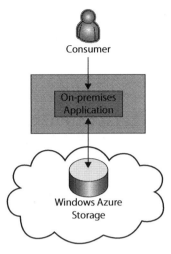

FIGURE 6-3

Cloud Service Integrated with Confidential Data Storage

Another scenario worthy of consideration is when a cloud-based application has to retrieve and store confidential data on-premises due to data privacy regulations. This scenario, illustrated in Figure 6-4, combines the benefits of public clouds, such as elasticity and cost efficiency, with the special requirements of confidential data.

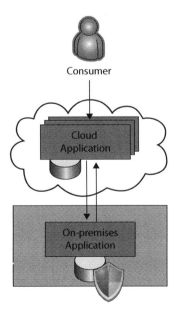

FIGURE 6-4

CLOUD BURSTING, OR BATCHING AT SCALE

A characteristic of cloud computing is the quick elasticity that it provides. This elasticity provides the capability to accommodate the following hybrid cloud option: An on-premises application designed for a certain average load can be enhanced on-demand by adding extra computing power in case of predicted additional load. When the need for extra computing power is over, the extra IT resources can be given back to the pool to reduce costs. As defined at SearchCloudComputing.com (`http://searchcloudcomputing.techtarget.com/definition/cloud-bursting`):

> Cloud bursting *is an application deployment model in which an application running in a private cloud on-premises data center bursts into a public cloud (Windows Azure) when demand for computing and/or storage capacity spikes. The advantage of such a hybrid cloud deployment is that organizations pay only for extra compute resources when they need them.*

This option, on-demand scaling to handle peak loads and illustrated in Figure 6-5, spawns batch scripts into many cloud processes to tackle a one-time job with brute force. One example of such a configuration is the intensive processing of images into multiple sizes and types being run in parallel on multiple Windows Azure Infrastructure-as-a-Service (IaaS) virtual machines.

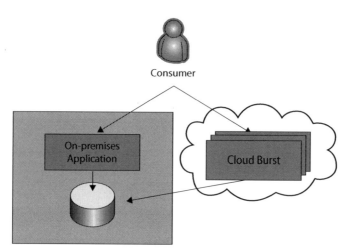

FIGURE 6-5

The hybrid cloud-bursting option can help organizations effectively use Windows Azure as an alternative resource when demand increases, without the need to interrupt services provided to users.

Figure 6-6 illustrates the conceptual reference architecture diagram for a hybrid cloud-bursting solution built by Microsoft Consulting Services (MCS).

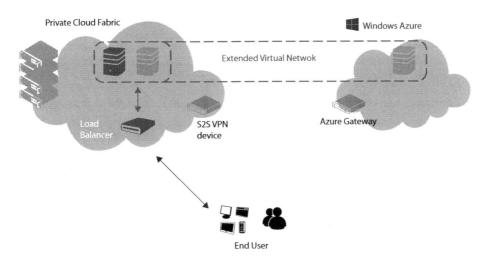

Private Cloud Fabric

Windows Azure

Extended Virtual Netwok

Load Balancer

S2S VPN device

Azure Gateway

End User

FIGURE 6-6

The Microsoft System Center Operations Manager constantly monitors performance of the compute VM nodes running the application web tier in the private cloud environment. When the resource utilization exceeds the pre-configured resource capacity threshold, a pre-defined alert is raised by System Center Operations Manager, which in turn creates an incident object that triggers a custom *runbook* (the term used by System Center to define an executable script of specific actions) executed by System Center Orchestrator. This runbook first checks within the private cloud resource pool to determine whether compute resources are available to provision an extra instance of the web tier application in the private cloud environment.

If the private cloud pool capacity is fully exhausted, System Center Orchestrator provisions an extra compute resource (for example, a Windows Server 2012 VM) in the Windows Azure IaaS public cloud environment. Once the demand for additional compute resources ends — which can also be automated via a pre-defined, low-utilization threshold in System Center Operations Manager — the newly provisioned virtual machine nodes in Windows Azure are removed.

Organizations can benefit from implementing a cloud-bursting hybrid option on Windows Azure in business scenarios with sudden, short-lived increased loads, such as websites launched specifically for public events (for example, the FIFA World Cup or the Olympic Games), as well as fixed yearly spikes for dates such as filing tax forms or holiday shopping. This scenario doesn't apply only to websites; temporary virtual machines could also be added for data processing and any other workloads.

DEVELOPMENT AND TEST CLOUD INFRASTRUCTURE

As a result of recent general availability of Windows Azure IaaS, development and test on the cloud infrastructure is likely to quickly become a key hybrid cloud scenario for using Windows Azure. These development and testing environments are only used for the duration of the project and have fewer service-level requirements than production environments. Using Windows Azure for their development and test environments, development teams can now quickly spin up or down resources in minutes without ever being bottlenecked waiting for resources from the IT department. This makes it really easy to start leveraging the cloud even without having to fully count on it yet for production scenarios. This cloud scenario is likely to gain even more momentum from many customers after a number of new enhancements were introduced at the latest Microsoft conference, TechEd, in New Orleans:

➤ When you now stop a VM, there will be no charge for any compute time while it is stopped — this is especially useful for Dev and Test scenarios, where you often want to cycle down environments in the evenings or on weekends if they aren't actively being used.

➤ You will now receive billing at a per-minute granularity — this is especially useful for Dev and Test scenarios, where you are often cycling up/down resources in a very elastic way. Now you can do so and save more money.

➤ You can now use your MSDN Dev and Test software licenses on Windows Azure for Dev and Test scenarios. You can also now install and use your MSDN Dev and Test server images for any number of Windows Server, SQL Server, SharePoint, BizTalk Server implementations etc., at no extra charge within Windows Azure VMs.

Because of their temporary nature, Windows Azure IaaS virtual machines and virtual networks are a wise choice, as these environments enable you to return resources to the pool after the project. The capability to keep a snapshot of the development and test environments for later use — for improvement or bug-fixing projects — is also a considerable benefit. Figure 6-7 illustrates this integrated Windows Azure development and testing environment.

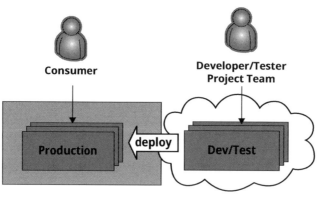

FIGURE 6-7

WINDOWS AZURE AS A DISASTER RECOVERY (DR) SITE

Many organizations are interested in using a public cloud service for temporary disaster recovery (DR) purposes. Planning for failure and disasters in the cloud requires you to recognize failures quickly and implement a strategy that matches your tolerance for the application's downtime. Additionally, you have to consider the importance of the current state of your data and how stale your data can be when it is restored. It's often important to get a DR site up quickly and cost-efficiently, so using a public cloud might be a suitable alternative to high-cost DR plans.

When discussing how to recover from a failure, it is often helpful to first define what disaster recovery really means in the Windows Azure context. For that, we will go back to the car analogy we started in Chapter 1. In the car scenario, an analogous disaster is when a car crashes and is no longer operational. Similarly, in a datacenter a disaster results from the systematic failure of critical capabilities. With respect to Azure, this could mean an entire datacenter is no longer functional (say, in the case of a hurricane). The strategic approach for dealing with the loss of a datacenter due to a true "disaster" is different from dealing with the loss of a specific node within a datacenter, as is the case with high availability. In this disaster case you need to have a plan to run your application or access your data outside of the datacenter. Execution of this plan revolves around people, processes, and supporting apps that enable the system to function. The level of the system availability during a disaster is coordinated among the business and technology owners who define the operational mode the system must run at that critical time. That can take many forms — from completely unavailable to partially available but running in degraded mode, with limited or delayed processing with respect to currency of the data.

There is no one-size-fits-all DR solution for the cloud, and your requirements can vary across different applications in your portfolio. The process, policies, and procedures related to restoring critical systems after a catastrophic event take a lot of commitment and time up front in order to manage this correctly — and once the process is established you just can't stop there. You should regularly analyze it and continually improve upon it.

In this hybrid cloud option, the backups or snapshots of the most important virtual machines and databases are replicated in an encrypted way to the Windows Azure IaaS and PaaS public cloud. As shown in Figure 6-8, if a disaster occurs, using either an automated cloud service "switch" or manual traffic redirect, these replicas can then be decrypted and mounted in the Windows Azure public cloud environment to quickly restore the most critical services.

NOTE *In Chapter 7 you can learn more about various DR implementation techniques, such as use of Windows Azure Traffic Manager in combination with Microsoft System Center Operations Manager either deployed in a private cloud or hosted in Windows Azure environment.*

Additionally, you may need to implement some of the Azure DR support yourself to supplement the native support from the Windows Azure platform, which you should exploit as much as possible.

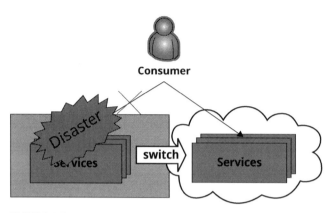

FIGURE 6-8

Part of a successful Windows Azure disaster recovery plan is architecting it into the solution up front. With the advent of the hybrid cloud, we now have additional options for failing over successfully during a disaster that are not available in a traditional hosting provider. Specifically, we are referring to the capability to dynamically and quickly allocate resources in a different datacenter without having to pay a lot for them to sit around and wait for a failure to occur.

Some common disaster scenarios include hardware and network failure, data corruption, and failover of VMs and connected services. Options exist to run the application in either full or partially degraded mode, offering limited functionality to users. Planning for this major type of failure requires active/passive data and cloud deployments.

SERVICE BUS AS AN INTEGRATION HUB

In this hybrid cloud option, shown in Figure 6-9, a Microsoft hybrid cloud integration layer provided by Windows Azure Service Bus off-premises and Windows Server Service Bus (or in some enterprise application integration [EAI] scenarios, Microsoft BizTalk Server) on-premises is used to easily integrate with other collaboration partners, suppliers, or communities in a standardized way without the need to rebuild on-premises connectivity, message transformation, and routing capabilities. This cloud-provided integration layer can be used to securely publish on-premises services to public-service consumers, such as medical benefits recipients, or to restricted consumers, such as department workers in other partner organizations.

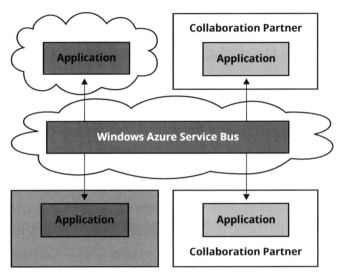

FIGURE 6-9

ENABLING MODERN APPLICATIONS

Modern applications take advantage of advances in technology (mobility, devices, cloud computing, the Internet) to enable new value opportunities for businesses across all industries, to scale their reach, and to grow their top/bottom lines. On-premises applications have traditionally been designed and implemented for local stationary users. However, as a result of increased mobility and the consumerization of IT, employees want access to their respective applications via their mobile and tablet devices from remote locations. A suitable way to enhance the accessibility of legacy applications might be to provision a web-based front end hosted in the Windows Azure Cloud Service that integrates with the on-premises legacy application (see Figure 6-10).

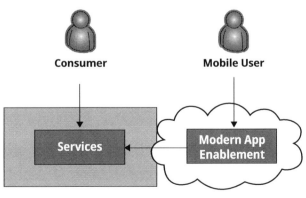

FIGURE 6-10

VIRTUAL DESKTOPS IN WINDOWS AZURE

The new Remote Desktop Services (RDS) feature, formerly known as Terminal Services, that can be turned on in Windows Server 2012 VM hosted on Windows Azure IaaS can also provide users such as consultants, partners, and suppliers with a virtual desktop for a limited period of time, such as for the duration of a project, during which employees can use their own devices (for example, tablets and smartphones). The new and enhanced architecture takes advantage of Windows Azure IaaS environment to make remote access a more flexible solution with new deployment scenarios. RDS enables organizations to provide access to Windows Azure VMs from virtually any location, any Windows device, from the Internet or an intranet. Applications running on these VMs, when accessed remotely through RDS, appear as if they are running on the end user's local computer. Figure 6-11 shows what the configuration of low-cost virtual desktops in Windows Azure looks like.

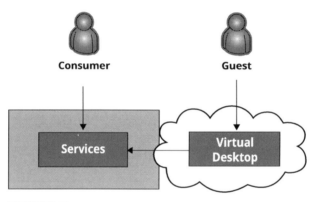

FIGURE 6-11

SUMMARY

In discussions with customers about hybrid cloud, we have often seen the perception that hybrid cloud use cases are mostly seen from the academic point of view, assuming that hybrid cloud scenarios are rare in today's IT reality and will only be dominant at some point in the future.

Well, we have news for you. Hybrid cloud scenarios are already here, whether you know it or not. If you are only planning for implementing hybrid scenarios down the road, we have a wake-up call for you — you most likely have already implemented at least one of the scenarios described in this chapter.

If your company has even a single public cloud application in use today, whether it is SaaS, PaaS or IaaS, we can almost guarantee you that it is connected to something inside your datacenter giving you a hybrid cloud scenario.

So the real questions are how aware are you of these hybrid cloud scenarios or options, and what are you doing about them? If they are being conducted below your radar, you'd better add investigating these scenarios to your next week's agenda. Chances are you don't have a clear and consistent enterprise reference architecture in place for hybrid cloud integration. And so, understanding and looking at each of the hybrid cloud scenarios described in this chapter through the lens of a business process will give you a better sense of what integration challenges lie ahead of you and how to manage them.

And don't think hybrid cloud integration is just a cloud problem. As your organization starts to build out more modern application designs, hybrid cloud scenarios will only start piling up. Per the "The Future Of Mobile Application Development" analysis recently completed by Forrester analyst, Jeffrey S. Hammond and Julie A. Ask, "the new model is omni-channel application architectures where discrete applications components talk to each other through RESTful service interfaces — an API management and integration challenge without having to be in the cloud." (http://www.forrester.com/The+Future+Of+Mobile+Application+Development/fulltext/-/E-RES89181).

Better be ready for this new modern world.

7 Designing for Resiliency and Scalability

To create a hybrid cloud resilient architecture, it's very important first to understand the nature and cause of all failure points for an application that can cause an outage. This has always been true, by the way, for a traditional on-premises architecture. It is also true for private or public cloud architecture, but its importance for a hybrid cloud architecture is immensely multiplied by the large number of potential failures and modes inevitably present in every hybrid cloud architecture.

NOTE *Understanding the failure points and failure modes for a hybrid cloud architecture and its related workload services enables you to make informed, targeted decisions regarding strategies for resiliency and availability.*

A *failure point* can mean many things — such as network, power, Internet connectivity, and so on — but in the architecture design, a failure point often means a design element that can cause an outage. Examples of design elements that can cause an outage in a hybrid cloud architecture include the following:

➤ DNS name resolution (especially when a DNS server is used to resolve VM names hosted in dispersed network environments, i.e., private and public clouds)

➤ Database connections

➤ Website connections

➤ Web service connections

➤ External interfaces connectivity

➤ Environment configuration changes

➤ Load balancing

➤ Operational tasks (e.g., deployment, testing, monitoring)

A *failure mode* refers to the root cause of an outage at those failure points. Examples of failure modes include the following:

➤ Overutilization of compute or database resources

➤ A significant peak in traffic that exceeds resource capacity

➤ A missing assembly DLL or configuration file

This chapter examines key considerations across Windows Azure and Windows Server hybrid cloud platforms and services you need to understand when building resilient and scalable hybrid cloud solutions.

BUILDING RESILIENT SOLUTIONS

You gain some noticeable advantages when you run applications in Windows Azure — namely, high availability and fault tolerance achieved by *fault domains* and *upgrade domains*. The following sections describe these two important strategies that should be adopted by hybrid cloud architects when designing and building resilient solutions on Windows Azure.

Fault Domains

The scope of a physical unit failure is a fault domain, which is in essence a single point of failure. Therefore, the purpose of identifying fault domains is to prevent a single point of failure. In its simplest form, a fault domain is a computer by itself connected to a power outlet. Clearly, if the connection between a computer and its power outlet is off, then this computer is down. A rack of computers in a datacenter is also a fault domain, as a power outage of a rack will take out the collection of hardware in the rack, similar to a single computer's power outage. In fact, Windows Azure datacenters are designed and built with the assumption that a fault domain is indeed a rack of computers. The allocation of a fault domain is determined by Windows Azure at deployment time.

Upgrade Domains

Conversely, an upgrade domain defines a strategy to ensure that an application stays up and running, that is, is highly available, while undergoing an update. When possible, Windows Azure evenly distributes the role instances of an application into multiple upgrade domains, with each upgrade domain serving as a logical unit of the application's deployment. When you upgrade an application, that upgrade is then carried out one upgrade domain at a time.

The upgrade steps are as follows:

1. Stop the instances of an intended role running in the first upgrade domain.

2. Upgrade the application.

3. Bring the role instances back online.

4. Repeat the preceding steps in the next upgrade domain.

An application upgrade is completed when all upgrade domains are processed. By stopping only the instances running within one upgrade domain, Windows Azure ensures that an upgrade takes place with the least possible impact to the running service. This is why it is so important to place, for example, two or more load-balanced web front-end virtual machines into a single affinity set when configuring Windows Azure virtual machines in an IaaS/Virtual Network, which puts these VMs into separate upgrade domains.

You can optionally control how many upgrade domains you have with an attribute, upgradeDomainCount, in the service definition file of a cloud service application. You cannot, however, specify which role is allocated to which domain.

In addition to fault domains and upgrade domains, to ensure fault tolerance and high availability Windows Azure also has network redundancy built into routers, switches, and load balancers that is completely transparent to any applications, cloud services, or users deploying their services to the cloud. Windows Azure Fabric Controller also sets checkpoints and stores the state data across fault domains to ensure reliability and recoverability.

Although you cannot control the allocation of fault and upgrade domains, you can either visually or programmatically find out which fault and upgrade domain a service is running within, as shown in Figure 7-1.

NAME	STATUS	ROLE	SIZE	UPDATE DOMAIN	FAULT DOMAIN
WAMS.CleanWorker_IN_0	Running	WAMS.CleanWorker	Small	0	0
WAMS.CleanWorker_IN_1	Running	WAMS.CleanWorker	Small	1	1
WAMS.JobWatcher_IN_0	Running	WAMS.JobWatcher	Small	0	0
WAMS.JobWatcher_IN_1	Running	WAMS.JobWatcher	Small	1	1
WAMS.JobWatcher_IN_2	Running	WAMS.JobWatcher	Small	2	0

FIGURE 7-1

Notice how a fault and upgrade domain index changes for each instance of the same cloud service (WAMS.CleanWorker or WAMS.JobWatcher).

Private Cloud Fault and Upgrade Domain Considerations

If you thoroughly read Chapter 5 and followed the recommended reading, then you already know that the architectural patterns suggested for on-premises private cloud deployments are similar to those for public or hybrid scenarios. If not, here are the two main links for these patterns:

➤ **Fault domains** — http://social.technet.microsoft.com/wiki/contents/ articles/4346.private-cloud-principles-concepts-and-patterns .aspx#Physical_Fault_Domain

➤ **Upgrade domains** — http://social.technet.microsoft.com/wiki/contents/ articles/4346.private-cloud-principles-concepts-and-patterns .aspx#Upgrade_Domain

As you can see from the rest of the content in that series, Microsoft has worked very hard over the past few years to bring the knowledge and experience gained from designing and operating its cloud-scale datacenters to its products, providing guidance that you can leverage in your own private cloud environment. How far you take these concepts toward an implementation is up to you.

Fault domain planning is a very different exercise in your own datacenter versus the public cloud. Typically, the hypervisor is used as the abstraction layer between physical faults and application availability, the application being the virtual machine. Therefore, your goal is to understand all the failure modes in the datacenter that could potentially bring down the hypervisor layer. A scale unit is usually a virtualization cluster and all the dependencies that comprise that cluster, such as storage, network, and *n* number of servers. The first point of failure to consider is power, as this affects all aspects of the scale unit. Typically, two power sources feed two large UPS systems in a medium-size server room. All racks in the room would then have power feeds from each UPS, and each physical server would have dual power supplies connected to each UPS.

But what if this is not the case? Maybe half the server room is served by one UPS and the other half is served by the other UPS. In this case, you would want to design your scale unit so that roughly 50 percent capacity is residing on each side of the room. For the virtualization cluster this would mean physically placing nodes in different racks; and for large SANs, which are not typically modular, you would need to find a way to get power to the SAN from each UPS. This is an oversimplification, but you get the idea.

That's just an example thought exercise related to power. You'll want to repeat this process up the technology stack for each system dependency that might fail — for example, air conditioners, physical network and storage devices, and even logical items such as DNS servers. After you have listed all these items, where do you start? Well, a good way to prioritize what you should give attention to first is to look at your outage history, or if you're designing a new datacenter, perhaps you can look at industry averages.

After identifying all your fault domains, you want to design IT services so that they are resilient to failures. This may mean that instead of investing in keeping your virtualization clusters up, you invest in designing applications that can tolerate the failure of a cluster, which is more typical in public cloud applications. Oftentimes this is not feasible with many line-of-business applications using off-the-shelf software because you don't have the luxury of deciding the design of the application. Therefore, it may be advantageous to work on the infrastructure layer, making it as highly available as possible but also having quick recovery techniques in place in the event of an outage.

How much should be invested in which layer will be made clear by this process of identifying the faults in the environment and then determining how you can design to tolerate them, or not. In general, you want to start thinking in terms of being resilient to failures versus trying to prevent them, which is much more costly.

Identifying upgrade domains within your own datacenter enables you to perform maintenance on infrastructure and services in an automated and predictable way without causing service interruption. Using the earlier example, suppose you have 10 virtualization clusters with 10 nodes per cluster, with 20 percent reserve capacity in each. In this case you can safely take down a maximum of two nodes in each cluster for hardware or software maintenance without causing service degradation or outages. However, it's advisable to reserve a node in case of failure. Therefore, you can plan for one node per cluster across all clusters. This means you can service 10 servers at a time, one per cluster. The resulting upgrade domain looks like what is shown in Figure 7-2. All servers in an upgrade domain can be removed from the pool simultaneously without disrupting service or diminishing performance.

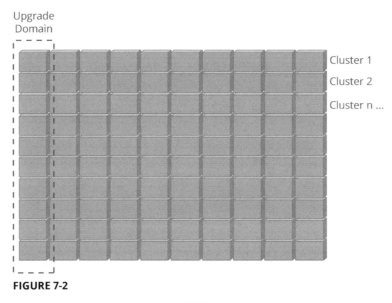

FIGURE 7-2

What Does High Availability Really Mean?

Understanding what high availability of your cloud service really means will help you determine the anticipated service-level agreement (SLA) that you'd like to deliver. Even if an SLA is not provided for your service publicly, this is the baseline to which you'll aspire to meet in terms of availability, which is typically expressed as a percentage of uptime in a given year. This availability percentage is referred to as the number of "nines." For example, 99.9 represents a service with "three nines," and 99.999 represents a service with "five nines."

For example, assume you have a hybrid cloud application that consists of Windows Azure SQL Database, an Azure storage account, IaaS Virtual Machines, and Virtual Network, which connects your Windows Azure services back to the on-premises infrastructure. Microsoft's public Windows Azure SLA page states that SQL Database customers will maintain availability of 99.9 percent of connectivity between the database and Windows Azure Internet gateway. The same 99.9 percent SLA is guaranteed also for a Windows storage account you use in your application. At the same time, for virtual networks and Windows Azure virtual machines, Microsoft guarantees that when you deploy two or more role instances in different fault and upgrade domains, your Internet-facing roles will have external connectivity at least 99.95 percent of the time.

One common misconception is related to the number of nines for a composite services application. Specifically, it is often assumed that if a given application is composed of a number of services, as in the example, each with a promised 99.9 percent uptime or higher (99.95percent) in its SLA, then the resulting composite service's availability is no less than 99.9 percent. This is not the case.

The percentage is actually a calculation that considers the amount of downtime per year. Both SQL Database and storage services with an SLA of "three nines" (99.9 percent) can be offline up to 8.76 hours; and the virtual machine and virtual network services, with an SLA of 99.95 percent, can be offline up to 4.38 hours For more detail see the table mapping availability to downtime at http://en.wikipedia.org/wiki/Nines_(engineering).

The catch is that the calculation formula for getting the downtime of composite application is the sum of all services' downtime:

```
Composite Service Downtime = Sum(Service(1) +  Service(2) + … + Service(n)
```

Incorporating all these four services into a composite application introduces an identified SLA risk of 21.9 hours, which reduces availability to 99.75 percent before a single line of code is written!

You generally can't change the availability of a Windows Azure service; however, when writing your code, you can increase the overall availability of your application using the resiliency patterns and considerations laid out in this chapter. When leveraging external services, the importance of understanding SLAs — both individually and in terms of their impact on the composite — cannot be stressed enough.

Resiliency Patterns and Considerations

This next section discusses the key patterns and considerations that you need to understand in order to create resilient architectures. Understanding the most common architecture patterns and the related recommended best practices will help you make informed, targeted decisions on strategies for resiliency and availability.

Asynchronous Communication Pattern

One of the ways to achieve resiliency is by making communication asynchronous. A resilient hybrid cloud architecture should default to asynchronous interaction, with synchronous interactions happening only as the result of an exception.

Imagine an event that occurs as the result of some interaction with a website. That event might require some data to be saved, an e-mail to be sent, a log service to be called, and a bunch of other things. You never want this to happen all in the original request. You want your UI to be responsive; otherwise, the user is just going to press the submit button again and again, right? This will result in either your website crashing due to the overload of processing requests or the original request being processed more than once (think of the credit card transaction, oops!) — neither of these two options is good for us.

To get around this problem, asynchronous messaging ensures that the message is processed only once and that the proper acknowledgement is sent back to the user right after the request button was pressed. The equivalent of this in Windows Azure would be use of the Cloud Services Worker role with multiple instances and Windows Azure Queues. In essence, the Windows Azure Queue service was designed specifically for asynchronous work distribution. Each retrieval of a work item from the Queue is guaranteed to be unique, except where the worker fails to notify the Queue of successful processing, in which case the work item is automatically re-enqueued after a certain amount of time. This ensures the work item is not lost due to a worker failure. Also, Windows Azure Queues are at least three times redundant (we talked about it in the Chapter 4), ensuring no work item is ever lost. The primary advantage of this approach is that it scales extremely well.

Transient Faults

In this section we will talk about transient faults that commonly occur in Windows Azure and how to be ready for them. Per Wikipedia, a "transient fault is a fault that is no longer present if power is disconnected for a short time and then restored" (`http://en.wikipedia.org/wiki/Transient_fault#Transient_fault`).

Many faults in connectivity to cloud services are transient in nature. Transient faults commonly occur where your architecture connects to a service or a resource such as a database. When consuming these services, it's a common practice to implement logic that introduces the concept of a timeout. This logic identifies an acceptable time frame in which a response is expected, and will generate an identifiable error when that time frame is exceeded. Depending on the timeout error, appropriate steps will be taken based on the context in which the error occurs. Context can include the number of times this error has occurred, the potential impact of the unavailable resource, SLA guarantees for the current time period for the given customer, and so on. Because no service has 100 percent uptime, it's realistic to expect that you might not be able to connect to a service on which a workload depends. The inability to connect to or faults seen from one of these services may be fleeting (less than one second) or permanent (a provider shuts down).

There are several key considerations for the implementation of transient fault handling, as detailed in the following list:

➤ **Retry logic** — The retry logic typically attempts to execute the action(s) a certain number of times, registering an error and/or utilizing a secondary service or workflow if the fault continues. Note that the design should limit the number of times the logic will be retried.

➤ **Exponential back off** — If the transient fault is the result of throttling by the service due to heavy load, repeated attempts to call the service will only extend the throttling and impact overall availability. It is often desirable to reduce the volume of the calls to the service to help avoid or reduce throttling. This is typically done algorithmically, such as immediately retrying after the first failure, waiting one second after the second failure, waiting five seconds after the third failure, and so on until ultimately succeeding or hitting an application-defined threshold for failures.

➤ **Idempotency** — In cases where retry logic is implemented, there is the potential for the same message to be sent more than once, for messages to be sent out of sequence, and so on. Operations should be designed to be idempotent, ensuring that sending the same message multiple times does not result in an unexpected or polluted data store.

Circuit Breaker Pattern

A circuit breaker is a switch that automatically interrupts the flow of electric current if the current exceeds a preset limit. Circuit breakers are used most often as a safety precaution where excessive current through a circuit could be hazardous. Unlike a fuse, a circuit breaker can be reset and reused.

NOTE *For more on the Circuit Breaker pattern go to* http://en.wikipedia.org/wiki/Circuit_breaker_design_pattern.

The analogy of a circuit breaker can be brought to a hybrid cloud architecture design in the form of a software pattern, where it is particularly applicable to services for which availability and resiliency are key considerations.

A common implementation of this pattern is related to accessing databases or data services. If a call to a database resource fails after 100 consecutive attempts to connect, there is likely little value in continuing to call the database. A circuit breaker could be triggered at that threshold and the appropriate actions taken.

Using Automation

People make mistakes. Whether it's a developer making a code change that could have unexpected consequences, a DBA accidentally dropping a table in a database, or an operations person who makes a change but doesn't document it, there are multiple opportunities for a person to inadvertently make a service less resilient. To reduce human error, a logical approach is to reduce the amount of humans in the process. Through the introduction of automation, you limit the risk of ad hoc, inadvertent deltas from expected behavior jeopardizing your service.

> ➤ **Using scripting as much as possible** — In the cloud, most services are exposed with an API. From development tools to virtualized infrastructure to platform services to solutions, most things are scriptable. Scripting is highly recommended. It makes deployment and management consistent and predictable and pays significant dividends against the investment.

> ➤ **Automating deployment** — One of the key areas of automation is in the building and deployment of a solution. Automation can make it easy for a developer team to test and deploy to multiple environments. Development, test, staging, beta, and production can all be deployed readily and consistently through automated builds. The capability to deploy consistently across environments works toward ensuring that the production environment is representative of what has been tested.

> ➤ **Automating data archiving and purging** — One of the areas that gets little attention is that of data archiving and purging. For resiliency plans that include one or more replicas of a data store, removing all but the necessary data can expedite management activities such as backing up and restoring data.

Redundancy and the Public Cloud

On-premises, redundancy has historically been achieved through duplicate sets of hardware, software, and networking. Sometimes this is implemented in a cluster in a single location or distributed across multiple datacenters.

When devising a strategy for the hybrid cloud, you must rationalize the need for redundancy across three vectors: deployed code within a Windows Azure environment, redundancy of Windows Azure compute and storage services, and redundancy between the public cloud and the private cloud.

When designing hybrid cloud architectures, you should establish one of the following redundancy strategies for the deployment of architecture components into the Windows Azure public cloud:

➤ **Deploy multiple VMs within a datacenter** — By deploying to multiple nodes, the solution can limit the downtime that would occur when only a single node is deployed.

➤ **Deploy across multiple datacenters** — While deploying multiple nodes in a single Windows Azure datacenter will provide benefits, architectures must take into account that an entire datacenter could potentially be unavailable. While this is not a common occurrence, events such as natural disasters, war, and so on could result in service disruption in a particular geo-location. To achieve your SLA, it might be appropriate to deploy your solution to multiple datacenters or to use the geo-replication option for services, such as an Azure storage account, that enable this functionality.

NOTE *With geo-replication, Windows Azure storage keeps your data durable in two locations hundreds of miles apart within the same region (for example, between North and South United States, between East and West United States, between North and West Europe, and between East and Southeast Asia). In both locations, Windows Azure Storage continuously maintains multiple healthy replicas of your data.*

Redundancy and the Private Cloud

While having a dependency on a Windows Azure may make fiscal sense, your organization may have certain business considerations that require on-premises redundancy for compliance and/or business continuity.

Based on the SLAs for a solution, it may be desirable to also incorporate on-premises redundancy. To realize this, you need to identify private cloud-deployable products or cloud services that will work across multiple cloud types. Microsoft SQL Server is a good example of a product that can be deployed on-premises or in an IaaS offering.

Traffic Management

Whether network traffic is always geo-distributed or routed to different datacenters to satisfy business continuity scenarios, traffic management functionality is important to ensure that requests to your solution are being routed to the appropriate instance(s).

Windows Azure Traffic Manager (briefly mentioned in Chapter 4) enables you to load balance incoming traffic across multiple hosted Windows Azure services, whether they are running in the same datacenter or across different datacenters around the world. By effectively managing traffic, you can ensure the high performance, availability, and resiliency of your applications.

Traffic routing occurs as a result of policies that you define and that are based on one of the following three criteria:

➤ **Performance** — Traffic is forwarded to the closest hosted service in terms of network latency.

➤ **Round robin** — Traffic is distributed equally across all hosted services.

➤ **Failover** — Traffic is sent to a primary service and if this service is not online, to the next available service in a list.

Traffic Manager continuously monitors hosted services to ensure they are online and will not route traffic to a service that is unavailable. Using Traffic Manager, you can create applications that are designed to respond to requests in multiple geographic locations and that can therefore survive entire site outages. Prior to the general availability of a production version of Traffic Manager, you could implement third-party DNS routing solutions such as those provided by Akamai or Level 3 Communications to build applications that are designed for high availability.

Note that relying on a traffic management service introduces a single point of failure. Therefore, it is important to investigate the SLA of your application's primary traffic management service to determine if alternate traffic management functionality is warranted by your requirements.

DESIGNING FOR BUSINESS CONTINUITY

The general approach to business continuity in the hybrid cloud is no different from any other clouds or on-premises environments. The same principles and metrics apply, but the implementation and process are different. This section explains how to plan for business continuity in the hybrid cloud when using Windows Azure and Microsoft private clouds.

On top of a secure and highly redundant infrastructure, Windows Azure provides services that act as building blocks for designing highly available deployments that span multiple datacenters. These services can each be used on their own or in combination with each other, third-party services, and application-specific logic to achieve the desired balance of availability and recovery goals. The following sections cover the three key services that should help you in planning resilient and scalable hybrid cloud architectures.

Infrastructure Redundancy

The majority of hybrid cloud scenarios are based on the general assumption that connectivity between on-premises private cloud and Windows Azure public cloud services is always on, so the first and fundamental requirement for hybrid cloud business continuity is the availability of a well-managed datacenter infrastructure in diverse geographic locations. If individual datacenters are not properly managed, the most robust application designs may be undermined by gross failures at the infrastructure level. With Windows Azure, you can take advantage of the extensive experience Microsoft has in designing, managing, and securing world-class datacenters in diverse locations around the world.

These are the same datacenters that run many of the world's largest online services. These datacenters are designed and constructed with stringent levels of physical security and access control, power redundancy and efficiency, environmental control, and recoverability capabilities. The physical facilities have achieved broad industry compliance, including ISO 27001 and SOC/SSAE 16/SAS 70 Type II, and within the United States, FISMA certification.

To ensure recoverability of the Windows Azure platform core software components, Microsoft has established an Enterprise Business Continuity Program based on Disaster Recovery Institute International (DRII) Professional Practice Statements and the Business Continuity Institute (BCI) Good Practice Guidelines. This program also aligns to FISMA and ISO 27001 Continuity Control requirements. As part of this methodology, recovery exercises are performed on a regular basis, simulating disaster recovery scenarios. In the rare event that a system failure does occur, Microsoft uses an aggressive, root cause analysis process to deeply understand the cause. Implementation of improvements learned from outages is a top priority for the engineering organization. In addition, Microsoft provides postmortems upon request for any incidents that affect customers.

Data Durability and Backup

Data durability for Windows Azure SQL Database and Windows Azure Storage (Blobs, Tables, and Queues) is facilitated by maintaining three copies of all data on different drives located across fully independent physical storage subsystems.

NOTE *Copies of data are continually scanned to detect and repair bit rot, an often over-looked threat to the integrity of stored data.*

Additionally, with the Windows Azure Backup service, Microsoft added support to enable offsite backup protection for Windows Server 2008 R2 SP1 and Windows Server 2012, Windows Server 2012 Essentials, and System Center Data Protection Manager 2012 SP1 to Windows Azure. You can manage cloud backups using the familiar backup tools that administrators already use on these servers, providing similar experiences for configuring, monitoring, and recovering backups — be it to local disk or Windows Azure storage. After data is backed up to the cloud, authorized users can easily recover backups to any server; and because incremental backups are supported, only changes to files are transferred to the cloud. This helps ensure efficient use of storage, reduced bandwidth consumption, and point-in-time recovery of multiple versions of the data. Configurable data retention policies, data compression, encryption, and data transfer throttling also offer you added flexibility and help boost efficiency.

Point-in-time backups for SQL databases are achieved with the Windows Azure SQL Database Copy command. You can use this command to create a transactionally consistent copy of a database on the same logical database server or to a different server. In either case, the database copy is fully functional and completely independent of the source database. Each copy you create represents a point-in-time recovery option. You can recover the database state completely by renaming the new database with the source database name. Alternatively, you can recover a specific subset of data from the new database by using Transact-SQL queries.

Geo-Replication

Geo-replication is designed to provide additional durability in case of a major datacenter disaster. It is an optional choice that you can select when you first create a new Windows Azure storage account, automatically replicating all Windows Azure Blobs and Tables associated with your storage account between paired datacenters hundreds of miles apart within a specific geographic region (for example, between East and West in the United States or between North and West in Europe).

With this first version of geo-replication, Microsoft controls when failover occurs, and failover is limited to major disasters in which the original primary location is deemed unrecoverable in a reasonable amount of time. In the future, Microsoft plans to provide customers with the capability to control failover of their storage accounts on an individual basis. Data is typically replicated within a few minutes, although the synchronization interval is not yet covered by an SLA.

Geo-replication of SQL Database data can be achieved by exporting the database to an Azure Storage Blob using the SQL Database Import/Export service.

PLANNING HYBRID CLOUD SITE DISASTER RECOVERY

We briefly touched on disaster recovery in Chapter 6; now we want to turn to planning for disaster recovery in more depth. Most IT organizations today have at least one plan for disaster recovery that greatly reduces what it needs to worry about to ensure high availability within its own datacenter. However, even the most well designed datacenter could be rendered inaccessible in the case of a true disaster. Moreover, for hybrid cloud scenarios in which your application is deployed in both an on-premises datacenter and a Windows Azure datacenter, your disaster recovery plan must include the case where either your on-premises services or the services deployed to Windows Azure become unavailable, or both. To plan for such disasters, you must think through both the technical and procedural steps required to provide the level of hybrid cloud site availability you require.

There are some basic steps that all but the most trivial of applications should take to ensure that they can be deployed in a different datacenter in the event of a site disaster. For many applications, redeployment from scratch is an acceptable solution. For those that need a quicker and more predictable recovery, a second deployment must be ready and waiting in a second datacenter. For an even smaller set of applications, true multi-site high availability is required. This section looks at each of these classes of applications, in order from the least complex and costly to the most complex and costly. Cross-site availability is a lot like insurance: You pay for protection that you hope you will never have to use.

NOTE *No two applications have precisely the same business requirements or technical design points, so these classes of applications are meant to serve as general guidance that should be adapted to your specific needs.*

Typically, for a hybrid cloud application that might include services deployed in at least two datacenters (for example, a private cloud and public cloud) to be available in the event of disaster, the following three requirements must be met:

1. The application and dependent services must be deployed in both on-premises and Windows Azure datacenters.

2. The necessary data must be available to the application (typically in the same datacenter).

3. Any external traffic must be routed to the application.

Each of these three requirements can be accomplished at the time of a disaster or ahead of time, and each can be accomplished manually or automatically. Every application is different, so there may be other application-specific requirements, such as availability of a dependent service. The rest of this section describes several common patterns for recovering availability in the case of a disaster.

Redeploy on Disaster

The simplest form of disaster recovery is to redeploy your application and dependent services when a disaster occurs. Redeployment of applications is accomplished with the same method used when the application was originally created. This can be done manually via the Windows Azure Management Portal or it can be automated using the Windows Azure Service Management API, Windows PowerShell, or with Microsoft System Center Orchestrator. To mitigate data loss, the redeployment strategy should be coupled with data backup or synchronization to ensure that the data exists and is usable from a backup storage account or database. To meet the third requirement (traffic routing to the new deployment), the custom domain name can be configured to route to the new application name after the new deployment is completed.

Because no compute resources are reserved for recovery, this is the least expensive solution. However, low cost comes at the expense of increased risk and longer recovery time.

Active/Passive Deployment

The redeployment strategy described previously takes time and has risks. Some customers need faster and more predictable recovery and may want to reserve standby resources in an alternate datacenter. For example, you might keep your master copy of the application in a private cloud, on-premises datacenter and use a Windows Azure datacenter as your backup. Or have both parts, private cloud and public cloud services, backed up in another Windows Azure datacenter, preferably in the same region as the master Windows Azure datacenter. The active/passive pattern means keeping an always ready (potentially smaller) deployment of the application in a secondary datacenter, also known as a *warm standby*. At the time of a disaster, the secondary deployment can be activated and scaled.

When using a warm standby, you need to carefully think through data consistency implications at the time of the failover. You need to plan for any steps that must be taken before your application is brought online in an alternate location, as well as how and when to return to the original deployment when it becomes available again. Because the application is not designed to function simultaneously in multiple datacenters, returning service to the primary location should follow a procedure similar to the one you follow in the case of a failover.

This solution, because it requires two copies of the application to be stored in two places, could be too expensive for some organizations that would prefer the first solution we described earlier. However, since the motto "pay as you go" can be applied for services deployed to Windows Azure, you could actually lower significantly your monthly bill for storing the passive copy of your application — especially if you employ automatic PowerShell deployment scripts for your application components (for example, VMs). These scripts can help you in exporting and importing your cloud services on demand. And as long as you don't run any VMs in the Windows Azure environment, you don't pay for them.

Active/Active Deployment

To achieve full, multi-site high availability without downtime, another common pattern is the active/active deployment, so named because two deployments in two datacenters are both active. The active/active pattern is very similar to the active/passive deployment pattern, but the third requirement (traffic routed to the deployment) is always satisfied because both deployments now handle incoming traffic at all times. This solution is the most difficult to implement, as it requires the application to be designed to handle simultaneous requests across multiple instances of the application residing in distinct datacenters. However, it is more efficient than the active/passive solution in that all compute resources are utilized all the time.

This solution, while providing the best breadth out of all disaster recovery solutions described here, is also the most expensive solution. To enable Active/Active Deployment you must run in parallel two identical copies of your application, data, and services that must be ready to take over the application requests in the event of disaster.

DESIGNING SCALABLE HYBRID CLOUD SOLUTIONS

While many aspects of designing hybrid cloud applications that use Windows Azure cloud services are very familiar from on-premises development, there are several key differences in how the underlying platform and services behave. Understanding these differences, and as a result how to design for the platform — not against it — are crucial in delivering applications that fulfill the promise of elastic scale in the cloud.

This section outlines three key concepts that reflect the critical design points of building large-scale, widely distributed scalable hybrid cloud applications. Understanding these concepts will help you design and build applications that not only leverage Windows Azure public cloud services, but also thrive there, returning as many benefits of your investment as possible.

Scale-Out, Not Scale-Up

The traditional method of building scalable applications on-premises relies on a mix of scale-out (stateless web and application servers) and scale-up (invest in a bigger multi-core/large memory system and database server, build a bigger datacenter, and so on). In the cloud, scale-up is often very limited and capped to available resources and, therefore, not a realistic option; the only path to achieving truly scalable applications is by explicit design for scale-out.

As many of the elements of an on-premises application are already amenable to scale-out (web servers, application servers), the challenge lies in identifying those aspects of the application that depend on a scale-up service. Another challenge is to convert (or map) them to a scale-out implementation. The primary candidate for a scale-up dependency is typically the relational database (SQL Server/Windows Azure SQL Database). This means design challenges such as explicitly partitioning data into smaller chunks (each of which can fit in a data partition or scale-out unit) and managing consistency between distributed data elements. This achieves scale through partitioning in a way that avoids many of the drawbacks of designing to scale-up.

By adopting this design philosophy with both your on-premises applications as well as those in the public cloud, you will have a much easier time moving applications between the two environments.

Scaling-Out through Scale Units

In a world where you run your own datacenter, you have a nearly infinite degree of control, juxtaposed with a nearly infinite number of choices. Everything from the physical plant (air conditioning, electrical supply, floor space) to the infrastructure (racks, servers, storage, networking, and so on) to the configuration (routing topology, operating system installation) is under your control.

This degree of control comes with costs — capital, operational, human, and time. The cost of managing all the details in an agile and changing environment is at the heart of the drive toward virtualization, and a key aspect of the march to the cloud. In return for giving up a measure of control, these platforms reduce the cost of deployment and management, and increase agility. The constraint that they impose is that the size (capacity, throughput, and so on) of the available components and services is restricted to a fixed set of offerings. That means even cloud resources have a definite limit. Be it an individual cloud services role instance, a storage account, a virtual machine, or even a datacenter — every available resource in Azure has some finite limit. They may be very large limits, such as the amount of storage available in a datacenter, but they are finite.

With this in mind, a suggested approach for adhering to scale-out application design is to partition the load and compose it across multiple scale units. In the infrastructure world, a scale unit usually refers to a predefined set of hardware capacity: compute, storage, and network. These scale units are deployed, as opposed to adding individual components, in order to achieve predictable capacity planning and a standardized infrastructure that provides other benefits such as reduced complexity and higher availability. Similarly, in the Azure world a scale unit refers to a predefined set of cloud resources such as web roles, worker roles, and data access or storage accounts. By partitioning and composing applications across multiple scale units you gain advantages of the massive scalability inherent to cloud datacenters.

You can further implement partitioning granularly at many components within the scale unit, including the following:

- Queues
- Table storage
- SQL Databases and database sharding
- Storage accounts

NOTE *A scale unit is a group of resources that can handle both a defined degree of load and additional load when used in conjunction with other resources.*

Compress Density of Scale

With the elastic scale provided by the Windows Azure platform, the supply curve can closely match the demand curve (rather than having a large amount of extra capacity to account for peak load). The amount of work that can be performed for a given amount of capacity is known as the *density* of the application. Denser services and frameworks allow a greater amount of work to be performed for a given resource deployment; that is to say, compressing density enables reduction in deployed capacity (and cost) or the capability to absorb additional load with the same deployed capacity.

With elastic scale, density of scale is driven by the following:

- **How efficiently work is performed within a scale unit** — This is the traditional form of performance optimization: managing thread contention and locks, optimizing algorithms, tuning SQL queries.

- **How efficiently work is coordinated across scale units** — In a world where systems are composed of larger numbers of smaller units, the ability to efficiently stitch them together is critical to delivering peak performance.

SUMMARY

You can use a number of optimization techniques to provide scalability and resiliency for your hybrid cloud application. These can have varying costs and contain multiple layers. At an application level, utilizing all of them is unfeasible for most projects due to cost and implementation time. By decomposing your application to the service level, you gain a benefit in that you can make these investments at a more targeted level, the single service.

Even at the service level, you may not choose to implement every optimization option. What you choose to implement or not is determined by your requirements. Regardless of the techniques you choose, you should make a conscious choice that's informed and considers all of the options.

Meeting your availability and recovery requirements using Microsoft System Center and Windows Azure is a partnership between you and Microsoft. Windows Azure greatly reduces the number of things you need to deal with by providing application resiliency and data durability to survive individual server, device, and network connection failures. Windows Azure also provides many services for implementing backup and recovery strategies and for designing highly available applications using world-class datacenters in diverse geographies. Ultimately, only you know your application requirements and architecture well enough to ensure that you have an availability and recovery plan that meets your needs.

8 Optimizing for Performance

In this and the next chapter we're going to focus on concepts that are closely related: performance optimization, and operations and management. One of the fundamental trends we see going forward is that of planning for management and operations from the application's inception. This is imperative. Several new methodologies have emerged to close the gaps in the life cycle of an application — from inception to design and development on one side, to operating and managing (O&M) and finally deprecation on the other. Historically, the disparity between development and post-deployment has been systemic, a result of the way in which the organization is structured and made worse by the culture of the two IT camps: application development and infrastructure teams.

Developers tend to see infrastructure as plumbing; boxes and wires, nothing too complex and nothing to worry about too much. If post-deployment issues arise, the infrastructure people can handle it. The people involved on the infrastructure side, however, tend to view developers as not understanding the implications of proper planning and proper operations from the beginning. The infrastructure teams tend to get caught in a firefighting mode without having a clear understanding of how the application was designed and therefore how to detect and respond to performance-related issues.

To address this disconnect, this chapter and the next focuses on optimizing applications for performance in a hybrid scenario and how to formulate a holistic operations and management strategy. These two goals are closely related because we really have two primary points in the application life cycle to affect performance: during the design phase and at run time. However, if you make a fundamental mistake during the design phase there's only so much you can do at run time to mitigate the issue. Conversely, if the application is designed flawlessly but managed and operated poorly, well, you get the idea.

CLOUD APPLICATION PERFORMANCE FUNDAMENTALS

Because this book is focused on fundamental concepts for the hybrid cloud, we don't cover application programming techniques here, even though they are critical to a well-performing application. For that, you'll need to pick up a developer-focused book and get some training. This section assumes a basic understanding of such concepts.

When talking about cloud applications, we don't have the luxury of customizing the infrastructure any way we want. We have a constrained infrastructure within whose parameters we need to design applications. For example, in a traditional computing environment, if we have a database-driven application and the SQL calls aren't performing adequately, it may be possible to simply throw more hardware at the problem — add memory, processors, storage, and let the SQL Server go nuts. In the cloud, private or public, we are more limited in terms of this option, as each individual instance can scale-up only so far because it is highly standardized. In other words, we need to design for scaling-out from the get-go, as we touched on in Chapter 7.

You can achieve this by partitioning data into smaller chunks and managing the data's consistency. Between your on-premises resources and Windows Azure you have multiple mechanisms at your disposal for a scale-out architecture, but always keep this core principle in mind as it is one of the main ways to optimize for performance in the cloud. It does, of course, carry with it new management and operational considerations, which we'll dig into in the next chapter.

One technique to help transition to a scale-out architecture is to decompose your service by workload. *Decomposing* means to break apart the individual components that comprise the application such as the web front-end, search and indexing, transaction processing, data storage and archival, etc. By doing this you can leverage specific optimization techniques suitable for each workload while also providing better manageability of costs and availability. An important aspect of this exercise is understanding the demand expected for the service. Considerations include total number of active users (not just registered, but actively using the service), the number of concurrent users, and acceptable response times. This is not always an easy exercise. For example, a start-up company may not yet know how many users to anticipate and therefore doesn't want to sink too much capital into the service, but at the same time wants to be ready for success in case the service becomes popular very quickly. In this scenario, you'd want to be more conservative in your initial deployment but leverage the elasticity of the cloud to dynamically meet demand as it increases. However, if the application's individual workloads are not properly optimized for scaling-out, it may soon encounter bottlenecks, such as used to be commonplace when an Internet site went "viral" and began receiving large amounts of unprecedented traffic. User tolerance for these types of outages has decreased rapidly over the past few years and you must have an approach that can scale to meet demand in order to prevent losing users to competitors.

When decomposing your service, consider the dependencies, both internal and external. If you're using external services, such as a URL shortener, be aware of the SLA provided for that service and the limitation it will impose. The limitations of Microsoft technologies are well documented and easy to build into your design, but external dependencies may be more challenging. Some Windows Azure services may impose throttling in order to ensure service quality for all subscribers and prevent denial-of-service attacks, etc. For example, Windows Azure SQL Database will throttle connection attempts in different ways under different circumstances (see SQL Database Engine Throttling, http://social.technet.microsoft.com/wiki/contents/articles/3507.windows-azure-sql-database-performance-and-elasticity-guide.aspx#SQL_Azure_Engine_Throttling). There are known techniques to avoid or reduce throttling such as "exponential back-off" which is usually done algorithmically in order to manage the connection retry attempts in a way that is aware of the throttling event.

It should always be assumed that in a cloud application architecture the services you are utilizing will not be available 100 percent of the time. Transient fault handling with retry logic is a core implementation approach. These concepts are covered in good detail in a series of work named "failsafe." The failsafe work was done by a number of people within the Azure product team and in Microsoft Services to analyze common and high-profile customer issues and bring the practices to avoid them into the public domain. Please see http://msdn.microsoft.com/en-us/library/windowsazure/jj853352.aspx for more information.

Storage Types and Data Location

The next important aspect affecting performance is storage. As you learned earlier in the book, compared to traditional storage, cloud-based storage has some key differences that result in unique performance characteristics. Again, the primary storage types in Azure are the blob, table, queue, and SQL database. However, within an Azure Virtual Machine, local storage is also available in the system drive and in the form of virtual hard disks (VHDs), which are presented as logical drives. These VHDs are actually stored on blob storage and are persistent, meaning they are sustained throughout the life of the Virtual Machine. Selecting the right storage type for the right purpose is the first major decision to affect storage performance. At a glance, the different storage types are best used as follows:

- **Local** — Data on the local VM in the system drive (C:)
- **Drives** — Data requiring local access from VMs
- **Blob** — Large binary objects such as video or audio
- **Table** — Structured data
- **Queue** — Inter-process messages
- **SQL Database** — Relational database management system

In a traditional data storage scheme you might place all application data — user information, pictures, and the like — into a SQL database; but to correctly leverage Azure storage you need to partition your data access according to the appropriate, fit-for-purpose storage type, such as tables for user accounts and blobs for pictures. Selecting the right storage for the right job can have a major impact on performance and service availability. Cloud-scale application development has shown that the majority of application operational issues originate in design and development. Therefore, it's critical to formulate design and development practices that will either directly address identified issues or lead to the identification of yet unknown issues. Having a testing methodology that reflects this knowledge cannot be overstated.

The quickest way to compare your storage options and their implications is to consult a table you can find at MSDN:

`http://msdn.microsoft.com/en-us/library/windowsazure/jj156168.aspx`

As you can see from the table at MSDN, they consider storage types and data location issues from the perspective of nine criteria. The criteria you prioritize in your own situation will drive your decisions regarding storage and data locations. The best choices for data storage are also dependent on your application architecture. One example would be whether or not the application is comprised of Windows Azure Virtual Machines.

- ➤ **Durability** — If durability is a top priority, then your best options will be Azure Drives, Tables Storage, and Blob Storage. Local storage obviously is the least durable although data stored within the C: partition will be persistent to an Azure Virtual Machine. Azure Drives are durable, but consider that if the Virtual Machine using it fails, the Drive must be manually mounted on another Virtual Machine. This means some downtime will be incurred.

- ➤ **Data Access and Concurrency** — The best solution for those prizing data access above all else will likely be Table Storage and Blob Storage. Tables and Blobs are designed to be accessed by multiple instances simultaneously via the REST APIs. Azure Drives are accessible for read and write operations to only one instance at a time, but can be accessed for read-only operations by multiple instances. Local storage is only accessible to the one instance for which it is local (hence the term "local storage").

- ➤ **Pricing** — You'll likely know if pricing is a top priority for you (and who among us is free from considering price?). There are multiple considerations for estimating price. The main difference is that local storage is included in the price of the Azure Compute account, and all other types are priced separately. However, there are obviously big trade-offs to using local storage vs. all others, and it should only be used when appropriate.

- ➤ **Latency** — Latency is addressed in more detail in the next chapter. The main difference here again is that local storage is co-located with the runtime environment and therefore has the lowest latency. However, again consider the trade-offs and use local storage judiciously.

- ➤ **Scalability** — Both Table and Blog storage are built to be massively scalable using techniques such as automatic partition distribution for Tables and the Windows Azure CDN for Blob. Azure Drives are less scalable, although they do benefit from residing on Blog Storage. Again consider the single instance write-access limitation. Local storage does not provide scalability.

➤ **High Availability/Fault Tolerance** — Table Storage, Blob Storage, and Queues are all replicated to three locations within a Windows Azure datacenter by default providing a high level of resiliency to failures. Azure Drives reside on Blob Storage so they also inherently have this attribute. Local storage provides no high availability functionality.

➤ **Disaster Recovery** — Table Storage, Blob Storage (and consequently Azure Drives) all have the ability to be replicated to an additional datacenter via Geo-Replication. Local drives do not.

➤ **Security** — Local storage is only accessible from its own virtual machine. Azure Drives have the read/write limitations stated in the earlier bullet. Table Storage and Blog Storage both require authentication for each request made, except in the case of using public container resources and anonymous access.

NOTE *You'll notice the bulleted list just presented does not include SQL database, which we mentioned as a storage type earlier. Using a SQL database usually comes as a choice dictated by the application. Whole books have been written on the topic of SQL databases, so we won't go into them here. The scope is just too large and developer-heavy. The afore-mentioned concepts should help you in case you're using SQL databases, and further reading about SQL Database development techniques is a must. Start with "Windows Azure SQL Database and SQL Server — Performance and Scalability Compared and Contrasted," found at* http://msdn.microsoft.com/en-us/library/windowsazure/jj879332.aspx.

In Chapter 4, we previously discussed the use of caching, queuing, and content delivery networks (CDNs) and their impact on performance. These are important techniques to include here as you consider how your application will scale and handle cloud-centric compute models.

NOTE *Remember: Decompose the application into smaller chunks and design with individual component failure in mind. Partition the data access across scale units using the right data storage type for each classification.*

In a hybrid cloud model you may choose to stretch certain components between public and private cloud environments. In this case, the most important element becomes the network's ability to provide resilient and low-latency throughput.

OPTIMIZING NETWORK THROUGHPUT AND LATENCY

We have previously touched on the high-level network components of Windows Azure. This section focuses on some important details for performance considerations in a hybrid environment. Two important key performance indicators (KPIs) of the network topology are *throughput* and *latency*. Depending on the architecture of the service or specific application component, different network elements are more important than others. For example, if you have determined that your application needs to keep its data within your own datacenter, then access between the front-end tier and the data tier takes center stage. However, if all application components are in Windows Azure, then network access characteristics within the Azure layers themselves become paramount.

Take a look at a scenario with Azure VPN Site-to-Site. This network topology extends the trust boundary of your datacenter to include your Azure Virtual Network. It is performed via a gateway device at each endpoint. Of course, the network traffic that will traverse this tunnel is highly dependent on the scenario and workload. You'll want to carefully plan and thoroughly understand each network communication that will use the site-to-site tunnel. Throughput requirements and latency tolerance are products of the application itself. It's important to understand the network topology of the application components and what latency they can tolerate.

> **NOTE** *For an interesting example of a hybrid application (an ASP.NET application in Azure leveraging a FAST Search environment on-premises) that achieved an approximately 66 percent reduction in latency by simply using Azure Connect (Site-to-Site) rather than the Azure Service Bus, see "Using Windows Azure Connect to Integrate On-Premises Web Services"* (http://msdn.microsoft.com/en-us/library/windowsazure/hh697512.aspx). *Of course, you can infer that the specific application and its hybrid network topology are the key factors in selecting the correct network type.*

A site-to-site tunnel is also dependent on your physical proximity to the Azure datacenter you will utilize. Physics does become a factor here. The earth is large, and Ethernet can only travel so many miles per hour, even on a fiber-optic backbone, as the speed of light, approximately 186,282 miles per second, is a constant we can't change (didn't think Einstein's special theory of relativity would come into play here, did you?). Therefore, you should consider both the physical proximity and connectivity between your datacenter and the Azure datacenter.

What about the clients, the folks who will actually use the application? From where will they connect? Well, if it's from the Internet, also known as an unknown network location anywhere on earth, then you should consider using the Azure Traffic Manager, which can automatically detect and route your client connections to the best location based on performance. In this case, you'll need to have deployed your application in more than one Azure datacenter, but it is an attractive option to have available when you need it. If your clients are in known locations, such as corporate offices, then you'll want to test and measure the network connectivity from those locations and plan accordingly.

Here's a handy way to think about total latency:

Network latency is the total round-trip between user and application, between application and data access, and back to the user. The actual performance experienced by end users is the total response time, calculated as follows:

```
2 (user to app + app to data) + App_Time + Data_Time
```

For optimization:

➤ Select datacenter(s) closest to the majority of your users.

➤ Co-locate data with the application (when feasible).

➤ Minimize network round-trips.

The Azure Throughput Analyzer is a free utility produced by Microsoft Research. You can use the Azure Throughput Analyzer to measure "the upload and download throughput achievable from your on-premise client machine to Azure cloud storage (blobs, tables and queue)." See `http://research.microsoft.com/en-us/downloads/5c8189b9-53aa-4d6a-a086-013d927e15a7/default.aspx`.

Another option is Point-to-Site, which enables on-premises computers to connect to the Azure Virtual Network without the need for a VPN gateway device. This is useful to connect to Azure Virtual Networks from behind a firewall without usually needing to involve network infrastructure folks. The same throughput and latency concerns apply, of course — it's just another configuration option.

Affinity Groups

Another important consideration is the proximity of your Azure Services to one another. Whether you are utilizing Azure Compute, Azure Storage, Azure Virtual Machines, or other services, they all have the potential to be deployed in a less than optimal way. For example, suppose you were deploying a web role in the US West Azure Datacenter and wanted it to use an existing storage account that happens to be located in the Europe North Azure Datacenter. Those two points are thousands of miles apart. Again, physics. Therefore, the first rule is to ensure physical proximity between application layers by deploying them in the same datacenter. However, consider that a single Azure datacenter can be many (American) football fields large, with thousands of miles of cabling. If you deploy two virtual machines, they may end up on physical infrastructure quite far apart.

Affinity groups address this potential problem. By locating your services within the same affinity group, you are basically telling the Windows Azure Fabric Controller to provision your services as near to each other as possible. It looks for an Azure container that has capacity within a cluster to locate these services together, thereby decreasing latency.

As shown in Figure 8-1, virtual machines have the option at deploy time to "connect to an existing virtual machine." You'll notice that when selecting this option, the affinity group is automatically chosen for you based on the location of the virtual machine you selected.

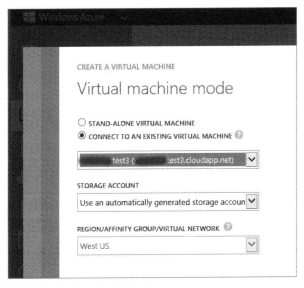

FIGURE 8-1

In cases where you're not able or don't want to deploy a virtual machine connected to another, you can select the "stand-alone" option, shown in Figure 8-2. You'll need to be aware of the location of the storage account and the affinity group selection. In this example I've previously created an affinity group that I can select.

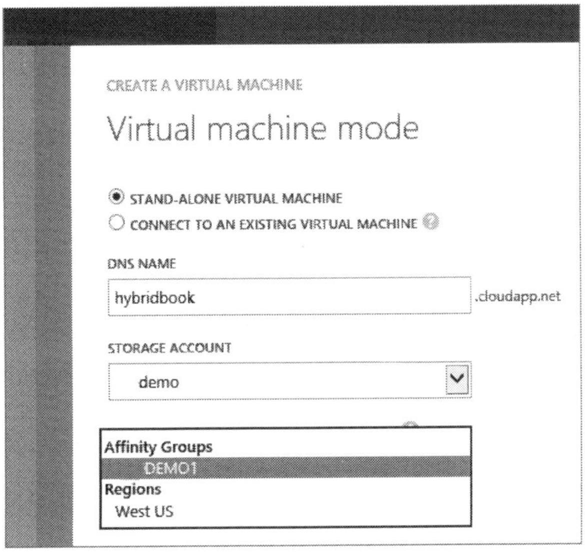

FIGURE 8-2

To summarize, affinity groups provide a way to aggregate resources, providing lower latency between the application tiers, which is especially important for high-speed data access.

SUMMARY

Remember much of what determines a cloud application's performance is highly affected by new application development design techniques, such as database sharding, transient fault handling, back-off/retry logic, throttling, and more. Please ensure that you thoroughly understand these techniques and incorporate them into your optimization strategy.

What we hope you'll take away here is information that helps you determine the important performance considerations for your hybrid cloud endeavor. Cloud adoption does require some rethinking of the way things have been done over the past couple of decades from an enterprise IT perspective. The rewards are worth it!

In the next chapter we'll dig into some concepts related to management and operations in the hybrid cloud, to help solidify how feasible and achievable it is to take advantage of the many possibilities the cloud provides.

Monitoring and Management for Successful Operations

9

CHANGE IS THE NEW NORMAL

Working as a team lead of infrastructure in a live datacenter environment was an eye-opening experience. One of the first major lessons I learned was that it didn't matter how great the infrastructure runs if the business units and application owners it exists for are not part of the plan. Although I considered those servers my babies, I was not really their parent — I was just entrusted with them. I had to formulate a close relationship with the application teams and businesses they developed for in order to ensure the infrastructure my team was building and maintaining was in line with their needs and with the overall objectives of the corporation.

To that end, we implemented *service delivery plans*, which were basically binders documenting the application, the supporting infrastructure, and the overall plan for its well-being currently and in the future. This included SLAs, backup schedules, maintenance agreements, and so on. We met with application owners at least once per month to review, revise, and discuss. The IT department also decided to embark upon Information Technology Infrastructure Library (ITIL) training and implementation of some governance, such as change management. ITIL has received much attention and adoption over the past few decades; but as you know, the industry is undergoing a major overhaul. The importance of technology and the rate of change have been increasing at breakneck speed. As good as they are, ITIL implementations that worked 10 years ago aren't necessarily appropriate or suitable today. One of the main problems is that typically in large organizations, the teams responsible for governance often sit outside the application and infrastructure teams. They have proven excellent at increasing overall quality control and process maturity, but at the price of innovation and time-to-market. This is a price enterprises aren't willing to pay, and they are considering changes to the way developers and infrastructure operations communicate and collaborate throughout the application life cycle. One of the major emerging trends to address this challenge is known as *DevOps,* shown in Figure 9-1.

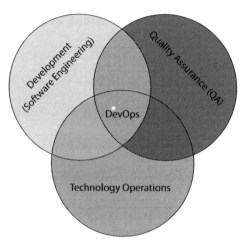

IMAGE SOURCE: DEVOPS.PNG: RAJIV.PANT

FIGURE 9-1

DevOps is typically characterized by adopting a more agile software release cycle that introduces smaller changes more frequently, which reduces the risks associated with less frequent releases of major changes. In addition, the coordination between development and operations teams is greatly increased, and sophisticated deployment automation techniques are often employed to reduce human error and increase the predictability and repeatability of software releases. These principles are brought to life by new tools on both sides of the equation.

You can tell this is an important shift at Microsoft, as reflected not only by the products they sell but also in the way the world's largest software company is changing its own development, release, and management practices. Because a hybrid cloud environment enables an agile and rapid software development, monitoring and managing this environment must evolve in kind. Microsoft's flagship software development tool, Visual Studio, has introduced several enhancements aligned with this trend, along with the datacenter management suite System Center.

MONITORING THE HYBRID CLOUD

As outlined in Chapter 5, a unified management experience (management capabilities that span multiple systems, both on-premises and in public clouds) is the key to a successful hybrid cloud environment. Another trend getting some attention these days is a phenomenon known as *shadow IT*. This basically reflects the fact that business units can now purchase IT capacity from public cloud providers directly, bypassing internal IT staff altogether. Instead of rallying against this trend, we suggest you attempt to understand the reasons behind it and embrace it. As IT providers, we really need to provide the benefits of this purchasing and deployment model, while maintaining the governance and control required for rock-solid operations. Processes and mentalities may need to change along with the management tools.

Unified Monitoring

I probably over-use the term "unified," but I do so for a reason. *Unification* is a persistent theme in a hybrid cloud environment because clouds can be very prone to fragmentation in terms of how they're managed alongside other IT assets. By definition, public clouds are not owned by you. How do you ensure that something you don't own is available, healthy, and well-performing? With System Center you can do it in the same way you would with your owned datacenter assets. That being said, there is also a case to be made for enabling just enough monitoring in a self-service capacity as to allow developers to achieve their rapid innovation goals. Windows Azure has some built-in and third-party monitoring capabilities that are just fine for development and testing cycles. When Enterprise Systems are brought into production, you can layer on your enterprise monitoring tools and processes. Figure 9-2 shows Azure's built-in dashboard view for a deployed virtual machine (VM).

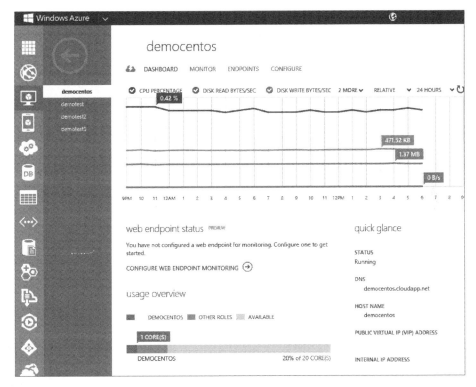

FIGURE 9-2

Taking this developer-centric perspective a step further, Microsoft has recently acquired MetricsHub, a free add-on service that enables deep and sophisticated web-based monitoring for Azure services. MetricsHub is quick and easy to enable and can enhance the Azure experience in a few key ways:

➤ Automatic scale-up and scale-down for PaaS services (not IaaS VMs)

➤ Detailed and consolidated billing information and projection

➤ Real-time health and performance monitoring

➤ Alerts and notification

When a service goes into production, you want to be able to monitor and respond to alerts with the same tools you use for existing assets, particularly for a hybrid application, which has elements in both public and private clouds. This is where System Center integration comes into play. System Center Operations Manager (SCOM) has advanced and sophisticated enterprise IT monitoring capabilities that also extend to Windows Azure. This component of the suite is designed to integrate with the others, such as Service Manager for automatically creating service incidents from alerts and automatically creating change requests from self-service requests. You certainly don't want to lose your carefully developed and refined operational practices; you want to extend them to include cloud-based resources — always keeping in mind the main drivers that led to leveraging public cloud resources. This is a balancing act that will require evaluation and reevaluation as you strive to continuously improve service delivery and service management.

In Chapter 5, we previously discussed the main integration points for System Center and the System Center Management Pack for Windows Azure Fabric. Note that just as monitoring the infrastructure and platform of your own private cloud is key, you may need insight into the application itself. If you are leveraging Windows Azure Virtual Machines, remember to weigh whether you need to deploy a monitoring agent inside the VM to gain that insight into the application.

Scenarios and Use Cases for Monitoring

Let's now look at some scenarios and use cases for monitoring. An important consideration when deploying any monitoring tool is its built-in knowledge — that is, the tool should have the built-in knowledge to understand what constitutes a healthy and well-performing service. But, let's face it, no tool can know everything. If it doesn't meet your current built-in knowledge requirements, it should be easily extensible to include the knowledge pertinent for your services. At Microsoft, one key differentiator is having the same teams that build the applications (Azure, hypervisor, platform, and line-of-business) also ship a management pack, including the KPIs for that application and associated knowledge. There is also a huge (numbering in the hundreds) and growing ecosystem of management packs available for free and for purchase to add knowledge for non-Microsoft technologies. Finally, if you need to monitor a service for which there is no management pack, you can build your own.

Many applications, known as *distributed applications*, span several layers of technology and have dependencies all over the place, including public clouds. You can model these as well in Operations Manager, providing a holistic view of health and performance. For example, consider a hybrid application that has a web tier in Azure, on-premises business logic and data, and maybe some dependencies such as authentication and DNS. This application can be modeled and monitored as a service, as opposed to monitoring each component independently with no understanding of the relationships and dependencies. This way, you can measure the SLA of the entire service by tracking the uptime of all its components together — a framework known as *service-oriented modeling*.

So, now you have a foundation for *holistic monitoring*: built-in knowledge plus hybrid integration along with service-oriented modeling. However, this is only the beginning; you must go much further to address some of the issues outlined earlier. One key investment area for Operations Manager is related to the idea of bringing together development and operations so that you can move toward managing the life cycle of a service (see Figure 9-3). First, you have the capability to do synthetic transactions. That means you can model end-user actions and have Operations Manager reproduce this experience, giving you a continuous real-time monitor that simulates the end-user experience. Even if you have insight into all the components that comprise the system (web servers, databases, infrastructure), you want to know what users are experiencing.

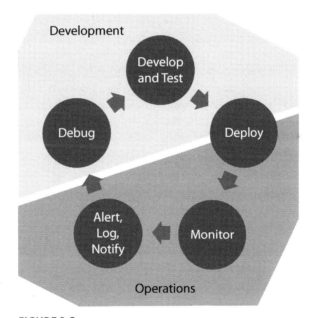

FIGURE 9-3

An example of this would be an online ordering system. To use the online ordering system, the user navigates to the website, does some shopping, enters data into a form, places an order, and receives a confirmation. A *synthetic transaction* can capture and perform this operation repeatedly and raise an alert if the process exceeds a time threshold. Suppose an alert is raised informing you that this transaction is taking too long. What do you do? The typical approach is to just fix it as soon as possible. Maybe Operations Manager is telling you that the latency is being caused by the web application. An IT administrator may troubleshoot for a while, but if the SLA is in jeopardy, the administrator's next step will likely be to reset web services or reboot the server. If this works, the immediate issue is resolved but will likely resurface, as the root cause hasn't been identified and fixed yet.

The next feature that comes into play here is the capability to monitor .NET applications. This provides insight into the actual code base and can identify the root cause of application issues: Take the case of a specific database query within the web application that's taking too long. So, now you know what's causing the issue, and you have restored the service via a reset of the application. But what is an IT administrator going to do with this information to ensure the issue does not reoccur going forward? By using Team Foundation Server Connector which integrates Operations Manager and Visual Studio, he or she can now send the error trace and debugging information directly to Visual Studio, where it can be triaged by developers using their own tools. Developers can track, assign, debug, and release a fix using this detailed information. Pretty cool, right? But what about adherence to governance?

Integration of Operations Manager and Service Manager

The final feature in this scenario is integration between Operations Manager and Service Manager. Via a connector, the Operations Manager alert has automatically raised an incident so that it can be tracked and folks can be notified. Lastly, when the fix is released, you naturally will want to enter a change request and get approval before implementing — and the reason you can easily do this via Service Manager is that it already knows about the application and has all its elements discovered as configuration items (CIs) in the Service Manager Configuration Management Database (CMDB). These are pulled into the CMDB via the Service Manager CI connector. Incidents and change requests can reference the exact systems and services affected.

This is a rather holistic develop, deploy, monitor, and remediate story. A couple of other unique elements may be of interest. When monitoring a service via a synthetic transaction, again, what you are really after is the end-user experience. In this scenario, the end users are not sitting in your datacenter; they're out there online somewhere. What you need is the capability to perform the transaction from multiple Internet locations globally, which is just what Global Service Monitor provides. Global Service Monitor is a feature that enables your synthetic transaction to be performed from Azure datacenters around the world, giving you an accurate view of the actual experience end users are getting from multiple points of presence on the Internet.

Another nice component to help pull all these elements together is the service dashboard. A couple of different dashboards are available in Operations Manager, such as the 360 .NET Application Monitoring dashboards, which give you an overall view of the health, performance, and reliability of your modeled distributed applications. You can see in a single view how your service is performing against its SLA via aggregated data collected from the following Operations Manager elements: .NET Application Performance Monitoring, Global Service Monitor (external end-user experience), and Web Application Availability Monitoring (internal end-user experience).

You can also easily create custom dashboards based on a management pack and its corresponding objects and data, and then use these for displaying real-time SLA performance or surfacing alerts, such as in the case of a network operations center (NOC).

By using the right tools for the job, it really doesn't matter whether the services you are monitoring are in your own datacenter or someone else's. The point of monitoring the service is to have all the data needed for successful operations in one place.

UNIFIED MANAGEMENT

Let's now look at some management strategies. In Chapter 5 we talked about the importance of automation. Let's dig into that a little further. The first thing people usually want to address is automating the deployment of resources, typically servers that are used for development, testing, and production applications. This is made available to consumers of the resources by means of a self-service portal, but what do you automate next? Honestly, that's what your management system should be telling you. Where are the most issues coming from? What are IT people spending the most time doing?

Automation is not so much a technology or technique as much as it is a philosophy. Think of automation as a way of life, which over time results in a more stable, predictable, healthy, and well-performing environment. One hurdle to adoption we often see is the fear that automation will result in the loss of IT jobs. In reality, however, that's rarely the case. Actually, automation allows the IT staff to take on more important responsibilities and focus on continual service improvement, rather than being forever stuck in "fire-fighting" mode. Industry surveys have consistently shown that more than 70 percent of IT budgets is spent just "keeping the lights on" — that is, keeping existing services up and running. That leaves a small slice of the budget to invest in innovating and engineering for tomorrow's opportunities.

Orchestration Considerations

After you have adopted automation as a philosophy, you'll want to consider orchestration. Orchestration takes multiple automation routines and management systems and ties them together in an end-to-end runbook. A runbook can contain logic beyond what's typically possible via scripting alone, and it lowers the barrier to entry by having many automated tasks already ready to use. System Center Orchestrator implements these in the form of integration packs. The integration pack contains activities that automate a granular task. You can then chain together multiple activities and automation scripts into a complete process to orchestrate complex scenarios. Consider building a runbook library over time so that you can reuse common automation tasks in multiple runbooks.

The other valuable thing System Center Orchestrator brings to the table is the integration of multiple management tools. Enterprise IT has often deployed many different systems and tools over time as a result of filling in the gaps that most management tools have. Purchasing decisions are either driven from a best-of-breed point solution for a specific need, such as Linux management, or are made at a strategy level that involves purchasing a large suite, which individual teams are then asked to make work. The Orchestrator component enables teams to drive scenario-based runbooks that cross-cut multiple tools and systems.

To position process automation with customers and constituents, you want to make sure you have an awareness of both higher-level systems, such as service management, as well as the lower-level tools that talk to endpoints, such as patch management, deployment, virtualization managers, and so on. Think of orchestration as the glue that binds these elements together. That being said, if the glue is not able to adhere to systems and tools both above and below, it will not be effective. A hurdle many face in this approach is the organizational structure preventing cross-cutting scenarios because teams that own those environments and systems don't trust an external connector to do the right things with their management system. This is where soft skills are important, such as interdepartmental campaigns that sell the benefits to those teams and invite their participation in order to get their buy-in and support.

Service Management Considerations

Service management is a critical layer in a cloud architecture, as this team and their systems often own the governance of IT as a whole. The rule of thumb is that you will need to understand their charter and often delegate or concede certain parts of the architectural decision making to them. Your main job in this case is to ensure that you have clearly articulated your requirements for the elements critical to your cloud initiative, such as self-service, standardized service requests and templates, and automated approvals and notification for standard changes. Without these elements, your goal of becoming a cloud service provider can become thwarted or severely slowed, which will again drive consumption of public cloud resources without IT involvement. Ideally, the service management system will be able to expose a service catalog with self-service capabilities that is directly tied to your orchestration engine.

If a decision has been made to adopt cloud services and have them work within the constructs of the IT methodologies, then you have a strong case with top-level support for driving the right decisions in this area.

Systems Management Considerations

Let's switch gears to systems management. We've already spent a good deal of time on monitoring, but there are other management considerations that you don't want to exclude in this realm. A few key focus areas for managing systems across private and public clouds are as follows:

➤ Configuration management, updates, and maintenance

➤ Capacity management and consumption

➤ Data warehousing and reporting

> ➤ Service-level management (private clouds vs. public clouds)

> ➤ Backups and disaster recovery

> ➤ Security, auditing, and compliance

> ➤ Identity and access management

Several of these have been covered throughout the book, but take a moment to consider a few in more detail, as they become more pronounced concerns in the hybrid cloud.

Again, you need a holistic management solution that can be leveraged regardless of where the platforms and runtime environments are located. I emphasize this only because it's easy to see how, if you lose sight of this, you quickly lose the ability to ensure that the preceding bulleted items are addressed as cloud adoption occurs. IT management is largely managing software. Once deployed, software must be consistently configured, updated, and maintained. It really doesn't matter whether it's an operating system, application, setting, or file. Once software is deployed, regardless of how mature the release process was, it has a tendency to change over time — a condition known as *configuration drift*. A good configuration management system will be capable of not only deploying operating systems and applications, but also watching their configuration over time and reporting on the drift from the initial or desired configuration. This is applicable regardless of whether you are using IaaS, PaaS, or SaaS deployment models, and it is likely your organization will eventually end up using a combination of all three. Again, System Center has investments in this area. A tool called System Center Advisor was recently announced as a free service that will help scan what you are managing and advise on best-practice configurations to proactively prevent issues. Of course, the heavy hitter in this space is System Center Configuration Manager, whose agent-based model enables tracking assets, deploying packages, and reporting on and even enforcing configuration compliance against a baseline that either you or Microsoft defines.

Now, as far as you're concerned, public cloud–based capacity is unlimited, or at least only limited by what you're willing to pay for. However, that doesn't mean it's a free-for-all, does it? For on-premises assets, you need to carefully watch resource consumption patterns so that you don't run out; but for public clouds, you need to carefully watch them to ensure they are responsibly utilized and don't break the bank. This is where data warehousing and reporting is key, as it enables you to monitor consumption behavior and run not only consumption reports but also predictive analyses to project what future demands will look like based on historical patterns. Consider developing a regular cycle to review reports proactively both for budget planning and to inform infrastructure teams what they need to be thinking about for the future.

SUMMARY

Holistic operations in a hybrid cloud environment are as much about people and processes as they are about tools and technologies. Advantages which impact the software development life cycle are a main driver for leveraging cloud-based PaaS and IaaS resources. You need to get to know your application teams and understand what leads to their success in order to select the right management strategy and implement the appropriate tools. New operational models, such as DevOps, are becoming more prevalent to address these challenges.

Stresses may be identified in the service management frameworks and tools implemented prior to the prevalence of public clouds. This can be addressed with awareness and acceptance of the fact that change is here to stay. Standardization, automation, and orchestration are key themes to operating as a service provider, especially when leveraging public cloud services in conjunction with your datacenter assets. Deep integration and built-in knowledge are important features to consider in your hybrid monitoring and management strategy. People who can embrace change and keep up with this rapidly changing IT landscape become the linchpin of these modern IT environments.

10 Final Hybrid Cloud Considerations

As we move into the final chapter of this book we would like to recap the journey you have just taken. At this point, you have examined in depth the process to understand and prioritize your business goals, determined the right solution for your needs, explored the capabilities of Azure and System Center, and hopefully crafted a way forward for deploying a hybrid cloud solution within your environment. Chances are good that you found certain parts of this book more engaging than others and spent more or less time in specific parts according to interest or need. If that is the case, don't worry — no one is an expert across every topic covered in this book. Frankly, it took the three of us working very closely together (not to mention the amazing editors) to ensure that each chapter flows logically and that you have the necessary information to build a hybrid cloud solution. Likewise, what will most likely happen in the real world is that you will need several resources with various skill sets to appropriately justify, design, build, and deploy a hybrid cloud solution.

We are not under the impression that one person alone will carry out all aspects of building a hybrid cloud solution. No doubt, it will take a team of resources with various backgrounds and disciplines to ensure a successful implementation. You will need at the very least skill sets that range from business value justification, applications development, infrastructure management, and service management, not to mention automation and orchestration. This is a wide-ranging set of skills that you may not have on tap; therefore, we did our best to arm you with the information you need to begin the journey on your own, supplementing any additional resources where you see fit. One point that we want to stress, however, is that adopting a hybrid cloud solution can potentially transform your IT department in terms of operations and management, and even its organizational structure.

A hybrid cloud solution brings with it a few elements that many IT departments may not be ready to embrace, such as the need to negotiate and partner with large service providers to deliver IT services to end users. Think about it — part of your IT environment exists not only on the premises (in your datacenter), it now extends to or leverages an external service provider's environment. This means that any service-level agreement (SLA) you provide to your end users must take into account the SLAs provided by a service provider. Essentially, you will be only as reliable as your lowest combined SLA. The good news is that most large service providers operate and offer services that are more reliable and stable than what most "in-house" IT organizations can offer. Just be aware of the partnership into which you have entered and how much is really in your control.

> **NOTE** *Be sure to inform your end users about any downtime or maintenance planned by Microsoft. You can typically find this information on the Azure subscription page.*

HOW DO I EXECUTE MY HYBRID CLOUD INITIATIVE?

So far we have covered the motivating factors, design principals, and overall approach associated with building your hybrid cloud solution. Going forward we want to ensure that these efforts aren't wasted, so we propose a very "light" set of exercises that will assist you in executing your hybrid cloud initiative. Following these exercises will enable you to not only quickly figure out who in the organization you want working with you, but also identify the motivators that will help bring on board those who might initially be opposed to moving to or leveraging the solution. Remember the saying: *Most people aren't afraid of change, they are afraid of being unprepared for change.*

Analyzing Skill Sets

As you start your journey, try to take stock of the different types of skill sets that exist in your organization. This information is critical in understanding what potential gaps you may need to fill before the solution can become fully operational. Additionally, this is also a great way to validate some of your design elements and find proponents for the solution.

Skills you need in the business adoption area include:

> ➤ **Identify business goals and investment objectives** — As stated earlier in the book, it is essential to ensure that executive leadership understands and believes in the benefits (both financial and nonfinancial) that a hybrid cloud solution will provide to the organization.

> ➤ **Benefits management\realization** — Once benefits have been stated and structured, assign an owner to the benefit that will follow through and look to realize any stated benefit of the hybrid cloud solution.

> ➤ **Organizational change** — Expect that the role of IT will change; however, also anticipate that business users will most likely have to change the way in which they consume IT services (for example, think of the change needed to adopt self-service).

Skills you need to address in the public cloud (Windows Azure) area include:

➤ **A new cloud architect discipline** — When building software solutions for the public cloud, the traditional clear separation between an infrastructure architect, application development architect, security architect, and operations management administrator is becoming increasingly blurred. You might think that when moving applications to a public cloud, your organization's need for the infrastructure or networking architecture discipline is deprecated. It's not! In fact, when you start constructing your hybrid cloud architecture as described in Chapter 6, you quickly realize that your cloud architects need to not only possess application development skill sets, but also need to know how to design and architect virtual networks, virtual machines, Active Directory, and DNS; have knowledge in PowerShell, OAuth, and digital certificates; and possess many more other skills that traditionally were required by infrastructure, networking, and security disciplines.

➤ **Architecting for scale** — To a cloud consumer, a public cloud should appear to have infinite service capacity. Just as when they are buying electricity from a utility company, consumers can use as much or as little of the cloud service as they need. This capability means that the most important principle of architectural design for the cloud is the solution's ability to satisfy requests on demand. Applying this principle reactively and in isolation often leads to inefficient use of resources and unnecessary costs. Understanding this and other best practice cloud principles described in this book is a very important part of any skill set.

➤ **Agility** — An increasingly agile infrastructure is great if you are an increasingly agile company. In case you didn't know, Windows Azure release cycle is every 6 months, and minor updates and new features are frequently pushed into the Microsoft Windows Azure datacenters. Compare that to older, more typical Microsoft product release cycles, which ranged between 2 to 5 years (e.g., SQL Server 2000, SQL Server 2005, SQL Server 2008, SQL Server 2012, etc.), and you will quickly realize that in order to keep pace with the cloud technology you must be almost as fast and agile as the technology on which your cloud services are hosted. Blink and you have just missed a train — while your competitor hasn't.

Skills you need concerning System Center 2012 include:

➤ **Fabric Administration** — The role of the fabric administrator requires more breadth than depth. Typically this role interfaces with storage, network, and server teams but may or may not directly administrate those systems. Responsibilities include:

  ➤ Formulating resource pools consisting of pre-allocated units of storage, network, and compute resources

  ➤ Formulating templates for VMs and services which have pre-determined size, performance, security, network, and SLA characteristics

  ➤ Assigning tenants and services to resource pools

➤ Capacity planning and cost containment

➤ Advanced virtualization skills along with a close partnership or direct responsibility for the cloud management platform

➤ **Service Management** — This discipline ensures alignment of business needs to IT capabilities. Service Management may encompass a wide variety of elements and dependent technologies depending on the organizational needs. For example, financial management may be critical to one organization and virtually irrelevant to another. Some of the more common aspects include: service catalog, service level agreements, service mapping, lifecycle management, continuity and availability management.

➤ **Management & Operations** — M&O skills are needed today as they always have been in traditional datacenters, but now we need to extend our skills to include some public cloud aspects. Key areas impacted may include: release and deployment, service health and performance, security and compliance, configuration, maintenance and patching, incident, problem & change management, reporting and dashboards.

➤ **"Infra-Dev"/Automation Engineer** — This is a somewhat new type of role that many forward-thinking organizations are developing which is why I use a new term: infra-dev. This competency requires a mix of advanced infrastructure along with scripting and automation experience, although the right orchestration engine may lessen the burden on advanced scripting. Most large IT shops will know instinctively who is best suited for this role, it's the person who loves to write scripts and automate IT systems. A successful implementation will grow this individual from a scripting guy or gal to an end-to-end runbook developer. In our new cloud world, this role becomes pivotal to the success of the design as automation, orchestration, and integration are lynchpins of cloud computing infrastructure.

You'll notice that many of these skill sets are covered in this book, so if you need a little brushing up on the subject just revisit some of the chapters and get reacquainted with the material you feel less comfortable with.

NOTE *You no doubt noticed that along with the technical aspects of a cloud solution we have emphasized heavily the operations and business value development of a hybrid cloud solution. The reason we keep bringing this up is because hybrid clouds (or any clouds for that matter) typically require some form of organizational change in order to properly leverage and truly realize its benefits. When you make organizational changes you typically also require executive sponsorship. Business leaders are always (or should be) keenly focused on setting up the right organization model to support their business processes and functions. IT is not excluded from this conversation. Although business operating models are not covered in this book, be aware that in order for an organization to realize a benefit, it must change its behavior: start doing something, stop doing something, or improve something.*

Moving toward a Converged Infrastructure

As organizations look to adopt cloud solutions and move these systems into operation, they may find that the typical server or network administrators will feel constrained in their ability to properly manage the new solution. Why? First and foremost these traditional admins and roles are typically siloed to a specific function or technology. Cloud solutions, however, are ushering in the concept of *converged infrastructure* (or software-defined networks/datacenters). All this really means is that specific resources that were once treated independently (think servers, networking, and storage) are now treated as a whole of interconnected parts. This whole is treated as a single unit of integrated resources.

Converged infrastructure is also just another term for resource pools (an essential cloud tenant covered in Chapter 1). Whichever term you use, because these resources are treated as a single unit, operating and managing this infrastructure and solution must also be done in an integrated fashion. What does this really mean? It means that a new role must be defined, and many organizations are labeling it *datacenter/hybrid admin*. This is not a new concept; large service providers have been staffing such a role for a number of years.

NOTE *For greater insight into, and examples of, agile organizations that running and offer services to customers, look into frameworks such as the Enhanced Telecom Operations Map (eTOM which you can find at* `http://tmforum.org/BusinessProcessFramework/1647/home.html`*). Although you may not leverage all the concepts covered in this framework, it will give you an overview of how a large organization can provide end-to-end services to its consumers regardless of the technologies or functional areas the services span.*

This approach will no doubt influence how many IT organizations reshape their structure, especially when it comes to adapting to hosting services and applications that span both private cloud and public cloud resources. As we move into this new era of computing, clearly defining the relationships, roles, and responsibilities of the support staff have never been more important. We cannot emphasize enough the change that will be required to properly set up and manage the services that will be hosted across both public and private cloud platforms.

Managing Stakeholder Objections

Earlier we highlighted the saying *Most people aren't afraid of change, they are afraid of being unprepared for change.* This observation stems from the many experiences we have encountered in assisting large and small organizations to adopt cloud solutions. Interestingly, the main blocker or issue that is encountered when an organization is adopting a cloud solution is resistance — specific individuals pushing back against that change. Why would an individual or a group of individuals knowingly and actively try to derail or delay an organization trying to adopt a cloud solution? Some of the main objections include the following:

➤ Fear of job loss

➤ Increased accountability/responsibility

➤ Unsure of potential benefits

➤ Confusion about terminology

Consider the following list of strategies we have compiled that can help you remove the potential blocker and ease some of the concerns that your staff may have about adopting a hybrid cloud solution. Many of these strategies can be used in cases where you are adopting a private, public, or hybrid cloud, but you have one main benefit when dealing with a hybrid cloud solution. Essentially, you are almost ensured that there will be on-premise elements to the solutions that will still require on-the-ground expertise of certain technologies and solutions. These strategies were born from a very simple methodology built around stakeholder management. The questions we try to answer pragmatically for stakeholders are as follows: "What are the concerns?" and "What measures can we take to address those concerns?"

First, you begin by identifying the potential stakeholders (or those affected by the solution) for your engagement. The following lists give an example of a few that we have identified for you (remember that the lists may vary based on the structure of your organization).

Role: IT Pro

➤ Who: Responsible for the administration and operations of IT services within an organization.

➤ What: Will most likely feel that their jobs are at risk because many associate outsourcing with the term cloud.

➤ When: Will assume ownership and maintenance of a cloud solution after it goes into production.

➤ Why: Hybrid cloud solutions typically also require the management of on-premises traditional IT elements in conjunction with public cloud resources.

➤ How: Should be involved with the initial conversations about adopting a cloud solution.

Role: Architects

➤ Who: Responsible for the overall design of technical solutions, their integration with existing platforms, and the organizational and business impact and applicability of technology within an enterprise.

➤ What: Concerned with organizational shift and the introduction of new technologies within the enterprise.

➤ When: Should be involved with the high-level design and envisioning of the hybrid cloud solution.

➤ Why: Provide deep insight into how an organization should begin to use the hybrid cloud and what tactics can be leveraged to begin the initial consumption of a cloud solution.

➤ How: Through engaging with various business stakeholders and soliciting the functional and non-functional requirements of a solution they provide the high-level design and approach to implementing Enterprise Solutions.

Role: Users

➤ Who: Application owners, Line of Business owners, Information Workers and any staff that leverages IT Solutions to perform their job functions.

➤ By leveraging technical solutions provided through the IT Department, users are the base audience for which technical solutions should be designed.

➤ When: Provide requirements for building technical solutions specifically around operational needs and future capabilities required within a solution.

➤ Why: As the primary users of technical solutions, application users should drive the acceptance criteria and should routinely provide feedback on the effectiveness of deployed services within an organization.

➤ How: Through the use of surveys, control groups, and feedback loops, application users can provide valuable feedback on the effectiveness of existing technical solutions as well as provide input to business leaders about trending issues, and provide insight to Architects and Business Leaders on areas to improve and optimize their core functions.

Role: Business owners

➤ Who: Comprised of Business Decision Makers, SVP's and Business Unit Presidents which are typically responsible for the performance, output and overall efficiency of business functions.

➤ What: By engaging with Architects and Technical Decision Makers, they provide the business need, drivers, and pain that IT Solutions look to support, enable, or relieve.

➤ When: A regular cadence should be set up, which allows Business Owners to share their thoughts, strategy, and plans to Architects and Technical Decision makers, which coincide frequently enough to capture changing business requirements, however not so often that meetings begin to introduce additional overhead without providing significant value to either parties.

➤ Why: Ultimately all IT Investments should be traced back to some form of business need. If this alignment cannot be made, then the IT Project, technology, or solution should be reassessed as required for the organization.

➤ How: Through regularly informing TDM of the priorities of the business and providing regular feedback on the effectiveness of IT Solutions.

Again, that's not an exhaustive list, but you can get the idea from what we provide here regarding what information you need to provide for the people in your organizations. All of the preceding roles need to understand how a cloud solution will affect them; therefore, we suggest a communication plan that spells out in detail (using the framework in the table) how their roles will change when the organization adopts a hybrid cloud model. We have carried this out through "brown bag" or "lunch and learn" sessions in which stakeholders in the solution spend 90 minutes or more discussing how the solution will be rolled out in the environment and how it specifically affects them. As simple as this sounds, many resources are often not included in large organizational changes (such as adopting a cloud solution), not because they are willfully ignored but because many organizations underestimate the impact that cloud solutions will have on their business.

The Hybrid Cloud Admin

This will most likely be a new role within your organization, but it is important to note that it leverages the skill sets and specialties of multiple resources into a single position. This new role will not replace your existing resources (at least not initially). To usher in this new role, you can look at creating a Center of Excellence/Innovation (CoE/I) whose charter is to manage and maintain the hybrid cloud solution and make clear the subtle nuances and differences required to manage a cloud solution versus a traditional on-premises solution. The hybrid cloud CoE/I's charter should also include creating operational guides and best practices and educating the rest of the organization of this information where applicable. Other fundamental purposes of this newly appointed team would be to seek new ways in which the business can leverage technology to differentiate itself from its competition, find new levels of efficiency within the organization, continuously seek ways to offload IT capabilities that can be provided either at higher availability and lower cost, and potentially provide a competitive advantage to the organization within their market and industry vertical.

Hybrid cloud admins are not a resource (or a set of resources) with deep expertise across a number of different technologies and products. Instead, they act more as generalists, with a comfortable set of management and operational capabilities across myriad technologies and solutions sets. They might, however, have deep expertise across a single product, and in conjunction with other resources round out the team's expertise across a broad set of products and technologies. We call this the T-shirt approach because resources would be expected to have a broad understanding of various technologies (horizontally) and a deep expertise on just one specific product or technology (vertically). This approach is actually fairly common in the consulting business, as it is difficult to staff a team of resources that knows everything about everything. Instead, consulting organizations build a base level of knowledge across a number of technologies, and various individuals assume the role of building deep expertise in specific product sets (messaging, virtualization, storage and etc.). This happens naturally in smaller IT organizations as well, and results in IT generalists who have to do it all because frankly they don't have a choice.

EMBRACING CONTINUAL IMPROVEMENT

After you begin consuming a hybrid cloud solution, does that mean you can sit back and coast? We wish we could say that were the case, but in fact you are just beginning your journey in leveraging your new cloud solution. Two factors are going to shape how you continue to leverage such a solution:

➤ The changing needs of your business

➤ New cloud capabilities

As your organization begins to become more comfortable in leveraging cloud solutions, you will find new ways to leverage them (many of which probably have not been discovered yet), and as cloud solutions mature you will find that some of the constraints that prevented you from leveraging them will be gone. You will also find that your organization has fewer reasons to manage and deploy hybrid cloud solutions, instead consuming purely public cloud offerings. That is a topic for another day, however.

We advise you to reassess the health of your hybrid cloud solution and its applicability to the business quarterly. At first glance you might feel that this is too frequent a time frame, but we suggest quarterly because the rate at which cloud solutions are maturing is quickening and only increasing in velocity. Also, many organizations, such as Microsoft, are shortening their update and software release cycles to as often as (you guessed it) every 3 months. What this means for you and your business is that new capabilities are going to be released by large service providers, so the complexity and burden associated with managing a hybrid cloud solution can be addressed though the increased integration and maturation of cloud offerings. Ideally, taking a service and completely shifting it to a public cloud model would free you and your business to focus on your core capabilities, leaving mundane or non-core activities to the service providers completely. This enables you to direct your smartest and most effective resources into continuously improving the services that your IT department delivers to the rest of the business, in addition to innovating and discovering new ways in which the organization can leverage technology to differentiate itself from its competitors.

WHEN IS IT TIME TO JUMP ONBOARD?

If you think your company is a good fit for hybrid cloud computing, there remains the question of when you should seriously start thinking about deploying it. Should you wait or should you jump onboard?

We recommend a third approach. Start by following these steps:

1. Build and optimize your own private cloud with the functionality you need.

2. Bring in a third-party cloud service provider as a partner.

3. After negotiating specific terms, move into the hybrid space when you're ready.

As with any technology, you need to prepare ahead of time to take full advantage of it in the future.

THE TIME IS NOW — THE TIPPING POINT

As you can tell from the previous section, we strongly believe that you should be thinking about and taking steps toward a cloud solution right now, and Windows Azure is a great place to start. As we stated, cloud solutions are going to be become much more mature and widely available with every passing day. The moment you are able to find a public cloud solution that meets the requirements of your business, we believe you should move to it as soon as possible. For many organizations it might be a slower or more gradual move (especially if you recently moved to a hybrid cloud solution), but offloading any and all IT capabilities to a large service provider should be the goal of almost all businesses (with the exception of true service providers, telcos, and some governments). The ultimate goal should eventually be the consumption of a public cloud solution, removing the burden from an in-house IT department. We all believe that like utility companies offer electricity, power, and water today through a publicly available grid, IT capabilities and technologies will also eventually fall into this model; and in the future, new businesses will probably be created without any IT footprint (save a few negotiators or managers who govern the technology services provided by service providers).

Every day large service providers, such as Microsoft, are making incredible strides in the public cloud arena to answer many of the concerns that organizations have about the public cloud (e.g., data sovereignty, encryption, site resiliency, and availability). One such team that Microsoft has created to deal with these concerns is Trustworthy Computing (TwC). You can learn more about TwC at http://www.microsoft.com/about/twc/en/us/default.aspx. We personally know many of the men and women in TwC, and they are working hard to ensure that Microsoft can enforce the security standards that our customers require when storing their data, such as the following:

➤ ISO 27001

➤ Safe Harbor

➤ SSAE16 SOC1 Type II

➤ FISMA

This list will keep growing, and TwC will no doubt introduce new methods and processes that will assure customers that their data is secure and accessible when they need it. Additionally, you can also expect to see many government organizations relax restrictions around leveraging public cloud solutions.

Microsoft will also continue to invest in bringing its cloud services to new geographic locations. Microsoft is investing billions of dollars a year in expanding the footprint of its datacenter and also optimizing and continuing to innovate around cloud services. The tipping point in the industry has been reached, and Microsoft will continue to invest heavily in its cloud services and platform.

SUMMARY

As you progress on your journey, you may find that not everything goes as planned and there will be some hard lessons learned along the way. However, always bear in mind the following saying, which should put the challenge you face in perspective: *Progress is the enemy of tradition, and tradition is the enemy of progress.*

If you face resistance on this journey, don't fret, for those people most likely don't want to change because they are more comfortable doing things the way they have always been done. These are the resources that will no doubt give you the greatest heartache. We hope that you will be able to apply the approaches laid out in this book to not only deal with those traditionalists but also give you greater insight and guidance as to what elements are required for a successful hybrid cloud deployment. The hybrid cloud really is that middle ground or sweet spot between the public and private cloud, and its immediate applicability is clear. We hope that you found this book insightful and helpful in your journey to hybrid cloud solutions. Remember, the tipping point has been reached. It's time to head to the cloud.

INDEX

Made in the USA
Lexington, KY
31 May 2018